Neo-Spiritual Aesthetics

Bloomsbury Advances in Religious Studies

Series Editors: Bettina E. Schmidt, Steven Sutcliffe and Will Sweetman

Founding Editors: James Cox and Peggy Morgan

Bloomsbury Advances in Religious Studies publishes cutting-edge research in the Study of Religion/s. The series draws on anthropological, ethnographical, historical, sociological and textual methods amongst others. Topics are diverse, but each publication integrates theoretical analysis with empirical data. The series aims to refresh the interdisciplinary agenda in new evidence-based studies of 'religion'.

A Phenomenology of Indigenous Religions, James L. Cox
A Sense of Belonging, Stephen Friend
American Evangelicals, Ashlee Quosigk
Appropriation of Native American Spirituality, Suzanne Owen
Becoming Buddhist, Glenys Eddy
Charismatic Healers in Contemporary Africa, edited by Sandra Fancello and Alessandro Gusman
Community and Worldview among Paraiyars of South India, Anderson H. M. Jeremiah
Conceptions of the Afterlife in Early Civilizations, Gregory Shushan
Contemporary Western Ethnography and the Definition of Religion, Martin D. Stringer
Cultural Blending in Korean Death Rites, Chang-Won Park
Free Zone Scientology, Aled Thomas
Globalization of Hesychasm and the Jesus Prayer, Christopher D. L. Johnson
Individualized Religion, Claire Wanless
Innateness of Myth, Ritske Rensma
Levinas, Messianism and Parody, Terence Holden
New Paradigm of Spirituality and Religion, Mary Catherine Burgess
Orthodox Christianity, New Age Spirituality and Vernacular Religion, Eugenia Roussou
Post-Materialist Religion, Mika T. Lassander
Redefining Shamanisms, David Gordon Wilson
Reform, Identity and Narratives of Belonging, Arkotong Longkumer

Religion and the Discourse on Modernity, Paul-François Tremlett
Religion as a Conversation Starter, Ina Merdjanova and Patrice Brodeur
Religion, Material Culture and Archaeology, Julian Droogan
Secular Assemblages, Marek Sullivan
Spirits and Trance in Brazil, Bettina E. Schmidt
Spirit Possession and Trance, edited by Bettina E. Schmidt and Lucy Huskinson
Spiritual Tourism, Alex Norman
Spirituality and Alternativity in Contemporary Japan, Ioannis Gaitanidis
Theology and Religious Studies in Higher Education, edited by D. L. Bird and Simon G. Smith
The Critical Study of Non-Religion, Christopher R. Cotter
The Dynamic Cosmos, edited by Diana Espírito Santo and Matan Shapiro
The Problem with Interreligious Dialogue, Muthuraj Swamy
Religion and the Inculturation of Human Rights in Ghana, Abamfo Ofori Atiemo
Rethinking 'Classical Yoga' and Buddhism, Karen O'Brien Kop
UFOs, Conspiracy Theories and the New Age, David G. Robertson

Neo-Spiritual Aesthetics

Embodied Transformation in the Israeli Movement Practice Gaga

Lina Aschenbrenner

BLOOMSBURY ACADEMIC
LONDON • NEW YORK • OXFORD • NEW DELHI • SYDNEY

BLOOMSBURY ACADEMIC
Bloomsbury Publishing Plc
50 Bedford Square, London, WC1B 3DP, UK
1385 Broadway, New York, NY 10018, USA
29 Earlsfort Terrace, Dublin 2, Ireland

BLOOMSBURY, BLOOMSBURY ACADEMIC and the Diana logo are trademarks of
Bloomsbury Publishing Plc

First published in Great Britain 2023
This paperback edition published 2024

Copyright © Lina Aschenbrenner, 2023

Lina Aschenbrenner has asserted her right under the Copyright, Designs and Patents Act, 1988, to be identified as Author of this work.

For legal purposes the Acknowledgments on p. xiii constitute an extension of this copyright page.

All rights reserved. No part of this publication may be reproduced or transmitted in any form or by any means, electronic or mechanical, including photocopying, recording, or any information storage or retrieval system, without prior permission in writing from the publishers.

Bloomsbury Publishing Plc does not have any control over, or responsibility for, any third-party websites referred to or in this book. All internet addresses given in this book were correct at the time of going to press. The author and publisher regret any inconvenience caused if addresses have changed or sites have ceased to exist, but can accept no responsibility for any such changes.

A catalogue record for this book is available from the British Library.

Library of Congress Control Number: 2022942236

ISBN: HB: 978-1-3502-7287-3
PB: 978-1-3502-7296-5
ePDF: 978-1-3502-7288-0
eBook: 978-1-3502-7289-7

Series: Bloomsbury Advances in Religious Studies

Typeset by Newgen KnowledgeWorks Pvt. Ltd., Chennai, India

To find out more about our authors and books visit www.bloomsbury.com and sign up for our newsletters.

To my family near and far

Contents

List of Illustrations	x
Lists	xi
Preface	xii
Acknowledgments	xiii
Introduction	1
Interlude: A Body-Focused Research Method	20

Part 1 Gaga Class: Aesthetics in Creation

1	Influential Culturescape	31
2	Ritual Environment Shaping Enactment	49
3	Body Topography in Discussion	88
4	The Power of Instructions	108
5	Transformation in Movement	119

Part 2 Gaga Participants: Aesthetics Perceived

6	Narrating Body Knowledge	159
7	The Wow of Gaga	178
8	Gaga's Therapeutic Impact	204
9	Gaga Goes Worldview	217
10	Concluding Thoughts	242

Notes	251
References	257
Index	269

Illustrations

Figures
1 Studio Suzy after the first and before the second evening class on April 23, 2017 — 54
2 Studio Varda before the evening class on April 24, 2017 — 57

Table
1 Observation Criteria during Participant Observation — 21

Lists

1	Body Knowledge Inventory	14
2	(Pseudonymized) Human Data Sources and Protagonists of the Book	25
3	First Grouping of Participants	67
4	Second Grouping of Participants	69
5	Aesthetically Effective Ritual Roles (Human)	72
6	Aesthetically Effective Kinds of Language	83
7	Metalanguage for Movement Description (LMA and LOD)	102
8	(Wording) Categories for Instruction Design Analysis	111
9	Characteristics of Wow-Moments' Narrations	182
10	Different Stages of the Practice–Participant Relation	222

Preface

In a framework of embodiment, every sensory involvement and every movement one undertakes change one's body knowledge, one's body scheme, one's perceptual order, one's experience filters—be it dancing or observing, be it reading or writing. Researching the Israeli movement improvisation practice Gaga meant sensory involvement and movement, which changed my body knowledge significantly. Not only did I find Gaga practice an apt ethnographic field and plentiful data resources to refine my research interest and research method on neo-spiritual aesthetics, researching Gaga significantly changed me. Partaking and observing changed my body image and body scheme, my movement (quality) range, my sensory monitoring level, and attention abilities. I am, I can say, a different person than before I started the research. As a researcher I say this without judgment, without wanting to judge. In this specific context, I am only observing. As a dance teacher and dancer and as a living and struggling human being, I am very delighted with the change. I gained a lot of knowledge and I like the changed version of myself.

I mention this self-reflecting, but I mention it also to make you, as my reader, as academic, or as nonacademic, aware of how you already are and will be changed by every sensory involvement and movement—be it moving, researching, or simply reading this book.

Also, just to make sure, this is an academic book. I do not claim any knowledge about the "true nature" of Gaga class. The Gaga instructions I cite are not, and do not want to be, exact reproductions and replications of Gaga instructions found in class. I am no Gaga teacher, member of the Gaga Movement Ltd., or whatsoever and do not aim to be. Instead, to me, Gaga becomes a social and cultural phenomenon of great interest in understanding the aesthetics of neo-spiritual practices. Thus, in this book, Gaga becomes an example. This is a book with Gaga, rather than a book about Gaga, if you want. My book is a book about neo-spiritual aesthetics.

I hope you enjoy reading, as much as I enjoyed researching and writing.

Acknowledgments

First, I want to thank my supervisor, Anne Koch, who inspired me to conduct research on Gaga (instead of following the path of ancient Ethiopian literature, which was offered to me by my master thesis supervisor, Loren Stuckenbruck—however, I have to thank him for allowing me to think about pursuing a researcher's career at all). You, Anne, opened my eyes to the possibility of researching Gaga from the perspective of a study of religion, and the Aesthetics of Religion in particular, and thus helped me to combine two important areas of my life, my main interests: dance and the study of religion. Not only did I learn much from you and draw inspiration from your own work, but you also always encouraged me to follow my own ideas and supported me during my journey. This book would simply not be without you!

Second, I would like to pay my special regard to Adrian Hermann and all members of the colloquium hosted by the department for the research on religion at the Forum Internationale Wissenschaft Bonn, in which I was invited to participate at the Annual Conference of the European Association for the Study of Religions (2018). Thank you for welcoming me so warmly in your midst—virtually and in person. Thank you for many inspiring discussions, the helpful feedback on my research, and the academic exchange, which helped me to stay focused and navigate more easily between my identity as a scholar and writer, a dance teacher, and, nowadays, a mom.

I wish to express my deepest gratitude to everybody in and around Gaga whom I met and talked to during my ethnographic fieldwork. Thank you for reflecting with me on my research, its purpose, method, and results. Thanks also to those who partook in my data collection and allowed me to be part of their Gaga experience. I appreciate your time and the enthusiasm with which you answered questions, discussed with me, and shared your experience. Thank you for welcoming me into your community, which made my participant observation simultaneously easy and pleasurable. Furthermore, thank you for the many coffee talks after class and the informal conversations, where I was able to gain further insights into your Gaga world. I am so grateful for all the friendships I made along the way, and I keep many happy memories from my research time in Tel Aviv!

I especially thank my younger sister, Marie. Thank you for every philosophical discussion, which broadened my academic horizon; for all the critical proofreading and questioning of abstracts, papers, and extracts from my work; and for your open ear to my theoretical and practical research problems and all my self-doubts. Without you, I would never have gotten this far on my academic path!

I want to thank Laura and Micaela for reading the manuscript and sharing their valuable opinions. Thanks goes out to the reviewers, too. Besides, I would like to thank Stephanie for sharing many hours in the library and for uplifting coffee-break talks and the exchange of a plentitude of memes.

I wish to acknowledge the immense support and great love of my partner Tao and, of course, the rest of my family, all my siblings, and especially my parents for emotional and economic support. I thank my daughter Ke'ala for spending so many hours patiently sleeping on my lap and in the sling, so I could finish writing up my research. Also, I thank you, Ke'ala, for showing me so much love and for making myself love you to an extent I did not know I could—it makes up for every difficulty of being a writing mom.

Last but not least, I am indebted to my grandmothers and grandfathers, Inge and Klaus Witting, and Elisabeth and Ernst Aschenbrenner, who will not be able to read this book, but who nevertheless provided one of the greatest motivations to finish it—I know you would not have expected and accepted anything less from me!

Introduction

Until quite recently, dancing literally defined my life. I could not live without it. It made me happy; it made me smile; it made me feel good, pretty, comfortable in my body, and self-confident. In a time of existential search, it gave me purpose and goals to achieve—getting better at dancing, getting better in shape for being able to dance according to self-set standards, accomplishing technical tasks. It helped me deal with sorrow; it helped me deal with stress. I went to take dance classes every day; I consumed dance classes as often as possible. I was definitely a dance insider, when it came to experiencing the aesthetics of practicing. I even went on to become a dance teacher myself—I professionalized my "passion." With time, dance became central to my world; it became central to my experience of everyday life and my behavior; it became central to my meaning-making.

Being who I am, a study-of-religion scholar with a particular interest in bodies, practices, embodiment, aesthetics, and experience, this dance journey sparked my scholarly interest. I became curious about what dancing did to me; how was it that dancing could gain such a centrality in my life? I knew partaking in dance classes changed part of my body; it triggered some body knowledge, which changed my social and cultural existence. I started to self-observe and analyze my embodied experience in dance classes and to compare it to the effect dance had on fellow dance class participants as well as to the effect of body and movement-focused leisure time activities in general. I concluded that neither was my experience singular nor unique in any way but instead many others shared it with me, and that it would be worthwhile to look at the creation of this physical-psychological effect of body and movement practices and its social and cultural function from a study-of-religion perspective. I kept on observing but let my research interest slumber until I came about a very particular phenomenon: Gaga movement practice.

Gaga Movement Practice

Originally developed by Israeli choreographer Ohad Naharin in the 1990s and instated as a training method for the Batsheva Dance Company in the 2000s, Gaga became a leisure time movement activity for people in Tel Aviv from 2001—though named Gaga only in 2003—and later advanced to a popular movement practice for professional and nonprofessional dancers worldwide (Friedes Galili 2015, 363–6). An official business was established, namely Gaga Movement Ltd., which oversees the organization of classes globally, marketing and public relations, legal and copyright issues, and the official education for those Gaga teachers who are not themselves former members of the Batsheva Dance Company. The practice itself has kept evolving and changing due to Naharin still playing an active part in ongoingly recreating and advancing it (while teaching it) and passing adjustments on to all the Gaga teachers of different nationalities.

The Gaga classes for nonprofessional dancers I participated in were one hour long. From an imagined bird's eye view, you would have been able to see a bunch of people, fifteen, thirty, fifty, or even a hundred, moving in space—remaining at one place, sometimes changing places quickly; moving fast, moving slow; moving small or big; moving with a lot of force and intention, or soft and dreamily; enacting a variety of different and ever-changing shapes with their bodies and body parts; never talking; never touching each other, though occasionally interacting with a smile. You would have recognized that each of the people moved in their unique way; still an underlying movement quality and form alignment happened, and common movement patterns existed. People clustered around one person, the teacher, who stood in the middle, surrounded. The teacher was constantly uttering instructions while moving and embodying the instructions themselves. Ongoing movement was demanded, and participants were told to always be aware of and attentive to what was happening within their bodies and their environment simultaneously. Moreover, because they were told to do so, people would look at and listen to the teacher attentively, trying to embody the instructions. Gaga class became a dance class mainly because people felt as though they were dancing. Music was playing, and movements sometimes went with the music, sometimes against it—not untypical for contemporary dance, where the music forms part of the sensory setting instead of the movement being composed to the music. Rather than following specific movement sequences demonstrated by a dance teacher, watching and listening and copying and enacting the movement to a particular piece of music and timing, participants were expected to incorporate awareness-focused movement instructions without a fixed form given by a Gaga teacher while constantly moving without "stopping to watch." In consequence, the main sensory information came from the visually and orally perceived instructions and was accompanied by sensory input from the environment, such as fellow participants and the sensescape of the location, and by the self-observation of one's own moving body; its muscular, postural, cardiovascular, thermal state; and its skin touching its nonhuman surroundings, such as cloth, floor, and air. Apart from the requirement for constant movement enaction, a Gaga class came with a variety of other rules, which were communicated to participants orally or written before their first class: no talking—questions could be asked after class, no leaving the room,[1] and no coming late. The space characteristically did not include mirrors.[2] Furthermore, a strict regulation was in place, overseen by Gaga Movement Ltd., regarding who was allowed to teach Gaga or call themselves a Gaga teacher.[3]

It is in this context of Gaga class that I witnessed something, a cultural phenomenon that reminded me of my own dance experience, and which I immediately came to be highly interested in: Gaga practice as a leisure time activity seemed to be of specific attraction to a particular group of people. People left class evidently bursting with euphoria, with smiles on their faces and expressing their gratitude toward the teacher, and they returned—every day, maybe even twice; every few days; or once a week. The practice seemed to be so important to some that they made a real effort to partake in class. In workshops in Germany or Austria, too, the same core group of people kept showing up frequently. Gaga practice seemed to affect all of them in a way that made them crave a repetition of the experience in and around class. They seemed to long for a lasting experience. All these people appeared to belong to a social subgroup homogenous not only because they were part of a single society and culture but also because they were all equally willing and able to spend time and money on Gaga practice.

I soon decided that what makes Gaga such an interesting and important object to study is not only its effect on participants but more so the fact that these effect and experience patterns form part of a bigger social and cultural trend of *neo-spiritualities*.

Neo-Spiritual Aesthetics

Gaga as a body and movement practice shares certain values and ideas not only about the body, body image, body use, movement, and embodied behavior, such as optimization, efficiency, betterment, and constant bodily awareness, but also about the importance of the center of the body for movement with broader social and cultural discourses and other contemporary practices such as yoga (Aschenbrenner and von Ostrowski 2022) and "free-form mindful dances" (Mazzella 2021). There is something that connects Gaga with other contemporary cultural and social phenomena: the aesthetics and, departing from a similarity between aesthetics, the embodied effect they create. In light of a "study of religion," it is to be mentioned that practices such as Gaga, which shall be subsumed under the "neo-spiritual" category, lack a distinctive aesthetic feature of other "religious" practices; they appear as secular leisure time activities. Different from traditional religious institutions known as world religions, charismatic movements, or New Age phenomena, neo-spiritual practices do not aim at salvation or connectedness with a higher being. Neo-spiritual practices, too, provide, at least implicitly, ethical advice by the social and cultural discourses that participants are made to embody. However, giving an ethical worldview is not their concern. Instead, they state their concern with different aspects of individual "well-being": emotional and physical welfare and health, longevity, and the optimization of individual capacities perceived as achievable. The well-being concern feeds from neoliberal demands such as self-optimization, on the one hand, and from a constant popularization of medical and neuroscientific knowledge, on the other. The basic tendency of this knowledge discourse is to hold the individual responsible for their own well-being and grant the individual the ability to transform their well-being by transforming the bodily state via food intake, exercise, or meditative practices. Bodily involvement remains the central requirement of neo-spiritual practices: The well-being of participants is reached via bodily transformation. Moreover, neo-spiritual practices pretend to offer a space of freedom or for breaking free from social and cultural demands. They pretend to offer a unique liberating experience resulting in well-being. Yet, naturally, by their aesthetics, neo-spiritual practices indeed reassure the same social and cultural values (Aschenbrenner and Koch 2022).

In this way, neo-spiritual practices offer an interesting field of research to an academic study of religion. These practices play an essential role in the lives of practitioners who are supposedly often substituting for or filling the niche formerly occupied by religious practices, whose practicing and effect are no longer seen and experienced as adequate. The development seems to be driven forward by social and cultural developments characteristic of a consumerist neoliberal society: "Consumption as an ethos and consumerism as a cultural backdrop are certainly among the salient features of our societies," write François Gauthier and Tuomas Martikainen (2013, 2). This includes the "commoditisation of more and more areas of life, the rise of lifestyles as loci for identity" and "the emergence of the consumer as an identity" (2). It is a setting in which "self-presentation and the promotion of the self" become crucial for cultural and social participation (3). In this setting, religious practices must compete to exist by offering "branded goods" as "experiential and social commodities. What is sold is not an object but an experience that must appear authentic if it is to be meaningful" (13). As Gauthier (2017, 447) observes, "Many of the novel religious phenomena are putting emphasis on experience rather than belief and can be understood as expressions of this ethics of authenticity." They become "more practical and experienced than represented and believed" (454). They also answer individual demands for identity creation or social values and goods such as "wellbeing," "healing," and self-optimization (Gauthier and Martikainen 2013, 3, 15). Due to their aesthetical design, neo-spiritual practices seem to have an advantage as goods on a neoliberal market compared to other religious practices.

Theorizing neo-spiritual practices as the research object of an academic study of religion needs a focus on the proclaimed effect of practice, the created experience, and the place these practices take up in a social and cultural context. Helpful theoretical considerations are provided, for example, by Heinz Streib and Barbara Keller (2015). These German scholars elaborate on "spiritual" and try to place "spiritual" within "religion" by building on various theoretical backgrounds: They combine Thomas Luckmann's "transcendence" and Paul Tillich's "ultimate concern" with Ernst Troeltsch's "mysticism" (28–35). For Streib and Keller, "'Spirituality' is a variety of religion" (27; translated by author). First, not all transcendences are to be connected to "religion." Rather, the interpretation of transcendences depends on the interpretative system to which the transcendence-experiencing individual is subjugated (29). Second, what "ultimately concerns" with Tillich does not necessarily make use of or be disguised by religious semantics (30). Third, spirituality is considered to form part of Troeltsch's "privatized" and "experience oriented" mysticism, which itself, along "sects" and "churches," forms part of "religion" (35). Transferring this to a theory of neo-spirituality would and could mean that neo-spiritual practices are researchable as "religion" because they offer (1) transcendences, though without religious interpretation, and (2) extraordinary experience, though without religious vocabulary. They also satisfy ultimate concerns as needs, which arise from a specific social and cultural context. The practices operate in the private sector, addressing individuals, and they are characterized by their experience orientation. However, when taking inspiration from Streib and Keller's work, it is important to highlight that in the field research on Gaga, the majority of Gaga practitioners restrain themselves from denoting Gaga even as "spiritual." Furthermore, "spiritual" does not necessarily enter the discourse evolving in and around a neo-spiritual practice like Gaga or a practice's semantics.

Gauthier's (2017) theoretical considerations on the new developments in the contemporary religious landscape are also worth mentioning: Gauthier, who, like Streib and Keller (2015), observes the experience instead of the belief orientation of contemporary religious phenomena, asks for a shift of research on religion toward a focus on the "sensory dimensions" of religion, along with a shift and establishment of a new definition of religion, defining religion by its aesthetical dimension, design, and function (Gauthier 2017, 447, 453). A definition of neo-spirituality as aesthetically "religious" phenomenon could potentially include experience-oriented neo-spiritual practices such as Gaga because of the particular aesthetics they provide to the practicing individuals.

Taking into account both theoretical perspectives, from Streib and Keller (2015) and Gauthier (2017), could lead to the elaboration of a practical theory of religion, where "religion" can function as an umbrella term for what is traditionally understood as religious, spiritual, or New Age practices, as well as for neo-spiritual practices. More importantly, this could pave the way for a study of religion that includes neo-spiritual phenomena such as Gaga. The study of religion could include neo-spiritual practices offering extraordinary experience to its participants regardless of the practice's open "belief concern." It could include neo-spiritual practices that shape senses and transform bodies according to particular cultural and social discourses such as self-optimization; that fulfill social and cultural needs such as well-being; and that, via senses and bodies, affect participants' worldview.

Bodies as Academic Matter

The book explores neo-spiritualities from an embodied perspective. It is assumed that the observed effect of practice, here Gaga, on its participants is inseparable from the effect of the practice on their bodies—the effect is created on a sensory and cognitive level affecting each other. In this sense, the effect is an embodied transformation of a bodily, and thus a cognitive, state. The effect of Gaga then is the direct result of practicing Gaga, which creates an embodied change in the implicit and explicit character of the experiencing practitioners.

This is a research framework influenced by the so-called body-turn, a research dedication and focus on the body across the social science and humanities. The body-turn departs from the work and thoughts of social and cultural researchers but also the science as well as the social and cultural events of the twentieth and twenty-first centuries. While the body became an inherent part, place, and mean of "individualization processes and post-materialistic values, ... aestheticization and eventization" as well as an item of interest to new technologies and biopolitics of neoliberal consumerist society and its culture (Gugutzer et al. 2017, v; translated by author), it moved to the center of discussion of social collectivities and their embodied, materialist, and performative conditions. A holistic and body-bound view of perception emerged (Koch 2012). Thinkers such as Maurice Merleau-Ponty ([1962] 2002), Marcel Mauss (1973), Pierre Bourdieu (1977), Michel Foucault (1995), Thomas Csordas (1993), and Judith Butler (1999)—to name just a few "milestones"— found that collective practices shape collective bodies and, via bodies, collective perceptual orders. The bodily state of social and cultural individuals has come to be understood and acknowledged as forming the glasses through which to perceive the world, while at the same time these glasses being tainted, the body being formed, and the bodily state being created by their social and cultural embeddedness (Merleau-Ponty [1962] 2002). Collectivities are made, demarcated, and held together and on the level of the body of those of whom they consist, embodying particular "techniques of the body" (Mauss 1973), "habitus" (Bourdieu 1977), "somatic modes of attention" (Csordas 1993), or certain self-conceptions such as gender (Butler 1999). Individuals are aligned on a body level; the body is the place where individuals are disciplined and governed, where politics and power are played out (Foucault 1995). Simultaneously, the reflections of phenomenologist Maurice Merleau-Ponty influenced scientific theories on embodiment: Embodied cognition has since become the basic principle to medicine, neuroscience, neurobiology, cognitive science, psychology, and other disciplines (Koch 2012). Considering all of this, the body becomes an important, if not *the* important, research object to understand social and cultural functioning.

Aesthetics as Academic Matter

As the body becomes an important academic matter, so do the senses as the interface between the body and its surroundings and as the part of the body, where the environment is perceived and where the environment can influence the body. To name this process, we can talk of aesthetics in its very reduced meaning of "sensory perception" derived from the Greek αἴσθησις, *aísthēsis*. Aesthetics highlight the role of the senses and their stimulation in meaning-making, in affecting worldviews and social and cultural participation, and in establishing power relations and dynamics (Mignolo and Vázquez 2013). Speaking of aesthetics thus comes with an understanding of cognition as embodied and situated. Bodies are framed, first, as shaped by culture and society and, second, as interdependent beyond individual body boundaries.

With its focus on aesthetics, my book is one among a growing quantity of publications and part of a particular recent branch of the study of religion: Aesthetics of Religion (AoR). The AoR approach attempts to bridge the gap between the theory and philosophy of cultural researchers and the practical and applied concepts and findings of scientists from other disciplines (Grieser and Johnston 2017a; Koch and Wilkens 2020). It builds upon philosophical elaborations on sensory perception while trying to incorporate theoretical concepts on the body in its materiality and an embodied cognition approach of medicine, neuroscience, cognitive studies, and psychology, all the while maintaining a cultural studies and study-of-religion perspective. AoR demonstrates the relations and interdependencies between the "sensory, cognitive and socio-cultural" effects of practice on "world-construction" (Grieser and Johnston 2017b, 2). AoR demands that the sensory effect of practice be set in the context of broader effects of practice on meaning-making and social and cultural actions. In consequence, there is no aesthetic research without interdisciplinarity, or, rather, aesthetic research is deeply interdisciplinary.

This book identifies, describes, analyzes, and explains neo-spiritualities as defined by their *neo-spiritual aesthetics*. By tracing the embodied transformation in Gaga from the sensory effective techniques applied in class to the experience as narrated by the participants, this book proceeds exactly along AoR's guiding idea while also making a contribution to further prove and develop AoR's theory and method in particular. As the book will demonstrate, Gaga indeed offers an effect on world construction, when participants are transformed and affected beyond their mere physical appearance and anatomy. This effect not only coincides with the social and cultural functions of practices traditionally termed religious, as discussed later, but also affects its participants similarly to the way in which religious practices affect their participants—via the senses until affecting perceptual orders. In addition, it is its aesthetic functioning and design, its techniques, that Gaga shares with neo-spiritualities, including those practiced in religious contexts. Practicing Gaga does not only align participants' bodies with a Gaga body or movement concept, but it aligns them with social and cultural ideas and values transmitted via practice. Investigating Gaga thus helps to understand the embodied effect and cultural and social functioning of a variety of other practices.

Core Term I: Aesthetic Cognizing Subject

The book is a detailed analysis of the triadic relationship between neo-spiritual practice, embodied transformation as the social and cultural shaping of practicing individuals, and its impacts on individual social and cultural participation. The first core term, which can help to illuminate these relations, is the *aesthetic cognizing subject*, introduced by Anne Koch (2020) as an ontology for researching aesthetics. For the aesthetic cognizing subject, cognition, and therefore behavior, evolves as a complex interplay between the processing of sensations and sensory information provided by environment or bodily states, and the constant updating of embodied perceptual orders guiding interaction with the cause of sensory information—an embodied cognition approach. Embodied cognition comes with several implications. Cognition happens in relation to sensory stimuli and is therefore intrinsically connected to the sources of sensory stimuli. Sensory information triggers sensomotoric reactions, which form the basis of sense-making. Sense-making and cognition thus depend not only on the sensory stimuli but also on the bodily perceived (re)action possibilities, which are bound to the anatomy and physiology of an individual body. The nature of the body as the interface between individual and sensation defines implicit cognitive mechanisms and activity and explicit cognition; sense-making is individual and body-bound (see Shapiro 2014). In this context, "culture" becomes a culturally specific "repertoire of bodily modes of interaction," which an individual gains through repetitive bodily participation in social and culturally specific actions and which comes to function as an underlying embodied norm provoking culture-specific, trained, and, therefore, easily accessible sensimotoric reaction (Soliman and Glenberg 2014). Practices can therefore, especially if repeated constantly, shape cognition and behavior by shaping the anatomy and physiology of bodies, by training attention and monitoring sensory stimuli, and by affecting the aesthetic cognizing subject's bodily modes of how to (re)act.

Core Term II: Body Knowledge

Theorizing the individual as an aesthetic cognizing subject and researching the cultural and social impacts of embodied transformation in practice now require a specific form of verbalization of embodied processes. The embodied can only be researched and analyzed with the help of a metalanguage, which offers descriptive tools and ways of verbalization. Here, I want to introduce Koch's *body knowledge* as a method for textualizing nonsemiotic data (see Koch 2007, 7, 11, 284). Body knowledge denotes the implicit, potentially explicit, or explicit actualization of the embodied state (117; 2015, 67). Moreover, it functions as a higher-order theoretical concept about the functioning of human bodies, as it connects embodied processes to emotional-habitual and cognitive output perceived by the individual (Koch 2020, 29). Body knowledge itself builds on lower-order concepts such as embodied cognition, where cognition is defined by bodily interaction with an environment (27); the existence of different sensory systems integrating information (28); or a body scheme, which structures and determines perception by providing perceptual guidelines (28-9). Koch proposes some concrete "religious aesthetical vocabulary" to talk about body knowledge. Her body knowledge vocabulary categories are, she accentuates, not thought of as a fixed manual, but rather an open one, which is open to being updated, specialized, and continued by further research (2007, 211)—this I did (for an overview see List 1).

First, I found (1) *body concept* and (2) *movement style* to be two crucial body knowledge categories as they could, in a second step via constant embodiment, influence the individual body scheme of Gaga participants. The body concept includes how the Gaga discourse understands the anatomy of the body and therefore influences how participants understand their bodies, whereas movement style denotes the movement that Gaga enables its participants to enact and that is presented to them directly and indirectly via movement instructions that are spoken as well as performed by the teacher. Moreover, while an embodied movement style can be observed by an outside viewer, the body concept is more likely to be caught by an outside listener. Both categories are united under the headline of *body topography*. Body topography becomes a carrier for the historical, social, and cultural discourses that Gaga practices incorporate into their own discourse and techniques and that are handed down to Gaga participants via enactment.

Second, I elaborated different categories to verbalize the implicit embodied transformation that participants undergo:

(3) *Proprioception:* Proprioception, also known as kinesthesia, is the sensory system that provides information about muscle tension, the positioning of body parts, and their placement in space. Sensory receptors are placed in muscles and tendons, and they work in combination with the vestibular sense situated in the ear (Koch 2007, 171).

(4) *Muscle tone and posture:* Muscle tone and posture is related to the experience of emotional states. Constant muscle tension or certain "bad" posture, for example, can be related to a situation of constant stress, constant arousal of the preparatory set, and the production of stress hormones. The embodied situation can be solved via the transformation of muscle tone and posture (see Gard et al. 2014; Payne and Crane-Godreau 2013).

(5) *Thermoregulation:* Thermoregulation is characterized as the "complex and mostly autonomous regulatory circuit" of elements such as blood flow or muscle tone (Koch 2017, 395). Like muscle tone and posture, thermoregulation is said to affect emotional states.

(6) *Tattooing:* Tattooing draws attention to the active *skin organ sense*, the organic nature and sensory function of the skin. Memories of sensation and attached experiences and individual interpretations are kept on the skin as tattoo but can also be revived by the skin. The skin is an organ, not a border (396).

(7) *Embodied imagination:* Verbal input as instructions given by the teacher in the form of a text and with a semiotic sense is not only processed explicitly—by thinking through and initiating action in consequence—but also directly and implicitly, as body knowledge is unconsciously created in reaction to the input. Not only because of the plentiful imagery used but also because of the metaphorical nature and embodied effect of language per se, Gaga instructions have an embodied effect (see Lakoff and Johnson 2003, 235). Or, as Einav Katan-Schmid (2017) writes, when evaluating the potential of Gaga instructions, "the body doesn't follow a metaphorical instruction, but rather enacts and realizes its comprehensive possibilities within a full engagement of body and mind" (277). Instructions appear to work via implicit imagination (see Traut and Wilke 2014): People sense what they are told before they enact the instruction—a mechanism as implicit as the functioning of covert imitation. Just perceiving by hearing is enough to provoke an embodied reaction. Instructions thus

come to function as sensational forms (see Meyer 2006), socially and culturally shaped perceptive patterns.

(8) *Covert imitation:* Social interaction and communication rely on covert imitation, the representation of others' perceptions within our own body, as it allows one to "sense" what others are feeling or about to do (Koch 2017, 395–6).

(9) *Embodied simulation:* Embodied imagination and covert imitation can be subsumed under the heading of embodied simulation. The observation of actions—be it visually or auditive, as well as the imagination of action—activates simulating mechanisms in "complex brain systems." At least the "low-level processing of observed actions" seems to be related to so-called mirror neuron brain areas. Mirror neurons, "rather than being immutable units from birth, … acquire their mirror properties through sensorimotor learning and change them by the same route" (Heyes and Catmur 2022, 161–3). They seem to help to simulate or map the actions "on the observers' motor representation of the same actions" and "on the same neurons controlling their execution in the observer's brain." Also, the bodily state and experience of empathy seem to be interrelated with embodied simulation (Gallese 2017a).

(10) *Prosthetic perception:* This is a special form of perception: the sensory perception of something distant or, better, the incorporation of a distant stimulus (outside the "reach" of most of the sensory organs, except the organs for exteroception such as vision or hearing) into the self-perception—perceiving as if the stimulus was directly happening to or, better, within the body. Koch specifies: "Prosthetic enlargement and the incorporation of tools, as well as the somatic activities of other actors … can all be displayed somatically in the embodied agent" (2017, 398). According to Koch, the embodied effect of rituals is to a large extent due to the body's ability to perceive prosthetically (2007, 283). For example, participants can perceive the actions of a ritual leader within their own bodies or even as their own (223).

(11) *Peripersonal space:* A special form of distal perception is the generation of perception in the so-called peripersonal space. The peripersonal space surrounds the human body and widens the body's direct sensory perception sphere, as, in this space, different sensory organs interact to build up an encompassing sensory system (222). "Body-ownership"

is extended beyond the physical body limits, and it can be extended or changed by the shift of sensory attention to specific areas of the body (Koch 2017, 399).

(12) *Flow:* Especially in the context of religious and cultural ritual studies, flow is a body knowledge category worth considering, as flow is what people experience as "enjoyable and intrinsically rewarding" (Csikszentmihalyi 2014, 233) and what becomes ascribed to an experience of "transcendence," for example. Flow, following Mihaly Csikszentmihalyi (2014), describes an experience phenomenon where people lose part of their self-sense—they feel as though they are part of the environment, and time and timing no longer matter to them—while they remain in control of their movement (137, 141).

The third and final body knowledge categories arose from the empirical data of participants:

(13) *Wow-moments:* As wow-moments, I label the highly positive emotional states that participants tell me about having experienced in the context of Gaga class.

(14) *Healing:* Participants mention the experience of physical and psychological "healing" provoked by Gaga practice. This means they experience their embodied state as better with the enactment of Gaga practice compared to how it was before. Gaga's healing effect consists of physical and psychological pain relief and an increase in physical and psychological well-being. Yet, not only is the embodied state "healed," as documented by the participants, but participants also create whole healing narratives around the embodied state. They explain both the causation of the healing effect in connection to Gaga practice and the life-changing impact of the healing experienced. The experienced embodied state of being healed and the healing narratives are apparently filtered by implicit and explicit, individual, and collective filters.

(15) *Central worldview:* Explicit and implicit body knowledge transformation itself seems to have the potential to become a "worldview"—not so much in terms of the extraordinary becoming an ontology, or epistemology, but indeed an axiology or praxeology to the ordinary (see Taves and Asprem 2016). Participants appear to take on different elements of Gaga practice as implicit and explicit perceptual cultural order.

List 1 Body Knowledge Inventory

(1) Body concept
(2) Central worldview
(3) Covert imitation
(4) Embodied imagination
(5) Embodied simulation
(6) Flow
(7) Healing
(8) Movement style
(9) Muscle tone and posture
(10) Peripersonal space
(11) Proprioception
(12) Prosthetic perception
(13) Tattooing
(14) Thermoregulation
(15) Wow-moments

I want to clarify that, on the one hand, because Gaga is a practice with set techniques, body knowledge is as individual as it is collective. Different bodies undergo a similar embodied transformation, leading to the creation of individual yet collective body knowledge. The general effect of Gaga practice on people, as introduced by the data generated in interviews, carries collective tendencies and similarities. This demonstrates the collective character of body knowledge, which is generated in Gaga practice and enforced and evaluated when experiences are exchanged in conversations. Talking of "Gaga body knowledge" therefore seems possible. On the other hand, some of the body knowledge production in Gaga practice is easily accessible, while other body knowledge and body knowledge dynamics, due to the mainly implicit embodied character, are more difficult to access.

More Terms

This leaves me to specify some more, perhaps not so core but very relevant concepts. By *practice(s)* I refer to situations of active bodily involvement in specific (religious) contexts, involving sensory stimulation, movement, and, consequently, bodily transformation. I understand practicing as having an extended social and cultural impact by generating "body groups" with a specific "style" produced in shared aesthetics (Blacking 1984). When I talk of *movement*, I very basically address all conscious and unconscious changes of the body state. To research, describe, and analyze practices, I need to capture them in their temporary and spatially fixed performances. Thus, I approach a practice's performance as *ritual* in the sense of Ronald L. Grimes (2014, 195): "embodied, condensed, and prescribed enactment." The term *technique(s)* is used in the sense of different technical methods applied to change the body and provoke body knowledge. Only with constant enactment, these technical methods can become embodied techniques of collectively shared body knowledge and embodied movement and behavior patterns of social nature and social value in the sense of Mauss's "techniques of the body" (1973) or Hamera's "dance techniques" (2007, 4–16).

As briefly mentioned above, when I talk of the *senses*, I do not refer to a traditional five senses model, but rather to an understanding of the senses as entangled systems dedicated to a specific task of sensing, such as proprioception and kinesthesia, nociception (pain perception), thermoception (temperature perception), humidity perception, or attached to specific body areas, such as the skin sensory system. Interoceptive sensory systems grasp body-internal sensations; exteroceptive sensory systems cover sensations provoked by a bodily outside. However, even talking of different sensory systems can be misleading. The bodily sensors, which capture the sensory information, while sortable "into electromagnetic receptors (photoreceptor, thermoreceptor), mechanoreceptors (hearing, touch, balance, osmoreceptor), and chemoreceptors (odorant receptor, gustatory receptor)" (Wicher 2010, 1), are not sortable into different clear-cut categories of sensation responsibilities. The systems are integrated, working together in the perceptive process—the sensory information of sensory receptors is cross-modally connected (Koch 2020, 28).

Finally, following Foucault (1972), you will find me talking of *discourses* to address all those collective, aesthetically effective practice elements, which are of social and cultural origin and of linguistic or nonlinguistic, semantic or nonsemantic, material and immaterial nature, and which stimulate the senses mostly indirectly, embodied in and as body scheme, or, in other words, techniques of the body, habitus, or somatic modes of attention. Discourses reflect in the sensescape of the practice environment, underlie the movement instructions, or other channels of communication. They are part of the individual preconditions of those practicing as well as perpetuated through practice itself.

Other Research on Gaga

My book is not the first scholarly writing on Gaga. However, it differs from the others not only by its research aim and research question but also by my scholarly background. My study-of-religion background provides a unique position in the academic discourse and adds a new research angle on Gaga's social and cultural impact. The book contributes to the conversation on Gaga, which until now has been dominated by dance studies scholars but has in the recent years started to spark interest in other humanities disciplines as well as in natural science. Dance scholar Deborah Friedes Galili, who has been working for Gaga Movement Ltd., provides the first important voice in terms of writings about Gaga. Not only did she, years ago, reflect on her Gaga experience in various blog posts on her web page, Dance in Israel (Friedes Galili n.d.), but she also wrote probably the most cited journal article on Gaga, "Gaga: Moving beyond Technique with Ohad Naharin in the Twenty-First Century" (Friedes Galili 2015). In her article, she characterized Gaga as a practice fitting the needs of the professional postmodern contemporary dancer.

Another important scholar to mention is dance philosopher Einav Katan-Schmid and her book, *Embodied Philosophy in Dance: Gaga and Ohad Naharin's Movement Research* (2016). Her work is of particular interest as she evolved Gaga as a philosophical practice—an "embodied philosophy." She departed from the similar assumptions about human perception and meaning-making and epistemology as myself and described dancing as a "perceptual process" (66, 88) and Gaga as a way to "enquire ... movement habits and ... schemata of perception" (25), provoking a "reformation" of implicit and explicit "habitual embodied knowledge" (55). Katan-Schmid accentuated the metaphorical functioning of Gaga instructions as "enactive" procedures (51): "The body doesn't follow a metaphorical instruction, but rather enacts and realizes its comprehensive possibilities within a full engagement of body and mind" (Katan-Schmid 2017, 277, cited from her article "Dancing Metaphors"). Apart from this, Katan-Schmid analyzed and pointed out how the increase in somatic attention and awareness in Gaga practice facilitates its "philosophical" and knowledge-reforming potential (2016, 14). Gaga, she mentioned, has the potential to become a physical habitus (165–9).

The third work of particular interest in the context of Gaga is the writing of Meghan Quinlan. As a scholar from the critical dance studies background, she approached Gaga using a methodology similar to that of my own research: ethnographic research focusing mainly on professional dancers at

Gaga classes in Tel Aviv, the main method being participant observation and conducting interviews. In her PhD thesis (2016), Quinlan investigated Gaga's incorporation of specific cultural and social discourses and values as explicitly discussed and implicitly practiced. She focused on the (de)colonial aspects and possibilities, the specific Israeli nature of Gaga in terms of culture, society, and politics, and the neoliberal characteristics of Gaga's aesthetics. Quinlan has continued her observations in several articles, where, for example, she framed Gaga as a "neoliberal metatechnique" (Quinlan 2017).

Short Outlook

The book is organized along a spatial metaphor: I start by describing the surroundings of aesthetical relevance and of sensory stimulant and affecting function, working my way, literally, from distant surroundings closer to the body of the aesthetically cognizing subjects participating in Gaga class, until taking into account the enactment of movement by the individuals themselves, and finishing with a close look at individual subjective experience and resetting this experience again into the broader space of "surrounding" aesthetics. Like the body knowledge categories, this is, of course, only one possible and exemplary way to deal with an encompassing aesthetic analysis. The readers of my book are encouraged to remind themselves throughout that, in the context of embodied cognition, "in real life," there is no such thing as a separation into surroundings like a ritual environment, the individual body, and the individually experienced and narrated, but all come together as aesthetics in body knowledge.

Before I start my journey along the neo-spiritual aesthetics of Gaga class, my readers will find a small "interlude" very dear to me. I dedicate it to my research method of body-focused ethnography in the hope that others can make use of it in their own research. I then turn to the elaboration of Gaga's aesthetics. Chapter 1 introduces Gaga as an Israeli, or at least an Israeli-originating, social-cultural phenomenon. Social and cultural discourses and the place of Gaga therein help to shed light on the historical origin of Gaga's aesthetics and the background of the participants entering class and being exposed to them, as the aesthetics are closely related to the social-cultural background. What follows is an aesthetic analysis of class and its most important aesthetically effective components: The focus of Chapter 2 is on the description of the ritual environment. Chapter 3 is dedicated to Gaga's body image and the movement possibilities offered to participants, explicitly in a discussed and enacted body image and implicitly in movement range and possibilities. The body topography is one way in which Gaga influences self-perception in the sense of body perception of participants. Chapter 4 then examines Gaga instructions and tries to answer how verbal and physical guidance affects body knowledge even before movement. This is followed by Chapter 5, which describes Gaga techniques and sheds light on how the enactment of guidance as animation and movement affects body knowledge. The analysis of aesthetic effect is completed in Chapters 6–9 by the embodied change as described by the participants. In Chapter 6 I take time for a close look at the characteristics of experience narration and the connection of modes of narration in aesthetics and experience. Chapter 7 depicts how body knowledge transformation in class produces wow-moments as individual yet collective emotions, and Chapter 8 shows how body knowledge changes bodies beyond the one-hour timeframe as a "therapeutic effect." Chapter 9 captures the narrative variations of how participants take on Gaga as their explicit perceptual-order worldview in biographical narrative episodes or when recounting experience. Finally, I end the book with a summary of the most important results and an evaluation of the value of such research.

The reader will find the book addressing three different issues: First, it establishes an aesthetic analysis hinting toward the different aesthetically effective elements that must be covered to understand the aesthetics of a particular practice. All the while, the book centers around the individual body—the body as body knowledge uniquely yet collectively preconditioned, the body that sensory perceives and transforms with perception and that, being the base of an individual's meaning-making, introduces changes to experiencing social and cultural participation. Second, quasi "on the way," the book demonstrates how bodies, practices, and aesthetics can and need to be researched with a body focus, and what can be gained from engaging the researcher's own body in order to be able to access the body in focus. Third, it addresses neo-spirituality and shows how neo-spiritual practices are characterizable and, in a society and culture that centers around experience, *only* sensibly capturable by their aesthetics. Ultimately, the research and the book that stems from it aim to be, above all, an encompassing analysis of neo-spiritual aesthetics, exemplified on Gaga practice, with a cultural studies and study-of-religion perspective—no more and no less. The hope is that the research results, as unfolded and conceptualized in the following pages, will help in understanding the effect of cultural and religious practices similar to Gaga and thereby moving beyond Gaga-centered research. My intention and dream are to pave way for an understanding of neo-spiritual phenomena by their distinct neo-spiritual aesthetics.

Meanwhile, in the language of Gaga, "enjoy the effort" of reading and "find pleasure" in it.

Interlude: A Body-Focused Research Method

Based on my own experiences, I propose and introduce a *body-focused ethnography* to gather the data needed for an aesthetic analysis. The body-focused ethnography combines the methods of *participant observation* and qualitative data provided by the *narration of participants*. Participant observation entails active participation in rituals accompanied by bodily self-observation of all kinds of sensory stimulations and impressions of body knowledge arising in this context guided by specific criteria (Table 1). This dataset is then set in relation to the narrated self-observations and experiences of others in the field.

My own body-focused ethnography took place in the field and focused on the aesthetics of daily Gaga/people classes held at the Suzanne Dellal Center in Tel Aviv. Data collection consisted of different stays in Tel Aviv and participation in nearly all available classes held in the mornings and evenings. The data collection period extended over one-and-a-half years, from December 2016 to June 2018, and was composed of four stays in Israel, three of approximately two weeks and one of a month. Participant observation meant that I actively participated in Gaga/people classes, and I observed the sensory effect of what was happening in class as it affected my own body. I looked for different kinds of aesthetic data that I could gain by sensing.[1] I performed the instructions as given by the teacher and tried to imitate the movement of the teacher as asked. My own body became a medium for the embodied effect of practicing Gaga.[2] I paid attention to incoming information via proprioceptive, interoceptive including nociceptive, visual, auditive, and skin sensory systems. Participant observation began with entering the field, arriving at the building, signing in for class, getting dressed, greeting and talking to other participants, entering the classroom, and waiting for class to start. The central part of participant observation was class itself. The relevant observation did not end at the end of class; after class, I continued to talk to people—still in the dance studio, the dressing rooms, on the way out, and outside the building. After morning classes, I usually went for a coffee with

Table 1 Observation Criteria during Participant Observation

Observation criteria	Content	Example
Basic facts	Date, time, teacher, place	Weather, studio, number of people, ...
Self-reflection (before and after)	Emotional-habitual state or sensory information on the embodied self at the beginning and end of class	Happy/sad/satisfied/..., sore muscles, injuries
Sensory information		
Exteroception	Interaction with the teacher	Not only what instructions are given and how the teacher moves but also the teacher's mood, the ability to connect to them via empathy, ...
	Interaction with participants	Exchange of smiles, how others move, extraordinary actions of others, ...
	Interaction with the environment	Air-conditioning, music, slippery/sticky floor, lack of space, ...
Interoception	Heart rate, body temperature, blood flow	Felt state of exhaustion/stress/calmness, sweating, fast/slow breath, ...
Skin sense	State	Sweating, cold/warm, stretched/soft, ...
	Touch	Cloth, floor, air circulation and temperature, body parts, ...
Proprioception	Body parts moving	Flesh/bones/skin, foot, hand, fingers, pelvis, chest, spine, shoulder blades, shoulder, elbow, head, ...
	Movement qualities ("inside observer")	Taking up a lot of/little space, moving through the room, effort, ...
Emotional-habitual transformation during class	Physical	Muscle tension, pain, headache
	Psychological	Happiness, relaxation, stress, sadness

Table 1 Observation Criteria during Participant Observation (continued)

Observation criteria	Content	Example
Ritual elements		
Actions	Instructions	What is said, …
	Side-actions	Going to the washroom, cellphone ringing, participants talking, …
	Movement qualities ("outside observer")	Fast/slow, staying in one spot/moving through space, taking up (or not taking up) a lot of space, …

some fellow Gaga participants, where I gained a great deal of additional insight into the experiences they had in the class we had all just taken or into their relationship to Gaga in general.

In consequence, the data was originally of a highly subjective nature connected to my own body as a participant observer. It gained in objectivity, comparability, and relevance, first, because I compared my data to the experience communicated by other participants. Second, I employed a standardized and preestablished observation method. Inspired by Koch's "aesthetic field record" (Koch in Laack and Tillessen 2020, 293–4), my notes on Gaga classes involved *observation criteria* (Table 1) divided into three parts. The first part contained basic facts such as date, time, number of people in class. The second part contained a self-reflection on how I felt on that day and on my psychological-physiological perceived state before and after class. In the third part, I kept track of

- the sensory information I perceived from different sensory systems, such as interoception, proprioception, and exteroception—a particularly important sensory system being the skin, as often addressed in Gaga practice;
- the emotions evoked by and connected to the sensory information;
- particular body parts involved in movement and sensory perception during class;
- my embodied state during class such as the ability to keep concentration on the task, mind-wandering, and "just being";
- the space in the sense of placing special focus on what I perceived as environmental stimuli, such as the cold air from an air-conditioner, construction work outside, or the beautiful sunset;

- the connections made with others in class, such as empathetic connections and embodied simulation, while also reflecting on feelings of disapproval and interpersonal communication via facial expressions;
- and the different ritual actions such as the instructions and movement of the teacher initiating movement actions, movements performed by participants in their different qualities, the course of different movements performed during class, and the movement "narrative."

I kept all the information in field notes, which I took after finishing each class, as class rules prohibited stopping throughout. With time spent in the field doing participant observation, probably due to the repetitive ritual patterns and the degree of embodiment that came with it, the amount and detail of information I could remember and was able to script down increased significantly. I tried different media for recording: typed notes on my laptop, oral notes recorded on my cell phone and only later translated to writing, and handwritten notes in a notebook—my remaining preference. I had enough time to analyze my field notes and start writing up my results during my time in Tel Aviv, still practicing Gaga daily. The simultaneous involvement in the field and evaluation seemed to help me sensorially "re-feel" and "relive" the notes and facilitate the aesthetic research aim. The in-field exchanges with other Gaga practitioners were as significant for the interpretation of my dataset as they were for its objectification. Participation in additional Gaga workshops in Munich and elsewhere allowed for a reassessment of the data when the time in the field was already over.

I find it important to reflect on some things that seem to have influenced the output of my participant observation: First, my somatic awareness I have developed over many years of dance training enabled me to remain (relatively) self-reflexive about what I sensed and what I felt and experienced in consequence. Second, my knowledge of contemporary dance and somatic movement practices helped me single out the body knowledge, which would connect Gaga to other practices. Third, by educating myself about anatomy and the embodied effect of movement, muscle tone, and posture on the emotional state through reading and observing, I became aware of the embodied processes and former tacit body knowledge and was able to locate and find ways to name embodied processes. Fourth, during my research, I went through different stages of participation. My body naturally transformed with participant observation of Gaga practice, which involved bodily participation in ritual actions. Through the enaction of movement and sensory awareness training exercises, I could observe how my explicit and implicit body knowledge changed. Not only did I become physically stronger, but I also became aware of body parts that I would usually not pay attention to. When walking down the streets of Tel Aviv, I would find myself enacting movements from class. I even woke up one night to find myself enacting the movements in my bed. Fifth, a specific task was to constantly separate my own experience from the experiences of others. This worked for the experience put into words by other participants; however, it was difficult to put into effect when it came to the implicit body knowledge that I received during class via embodied simulation from the teachers' movements and instructions. Sixth, along the same lines, I found it also especially challenging to not only script down the verbal instructions given by the teacher during class. I experienced a lack of words to describe my body knowledge beyond the vocabulary gifted to me in class and also failed to remember my experienced body knowledge wherein I perfectly remembered the instructions. Seventh, my full-body engagement helped me identify with experiences of my research objects, namely, the Gaga participants and their sensations and feelings, which they told me about, even though I might not have felt exactly the same in specific situations. Ultimately, I tried to copy down the given Gaga instructions as true in wording as possible. However, as I had to rely on my own memory and did neither audio- nor videotape classes, the Gaga instructions and vocabulary I list and harness in terms of fair academic use throughout this book are not, cannot, and do not want to be perfect reproductions and replications of what was said by teachers. I use them to hint toward and gain access to body knowledge, and by no means to canonize Gaga vocabulary, which constantly changes and evolves from class to class and teacher to teacher.

The data from participant observation was completed through *nine qualitative narrative interviews, four experience diaries*, and several *in-field conversations* (List 2). I recruited the participants of interviews and experience diaries in the context of participant observation and in the field of Gaga classes. All participants were participating in several of the same Gaga classes as myself. In-field conversations arose in the field—often before or after class in the changing rooms, in the classroom, or at a café close by over a cup of coffee, and I took the time to totally immerse myself in the field and in the community of participants. The combined sources provided me with information on the embodied effect of practicing Gaga as was perceived by the participants. In addition to participant-related data, I held three interviews with Gaga teachers, who mainly provided background information on the ritual characteristics of Gaga practice.

List 2 (Pseudonymized) Human Data Sources and Protagonists of the Book

(1) *Ada* (in-field conversation, April 2017)
(2) *Ariel* (interview, January 2017)
(3) *Ayala* (interview, June 2017)
(4) *Dafna* (experience diary, October 2017)
(5) *Dana* (interview, January 2017)
(6) *Eli* (interview, January 2017)
(7) *Ester* (interview, January 2017)
(8) *Hannah* (in-field conversation, December 2016; interview, January 2017)
(9) *Idan* (interview, June 2018)
(10) *Iris* (in-field conversation, September 2017)
(11) *Maya* (experience diary, June 2018)
(12) *Mira* (experience diary, October 2017)
(13) *Noam* (experience diary, October 2017)
(14) *Rahel* (in-field conversation, September 2017)
(15) *Sara* (interview, January 2017)
(16) *Shira* (interview, September 2017)
(17) *Talia* (interview, July 2017)
(18) *Tamar* (interview, October 2017)
(19) *Uri* (interview, December 2016)

Of the nine participants I interviewed, including the four participants who kept an experience diary, the youngest was twenty-six years old and the oldest was sixty-seven years old. At the time of data collection, all participants were living in Tel Aviv, holding an Israeli passport. Only some explicitly mentioned their Jewish background, but all of them could be characterized as Israeli-Jews.[3] Some participants would also mention their English, Russian, American, or Argentinian family background. They could be identified as Andrew Dawson's (2013) "new middle class": fully involved in society as consumers and producers, in search of individual fulfillment, engaged in an ongoing redefinition of "self" and identity, open to plural social and cultural diversity, and partaking in Israeli and global high culture and high-culture knowledge discourses shaped by education and the arts they consume (Dawson 2013, 124–37). Their professional occupations ranged from art, design, and other creative service offerings, high-tech industry, psychological and social services, to somatics and mindful movement practices such as yoga.

In *interviews*, I invited Gaga participants, in an open way, to talk about Gaga, their experience with it, and what Gaga "meant" to them. Interviews would often start from a situation where we had been already conversing about Gaga—especially in after-class interviews, due to the exchange in the studio, the changing rooms, or "on the way." If sensed and felt transformations, "changes" experienced in the context of Gaga, did not come up during their discussions, then I asked participants about them directly. Another topic I addressed was how participants experienced the enactment of body knowledge, different bodily states, in class. People were aware of my background as a researcher and often, while reflecting on their experience, contributed interesting and important thoughts to the research on their own, which helped to further elaborate the research question and focus. Talking in English seemed natural to all of them. English was the mother tongue or second or first language to some, and an often-used language to others. Interviews with participants were held in different contexts—four after class, one directly before class, and four outside the Gaga class context—and they were located in different places in Tel Aviv. Only one interview was conducted in a nonpublic space, a meeting room; all the other interviews were held in public spaces such as cafés, a park or square, or in the museum, but participants did not seem to be restricted at all by this fact. While the nine interviews with participants are definitely "illustrative rather than representative," as Grimes (2014, 119) formulates, the qualitative data was enough to help me single out the different facets of neo-spiritual aesthetics because similar data was found among different participants. All of those interviewed signed a consent form, in which they were informed about my study and the research-bound use and publication of the data. The audio-recorded data was gradually anonymized and pseudonymized. When quoting interviews throughout this book, the expression of emotional states or side information affecting text's understanding is noted within parentheses.

As a second set of qualitative narratives, I requested the participants to write out *experience diaries* by handing out experience diary consent forms similar to those of the interviews. To keep the experience data format open yet be able to fulfill the specific data purposes for which they were intended, the instructions for experience diaries were as follows:

Please write down after class: What did you experience in Gaga class?

Just to give an example, keywords used could be: body, different body parts, sensations, mind, emotions, feelings, teacher, other people etc.

You could write down only one sentence or many more—it totally depends on how you feel like …
A diary over five classes in a row would be ideal, but it will also help me a lot, if you keep it for only one. (Experience diary consent form, 2017)

The semi-structured aspect of the interviews was incorporated into the experience diary by providing keyword examples. Five classes seemed to be a useful number to gain an insight into the meaning system of the writing participant, as one class could be compared to another, and experience influences from outside of class appeared to be more likely to be detected. Data from the experience diary was pseudonymized upon reception. I kept the wording exactly as written and corrected misspellings only if necessary for understanding.

Finally, the Café Dallal, located close by, played the most important role in additional conversational data collection. It was popular among participants, teachers, and Batsheva dancers. After morning Gaga class, participants would decide to sit down together at the café for a coffee—or meet there incidentally, as everybody was going there—and I would usually join them. Sitting there, we often reflected and discussed experiences during the previous Gaga class or on Gaga in general. The situation at the café helped me become part of the field I was researching, and I made friends and got to know people closely while I gained insights and collected data from in-field conversations. The *in-field conversations* there, as well as in and around the Suzanne Dellal Center, such as in the changing rooms, washrooms, and the dance studio, and in the context of a Gaga workshop in the "desert" lasting several days, provided embodied experience "impressions," which completed the data from interviews and experience diaries. I did not audio-record the conversations but jotted parts of them down in my field diary.

The research method of body-focused ethnography acknowledges the impossibility of leaving out the body or, rather, an interdisciplinary and entangled understanding of the body in research focused on the effect of practice, yet—knowing that the researcher's expertise is as a cultural studies and study-of-religion scholar—attempts to evaluate and establish possibilities of how this can be done critically by using the methodical toolbox of a cultural studies and study-of-religion researcher and, in the case of this project, ethnographer. I hope I could demonstrate that body-focused ethnography is worthwhile and feasible.

Part 1

Gaga Class: Aesthetics in Creation

1

Influential Culturescape

Gaga's aesthetics are not of singular nature; practicing Gaga initiates embodied transformation whose experience is not exclusive to participants of Gaga classes. Other practices create similar effects, and it is presumed that participants could experience similar effects in other practices. This is because, on the one hand, Gaga answers or better reacts to the existing social and cultural state of the art—be it directly by its approach or indirectly by the way in which participants living in contemporary society understand it. On the other hand, Gaga practice grew from other body practices, whose techniques it employs and which therefore influence how the body is transformed. It implicitly carries these practices' historical baggage. Here, it is unimportant whether Naharin, for example, as the founder of Gaga himself, reflects on this baggage of historical discourses. Gaga's aesthetics have a history. In consequence, it is Gaga's aesthetics that place and relate Gaga in history and make it an active carrier of body-related discourses and a communicator of body images, especially via the creation of a particular body knowledge. Gaga's aesthetics become and create (body) archives. Thus, to understand the aesthetics of Gaga as a cultural and social phenomenon, it is not enough to describe a Gaga class; it is also not enough to question Gaga's body and movement concepts or the techniques it uses, nor to listen to what Gaga participants have to tell. Instead, it is important to establish the setting for Gaga, to describe the social and cultural context from which it arises and to which it contributes, and to understand its place within this context. The following pages are an attempt to point out the most important characteristics of this context within which Gaga is embedded and which define not only Gaga's aesthetics but also, to a certain extent, neo-spiritual aesthetics in general.

1.1 Ohad Naharin and the Gaga Story

The *Dance Magazine* mentioned Ohad Naharin (1952–) as one of "The Most Influential People in Dance Today" (Stahl 2017). The choreographic work of the former artistic director and now house choreographer of the Batsheva Dance Company, seated in Tel Aviv, is well known to dance enthusiasts around the globe. Naharin became artistic director of the Batsheva Dance Company in 1990. He developed Gaga "searching for a means of executing choreographic ideas with his dancers," and "anyone familiar with Gaga will, in some pieces, notice specific features and qualities of this unique language of movement" (Aschenbrenner 2019, 14). Only in 2001 public Gaga classes—for those other than the company members—began to be offered, and they quickly became popular (Friedes Galili 2015, 365) because of their relation to Batsheva and the "guru" Naharin, as participants call him. For many young professional dancers, the possibility of entering the Batsheva Ensemble or even the Batsheva Dance Company, or simply being skilled in Naharin's repertoire, continues a goal to be achieved, because it adds to their contemporary dancer market value. They partake in Gaga classes, especially Gaga intensives, where repertoire and "methodics" are taught in addition, because participation increases their value as dancers and their chance to be "seen" by Batsheva (see Quinlan 2016, 189–90, 193–7). For nonprofessional dancers, Gaga functions as a leisure-time activity with certain benefits—also here, the connection to Batsheva and Naharin makes Gaga particularly attractive. Practicing Gaga becomes the reason for both professional and nonprofessionals to travel to Israel. Though Gaga was visibly tied to Ohad Naharin, the company, Gaga Movement Ltd., had, during the years of my research period, been led by Yossi Naharin, Ohad Naharin's brother, along with a team that decided on organization, marketing, and finance issues.[1]

When the story of Ohad Naharin and Gaga is told, be it by scholars such as Friedes Galili (2015) or by popular media such as the documentary *Mr. Gaga* (Heymann 2015), different motifs or characteristics are pointed out, which influence how Gaga is seen and depicted in popular discourse and thus understood by the public. It is also these characteristics that connect and relate Gaga to its social and cultural environment: First, Gaga is strongly connected to Naharin's choreographic fingerprint. Friedes Galili states that Gaga primarily fulfilled the purpose of enabling Naharin his own movement research and development of ideas. More, "class of Ohad," later called Gaga, has functioned as Naharin's medium by which to communicate his choreographic ideas to the performing dancers (Friedes Galili 2015, 365–6). Second, the movement ideas behind Gaga are said to have been developed over a long time and in a natural, nontraditional way. Naharin did not gain his basic ideas on how to move from structured and professional dance training, which he only started quite late in his life compared to other dance professionals. Instead, he was most influenced movement-wise by the playful movement education he received from his mother, who was trained in music and dance (363). According to Friedes Galili, Naharin himself sees the establishment of Gaga "as a continuous process that started long before his first structured dance training" (365). Naharin is also generally presented as a natural movement and dance talent, who became a dancer without completing the traditional way of dance training. He became part of the entertainment troupe of the Israeli army and sang and danced as well as choreographed there without proper education. After his army time, he continued his dance career by entering the professional Batsheva Dance Company in 1974 in an unconventional way: His mother just arranged for him to partake in class (363). By a lucky coincidence, Martha Graham was choreographing for Batsheva at the time, and she seemed to have been so impressed by his ability to move that she not only chose him for the creation of a specific solo part but also paved his way to New York by an invitation (363). Third, Naharin, however, is never depicted as someone without sufficient expertise and knowledge in dance: He trained with Martha Graham and at the Juilliard School in New York. He was influenced by the modern dance Limón technique and took ballet classes (363). Naharin incorporated the following from them: "the elegance ever-present in ballet, the sense of weight that characterizes Limón, and the emphasis on moving from the pelvis along with the texture, stretch, and passion prevalent in Graham technique" (364). Untrained, yet natural as Naharin was as a ballet dancer, he even danced for famous ballet choreographer Maurice Béjart (364). As the "most influential choreographer I ever worked with," he mentions Gina Buntz with her "multilayered tasks" (364). Naharin gained additional body and movement knowledge in his recovery from "a severe injury that nearly paralyzed his left leg and his subsequent back surgery," where he practiced Pilates and t'ai chi and trained with a physiotherapist (365). Fourth, both written and oral discourses shared by Gaga teachers point out that Naharin is still constantly evolving his movement ideas and Gaga. Teachers will fill their classes with "new ideas" gained in a "class with Ohad." Friedes Galili cites Naharin himself: "It's still evolving, it's still so open; it's still so open to change its mind" (379). As a Gaga teacher said during a Gaga workshop in Munich in August 2016, "Nobody knows what will be if he is not there anymore." Fifth, though nowadays Gaga training is well established with high-culture concert dancers, it has been depicted as "an alternative approach," "moving beyond the confines of traditional technique and embracing an ethos of openness and evolution" (379). Sixth, the movie *Mr. Gaga* (Heymann 2015) highlights Naharin's injury as a milestone in his life and in the development of Gaga. Gaga, in consequence, was popularly connected to the healing narrative of Naharin and thus gains discursive healing potential itself. This occurred unaffected by quotes such as those by Friedes Galili, for whom "the causal claim that Naharin developed Gaga in response to a back injury" ranges under "perpetuated myths and misunderstandings" (2015, 361).[2] Seventh, Naharin's childhood in a Kibbutz is a biographical detail and personal characteristic that does not particularly impact the written discourse but impacts oral discourse on Naharin and Gaga. Participants claimed that his Kibbutz background gave Gaga a "local" touch. Others considered Naharin to have a "kibbutz arrogancy" and show-off nature— to him not only a "kibbutznik" but "very Israeli" trait. Eli saw Naharin's Israeli biography reflected in Gaga. He trailed of: "Also, it's a complex country and it's a state of it's in a constant state of war, it's open and liberal and it's closed and religious and all in the same time … I guess he would if he would have grown in a different atmosphere, he wouldn't have …" (Eli). Then, there were those such as Ester who revealed an ambiguous relation to "Israeli," underlining that even though Naharin developed Gaga influenced by his childhood environment in the kibbutz, Gaga itself was to be seen independent from it: "(very agitated) For me it has nothing to do with Israel! Now, I am sure biographically it does, but it doesn't really interest me" (Ester). Regardless of how controversially Naharin's kibbutz origins are discussed, they have been circulating as common knowledge, and thus influencing the talk on Gaga.

1.2 The Historic Origins of Gaga's Aesthetics

It is possible to understand Gaga in relation to a larger cultural and social historic movement concerning the body. Gaga inherited its aesthetics from body and dance practices, which had a significant moment of growth during the nineteenth and twentieth centuries and developed from and along particular ideologies, such as the worth of the healthy and strong body, the belief in primal movement and following the flow of movement, the promotion of a holistic body image, or the centralization of bodily awareness and body sense (von Steinaecker 2000). Perceptual orders were shaped alongside, thereby influencing how bodies of self and others were understood. Gaga carries aesthetical heritage of these developments. Gaga's body topography as well as its techniques function as archives, in the sense of repositories, and ongoing dispositifs of historic discourses and aesthetics.

Karoline von Steinaecker (2000) situates the beginnings of these aesthetics with Jean-Jacques Rousseau (1712–78). She writes that "'healthy' had been used until then almost only as an adjective. Healthy was something given by God. Now, however, man detached himself from his religious ties and health was transferred to the human being" (31; translated by author). Not much later, for example, Johann Heinrich Pestalozzi (1746–1827) and others called on for the recreation of an ideally balanced, healthy but also productive, holistic body state with the help of gymnastics and exercises, thereby already highlighting the importance of bodily awareness (32).

In their wake, "An unprecedented enthusiasm for athletic and gymnastic disciplines swept Britain and Europe during the nineteenth century," Mark Singleton (2010, 81) writes in his work, where he demystifies the historical origins of contemporary yoga practice. Furthermore, "The nineteenth century saw an eruption of European interest in the cultivation of the body as a means of regenerating the moral and physical mettle of the nation" (82). The body came into focus as a means to recreate strong nations built from strong bodies: "nationalistic 'man-making' gymnastics" (82). "States" also became obsessed with the improvement of collective national and racial bodies (84). On the other hand, popular European and North American discourse made the body important to the individual development as well: It was then that physical fitness, psychological well-being, and optimum physical and intellectual performance became connected. Health was redefined in the nineteenth century. Slim and sporty became healthy. The belief spread that physical and psychological healing could be reached through conditioning and training the body, and this led to the establishment of healing practices and the body being approached holistically (Merta 2003, 429–39). The term "physical culture" emerged at the end of the nineteenth century, and popular discourse promoted the individual "benefits of bodily cultivation through gymnastics and weight resistance exercises" (Singleton 2010, 83), while the "Lamarckian mythos" circulated "that the individual could manipulate his or her own evolutionary processes" and pass this genetic change on to his or her decedents (98). A man who had the willpower to change his or her body had positive characteristics and was a valiant citizen (Merta 2003, 525), while the bodily transformation allowed freedom from "bourgeois constraints and disease" (von Steinaecker 2000, 45; translated by author).

In her work, historian Sabine Merta (2003) focuses on the German "Lebensreformer" movement. She describes how "Körperreformbewegungen," body reformation movements such as the sports movement, or "Ausdruckstanz," expressive dance, were established at that time and how they participated in the body discourse. From what she writes, it is possible to discern the great impact the body practices had in establishing the new body paradigms as perceptual orders. The approaches of the practices in England and Germany, for example, differed slightly: In England, the creation of a fit and strong body and performance improvement of the individual became the reason to practice, whereas in Germany, the "hygienic, aesthetic, strengthening" body practices flourished. Furthermore, Merta points out that the transition and boundaries between gymnastics and dance at that time were fluent, and all body practices of the 1920s worked toward the creation of a beautiful "aesthetic-slim" and thus healthy body, and they saw a connection between bodily and mental states or rather worked with the body-mind unit as a whole (426, 470).

Of huge impact on the initiators of body practices at that time were the ideas of the French François Delsarte (1811–71) and his American pupils Genevieve Stebbins (1857–1934) and Steele MacKaye (1842–94), who asked for natural holistic movement and connected emotional-habitual states to the movement of different body parts. Delsarte established an order of movement, where the body was structured in three parts, namely, head, torso, and appendages, and the torso, for example, was structured in the subcategories of chest, back, inner organs, and pelvis (Merta 2003, 442–4). He also established connections between voice, breath, and movement (Singleton 2010, 144). Building on Delsarte, MacKaye believed that the body needed to be trained in a total way, so the "soul" could fully express itself through movement, and therefore established exercises practicing tension and its release. She promoted Delsarte's Aesthetic Gymnastics. Delsarte's pupil Stebbins, on the other hand, combined breath and movement; she taught that tension and relaxation could be reached by using the breath the right way. Her techniques were framed as Harmonic Gymnastics (Merta 2003, 444–5). As source for her movements and dances, Stebbins—other than Delsarte—used antique statues and the nineteenth-century fashion of statue-posing. In contrast to motionless imitation of postures, she opted for an imitation of the statues as living beings—for an imitation of body knowledge, one could say—beyond the visible surface (Mullan 2020, 106). Grounded in her studying of classical art and literature, Stebbins' solos were themed as personifying "ancient" female personalities, reinterpreting "ancient" dances from Egyptian and Greek realm (98). Stebbins was accredited with "a veritable Delsarte craze" in North America

(Singleton 2010, 144). However, most importantly, as Kelly Jean Mullan observes, "It is important to clarify more specifically that *Stebbins* created the actual framework for new dance, seeing as Delsarte did not work with dancers" (Mullan 2020, 109).

Seemingly inspired by Stebbins were Ruth St. Denis (1879–1968), who later founded a dance school with Ted Shawn (1891–1972) as well as dancer Isadora Duncan (1877–1927) (Mullan 2020, 99–100). In the United States, St. Denis and Shawn produced their own idea of "Oriental" dance and promoted orientalism in the world of dance at the same time as other "Asian-inspired techniques such as Transcendentalism, Theosophy, modern Vedānta, and, of course, yoga" arose (Singleton 2010, 144). Martha Graham (1894–1991), "the founder of modern dance," established her movement ideas in the same social and cultural environment of the 1920s, including Delsarte's ideas. In Europe, Bess Mensendieck (1864–1957) and the German Hedwig Kallmeyer (1881–1976) developed Stebbins' gymnastics further toward a practice producing female slimness as well as physical and psychological fitness of the degenerated female body. Besides, Kallmeyer seems to have shaped the still-persisting sports theory, which states that movement of the limbs is to be started from the center of the body, arms from the shoulder and legs from the hip area (Merta 2003, 445–50).

The second important player, after Delsartism, in the development of movement practices and dance, especially German expressive dance, was Swiss music teacher Émile Jacques-Dalcroze (1865–1950) and his Rhythmic Gymnastics. Jacques-Dalcroze's Rhythmic Gymnastics itself was influenced by Delsarte's Aesthetic Gymnastics and tried to improve bodily "defaults" and move away from standardized "mechanic" movements. He established the training of isolated limb movement and of the spontaneous movement reaction to music, and he developed rhythmic breath exercises (Merta 2003, 451–4). Traditional German gymnastics later originated from there, significantly influenced by Rudolf Bode (1881–1970), who proclaimed a strengthening of the weak body as a strengthening of the mental condition. The natural body power should be developed, and man should be trained to control his natural power. In these gymnastics, movement was originated from the pelvis (456–8).

In this environment, Duncan did not recognize a difference between gymnastics and dance. Instead, to her, gymnastics had preceded dance to come before to prepare the body "aesthetically-harmoniously" (Merta 2003, 461). For dancers such as Duncan, dance and body movement became a possibility to connect to oneself, and self-awareness came to be a source of inspiration. She focused on her solar plexus as the source of movement, which enabled a free movement of the upper body, arms, head, and facial expression (441). Three more important players in the field of historic aesthetics of dance should be mentioned: First, Rudolf von Laban (1879-1958). He was a body theorist and movement analysist who also aimed at the recreation of harmony between body and soul in movement. He spent time for movement research in Monte Verità, which became the meeting point for like-minded alternative and back-to-nature–oriented artists of all kinds. Second, Mary Wigman (1886-1973). The dancer, choreographer, and dance teacher spread the word and knowledge of German expressive dance globally and became Laban's assistant (462). Third and not least, Elsa Gindler (1885-1961). Gindler is accredited as the founder of somatics by the somatics movement itself. She trained in Stebbins' Harmonic Gymnastics via Kallmeyer, substituted for Kallmeyer as a teacher, and was involved in the foundation of the "Gymnastikbund," German Gymnastics Federation spanning schools of Kallmeyer, Bode, Laban, Dalcroze, Mesendieck, and herself and thus uniting all the different movement approaches. Gindler, however, traded Stebbins' emphasis on holistic expression via movement for a focus on interoception. Her school produced a very distinct strand of teachers focusing on bodily, somatic, sensory awareness. In contrast to Laban and Bode, for example, Gindler stopped running her school during the Third Reich, opposing Hitler's regime and refusing to adjust her teaching to Nazi values (Mullan 2017, 160-4).

Contemporaneously, with body and breath therapists, a body image emerged, which centralized awareness as bodily condition, as movement aim and impetus: First, the "body-soul unity" was to be perceived as "happening" and "becoming," as "movement" and "rhythm," instead of a fixed "state" (Karl Ziebler [1932, 16], "Singbewegung und Körperkultur," in von Steinaecker 2000, 45; translated by author). Second, movement had to initiate with "inner sensation ... consciously connected with the corresponding respiratory function" in order to achieve "more than pure muscular drill," "physical culture in the higher sense" (Marie Kuhls-Goslich [1912, 185], *Die Körperkultur*, in von Steinaecker 2000, 87-8; translated by author). Finally, the combination of flow, the "rhythm," and bodily awareness caused "a harmony of the mind, the body and the soul" (Alfred Spörr [c. 1920], *Harmonische Körperkultur*, unpublished text, in von Steinaecker 2000, 88; translated by author).

It seems important to mention that the zeitgeist of the nineteenth and twentieth centuries saw not only the emergence of certain body-related discourses and phenomena but also the development and establishment of different theosophy and esotericism-related currents. There were those who participated in these different movements simultaneously, enabled the evolution of both, and produced moments of direct interaction and interrelation—worthy of mention, for example, are Rudolf Steiner (1861–1925) and his expressive dance movement practice Eurythmy; and Georges I. Gurdjieff (1866–1949) and his Dalcroze-influenced movements and attention and monitoring exercises (Cusack and Norman 2012).

Historic body discourses, established practices, and aesthetics then paved the way for twentieth and twenty-first centuries' dance practices and, most important, for the so-called somatic movement practices or, in short, somatics, also denoted as "somatic studies"; "body therapies, bodywork, body-mind integration, body-mind disciplines, movement awareness, and movement (re) education" (Batson 2009, 1); or "movement-based embodied contemplative practices" (Schmalzl, Crane-Godreau, and Payne 2014, 1) and "body mind therapies" (Payne and Crane-Godreau 2015, 1). This category commonly includes well-known practices such as yoga, t'ai chi, Feldenkrais, qigong, the Alexander technique, meditation, and others such as Ideokinesis, Sensory Awareness, Body-Mind Centering, Bartenieff Fundamentals, Rolfing, Reichian Therapy, Formative Psychology, Somatic Experiencing, Trager, and Eutonia (see Schmalzl, Crane-Godreau, and Payne 2014, 1; Batson 2009, 1; Payne and Crane-Godreau 2015, 13–15). The practices share "movement awareness" as common characteristic, and their founders followed in the footsteps of "somatic pioneers" of the nineteenth and twentieth centuries, who explored movement from "listening to bodily cues arising from breath, touch, and movement" (Batson 2009, 1). The named founders of somatics are Frederick Matthias Alexander (1869–1955) with the Alexander technique, Moshé Feldenkrais (1904–84) with Feldenkrais, Mabel Todd (1880–1956) with Ideokinesis, Irmgard Bartenieff (1900–81) with Bartenieff Fundamentals, Charlotte Selver (1901–2003) with Sensory Awareness, Milton Trager (1908–97) and Gerda Alexander (1908–94) with Eutonia, and Ida Rolf (1896–1979) with Rolfing (Eddy 2009, 12). Though many practices were born in the early twentieth century and in the zeitgeist contact zone mentioned above, the term and category "somatic" is said to have emerged in the 1970s only, coined by philosopher Thomas Hanna, who first talked about somatics as derived from the Greek soma—"the body in its wholeness" (Batson 2009, 1). Some of today's practitioners of somatics are unified and organized under the "International Somatic Movement Education and Therapy Association" (ISMETA 2019), which self-defines as follows: Practices are concerned with "postural and movement evaluation, communication and guidance through touch and words, experiential anatomy and imagery, and the patterning of new movement choices, also referred to as movement patterning, movement re-education or movement re-patterning" (Eddy 2009, 8). The association claims to give people the opportunity to "listen to the body," offering an environment "freed from goal-directed effort." The practices generally emphasize an ongoing awareness of "proprioceptive signals." Somatic input might be given through touch, or verbally, using imagery (Eddy 2009, 6–7; Batson 2009, 1–2). Another scope of practice seems to be "to enhance human processes of psychophysical awareness and functioning through movement learning." Starting from there, practices train "perceptual, kinesthetic, proprioceptive, and interoceptive sensitivity" as well as exteroceptive sensitivity. In addition, "movement improvement" toward movement efficiency and the "experience [of] an embodied sense of vitality and extended capacities for living" (Eddy 2009, 8) is a goal to be achieved. On the one hand, somatics remain archives and dispositifs of historic techniques and aesthetics, which mutually influenced modern dance. On the other hand, they are also intrinsically connected of those dance forms subsumed under "contemporary" or "postmodern dance" of the twenty-first century: "Once considered esoteric and far removed from daily technique class, somatics is now a household word in a dancer's training" (Batson 2009, 1).

Of all somatic movement practices, Feldenkrais is said to have had the most influence on Gaga. The practice was developed by and named after "Israeli physicist and judo expert" Moshé Feldenkrais (Batson 2009, 3). Feldenkrais seems to share with Gaga the following discourses on movement and body ideals, aesthetics, body topography, and techniques: The Feldenkrais technique is aimed at improving movement efficiency and increasing well-being by realizing and overcoming restrictive movement habits, and thus "pain and limitations," and ultimately "redefining the body schema" (3)—"Feldenkrais [who was also involved in neuroscientific discourses at that time] believe[d] these changes will positively affect emotional and cognitive state[s]" (Payne and Crane-Godreau 2015, 14). The main technique to reach this goal is the creation of movement awareness via verbal instructions (in one strand of the technique and group sessions) or manual touch (in individual treatment), which invites "exploring the coordination between different body parts, by systematically varying postural and balance constraints, by guiding somatosensory attention to different aspects of a movement ... or by mental imagery" (Verrel et al. 2015, 2). The movement executed is described as playful:

> The movements often are akin to those in a baby's repertoire—where small-range, often idiosyncratic movements are explored in an effortless and playful manner with the goal of the movement achievement hidden. ...

The purpose of such a "playground" of movement is to disturb habitual movement patterns buried in the body schema. As the old habitual patterns begin to dissolve in an environment of ease and safety, new options for coordination become possible. (Batson 2009, 3)

To enhance the possibility to become aware, slow movement without overt muscular effort is used, balanced by moments of rest (Batson 2009, 3; Verrel et al. 2015, 2).

As Gaga is a body practice originating in an Israeli setting, it is important to reflect that the body discourses of the nineteenth and twentieth centuries are also closely related to the development of a national Jewish-Israeli identity: At the same time during which the new body approach and body practices started to dominate, pseudoscience, medicine, and propaganda implemented racist ideas in European and especially German society. The Jewish body was "proofed" to be weak, not fulfilling the demanded body image. It was constructed as the inferior "other" and served to underline national identity. The Jewish body contrasted and elevated the own strong Christian body (Gilman 1991, 38). The Jewish body was said to have a degenerated "Jewish foot" and a typical "Jewish nose," and it was proclaimed to be physically weak and of inferior condition, "bent-over" and "pale" (Spiegel 2013, 9). While this depiction of the Jewish body in relation to the promotion of the individual and collective benefits of strength and fitness played a major part in justifying the eradication of the Jews by German national socialists, it also provoked a counterreaction among people identifying as Jews. The Jewish body inferiority, as well as the need for a strong and fit body as the cultural perceptual order, seems to have been so established that, instead of trying to uncover these believes as a myth, the "Jews" self-defined with the inferior bodily state: "I had the typical ghetto boy's posture, with the round shoulders, and I was reading a lot. I was always with the books, so my head was always forward" (Ingber 2011b, 46), as Russian-born dancer Felix Fibich narrates. For him, dance became the way to overcome this bodily state: "I had very distorted posture but through exercises completely reconstituted my body" (46). Fibich thus also becomes a dispositif for the devaluation of the "intellectual" in comparison to a "physical" superior—a discursive practice used to discriminate not only Jews but also other groups in colonial contexts, for example. Jews unifying in the Zionist movement reacted to the perceived inferiority, while, at the same time, they followed the same goal as that of the already established nation-states of creating a representative and strong nation built of physically strong humans: "We must again create a strong, muscular Judaism ... with broad chest, strong limbs and valiant gaze—we shall be warriors," declared Max Nordau at the Second Zionist Congress in Basel 1898 (Spiegel 2013, 8). The Zionists aimed for a "new Jewish physique"; they did not want to identify as "people of the book" anymore, but rather as bodily strong (3). Mandatory Palestine, "Eretz Yisrael," where European Jews started to settle in the first half of the twentieth century, became the testing ground for a possible national identity. However, body practice was not central. European sports and gymnastics played no important role (see Kaufman and Galily 2009). Strength and health were established only as a side effect, when the "ideal pioneer" worked hard on the field (without monetary compensation) to shape a new land for the Jewish people (Weissbrod 2014, 19), while a new—mainly areligious—Jewish culture and Hebrew language was created (22–3). Dance played an additional and particularly important role in promoting and implementing the new Hebrew culture on a body level, creating new Jewish bodies meanwhile. This could be in the form of folk dances danced by the people: "In the nights after our work we would dance for hours, sometimes all the night through, joyful and proud, knowing we were reviving the land together" (Ingber 2011a, 106). Organized events fulfilled a similar function: In "Embodying Hebrew Culture," Nina Spiegel (2013) describes in detail how especially the "National Dance Competition for theatrical dance in Tel Aviv in 1937" and the "Dalia Folk Dance Festivals at Kibbutz Dalia in 1944 and 1947" were of importance in promoting the Zionist values and a new identity. High and low dance cultures were developed from scratch and designed to carry a "Jewish voice" and a new Hebrew narrative based on the bible as the historic document (Eshel 2003, 62). As Judith Brin Ingber observes, "They [people from the kibbutz] found in ancient Hebrew sources the reason for theirs holiday festivals, but as the original music and dance components had been lost in the 2.000 years of dispersal, these had to be constructed again" (2011a, 114).

The new dance culture was founded by dancers and choreographers such as Rivka Sturman, who immigrated to Palestine from Europe. Sturman explains her motivation to create dance: "I recognized that folk dance is worthwhile for educating our children to the special spiritual and rhythmic quality of our country; for me it is the best means of national and human expression" (Sturman in Ingber 2011a, 120). Early folk and concert dance choreographers who arrived in Palestine from Central Europe were all directly affiliated with German "Ausdruckstanz" and thus directly partaking in European body discourses, sharing their ideas and aesthetics (Eshel 2003, 63): Margalit Ornstein (1888–1973), "the founding mother of Israeli dance" (Aldor 2009), Gertrud Kraus (1901–77), "the 'first lady' of modern expressionistic dance in Israel" (Manor 2009), as well as Yardena Cohen (1910–2012) (Ingber 2009), Rivka Sturman (1903–2001), and Lea Bergstein (1902–89)—all "pioneers of Israeli folk dance" (Ronen 2009a, 2009b). Folk and concert dance choreographies were often filled with what the creators believed to be traditional and original Jewish rhythms—here the Yemenite Jews' culture often served as sources of inspiration—and biblical motifs. Eastern Europeans added the hora, a circular folk dance, as a choreographic base for folk dance (Eshel 2003, 62). Only later, the influence in the dance world shifted toward North America. Yet, part of the historic aesthetic influence shared with modern dance remained, now conveyed via foreign artists, such as Martha Graham, or Israeli artists studying abroad, such as Naharin (Friedes Galili 2013, 70-2; for details, see Eshel 2003).

A shift in national self-identity took place with the war of independence and the recognition of Israel as state (Weissbrod 2014, 38-9). It now included an explicit body image: "The Israeli was the Tsabar, the native-born, courageous, physically strong and aggressive individual, informal, self-assured, the upright warrior, who loved his/her country patriotically and was willing to defend it because it was his/hers by birthright, rather than because of having historical religious claims on it as a Jew" (Weissbrod 2014, 57). Military service has played an important role in the life of Israelis from 1984 until today; an Israeli identity, including physical strength, prevails (Quinlan 2016, 133-4). Though, as dance scholar Quinlan mentions, the contemporary Israeli body image promoted is different from that of the Zionists' "New Jew" insofar as it is now represented by "the sexy female sabras and the heroic masculine soldier" (135), "toned and flexible like the heroic and sexy images of contemporary Jewish physical ideals demonstrated in representations of young IDF [Israel Defence Forces] members" (139). Quinlan connects Gaga's aesthetics to this Israeli body image. Still, it should be underlined that Gaga's aesthetics, like the aesthetics becoming explicit in Gaga's body topography, are to be first and foremost connected to their historic origins in body discourses and practices for once and neoliberal ideals for second. Gaga does not seem to consciously perpetuate any Israeli body image—not least because Gaga shares its body topography with other neo-spiritual practices around the globe. Gaga's aesthetics came into being because of a network of relational social and cultural aesthetic influences, to which Naharin, on the one hand, and the Israeli Gaga participants, on the other hand, were and remain exposed to.

1.3 Gaga as a Neoliberal Well-Being Practice

Gaga as a cultural and social phenomenon becomes potentially explainable in the theoretical framework of a "consumer society" (Gauthier and Martikainen

2013; Gauthier 2017): Practicing Gaga enables and prepares individuals living in such a society for social and cultural participation. According to Uri Ram (2008), however, this cultural and social framework is only partially applicable to Israeli society. Twenty-first-century globalized Israel finds itself in-between "McWorld" and a "Jihad" society in a "bifurcation." On the one hand, Israeli society is a global-oriented neoliberal market society carrying on in post-Zionist tradition and constitutional-nationalism full of "globalization winners." On the other hand, Israeli society is a local-oriented "tribe" characterized as neo-Zionist and by neo-fundamentalism and ethnic fundamentalism (6–9). As Ram notes, "On the one hand Israel is a stable parliamentary democracy, it is highly advanced economically, and a Western-style consumer society; on the other it is a state of occupation, apartheid and social deprivation, and a place in which a separation between church (i.e., synagogue) and state hardly obtains" (6).

There is no arguing that the social and cultural phenomenon Gaga is interrelated with this Israeli setting, and that the Gaga Movement Ltd., as well as the Gaga participants belong to, or aim to belong to, so-called McWorld Israel. To participate, individuals need to overcome access obstacles such as payment. Gaga is associated with high-culture concert dance. Participation seems regulated by monetary and educational access. The movement practice is globally influenced and of global influence and orientation. Gaga practice does not promote any political orientation or Jewish values; it just claims an "openness to everybody." Practicing individuals self-characterize as fully involved in a consumerist social and cultural system not only by their reasons to practice, as well as by the effect of practicing described, but also by their biographical details and mindsets. They position themselves preferably in a global instead of an Israeli society. They are self-defined as inhabitants of Tel Aviv, open-minded, global, and ultimately "modern." They are artists, actors, writers, designers, entrepreneurs, informaticians, therapists, and movement practitioners. They might have come from a religious family but live a different life now. No one of the interviewed seemed to be identifiable as observing conservative Judaism or any form of Judaism apart from its popular version, such as the celebration of significant holidays. Independently from whether they grew up in an English-speaking environment such as the United States, or lived abroad in New York, or just frequently travel there, they all speak a suitable level of English. As shown above, to some, it is even important to look at Gaga as a global, and not explicitly an Israeli, practice.

Conducting the thesis in Tel Aviv and at the Suzanne Dellal Center meant observing the Gaga phenomenon and effect in and on a limited part of Israeli society: Westernized, neoliberal, and consumerist. While this means that the research results might not account for Gaga practiced anywhere in the rest of Israel,[3] they can apparently account for Gaga practiced under similar social and cultural conditions in the rest of the world, where participants belong to a "new middle class" of an "entangled late modernity," as Dawson (2013) establishes. This entangled late modernity's society and culture is characterized "by a *market-orchestrated, urban-industrial* and *techno-scientific* complex underwritten by structural and social *integration*" (131). In turn, the new middle-class members are characterized by "a liberal-capitalist mindset and its commoditised articulation of aspirational and meritocratic preoccupations"; "socio-cultural pluralism and value relativity"; "a mobile, expressive and self-oriented demeanour"; "unremitting and eclectic pursuit of aesthetic satisfaction, intellectual gratification, and psychophysical stimulation which finds its greatest pleasures in the new, different and exotic." Their identity is "permanently under construction" and "forged as a customised lifestyle and stage-managed presentation." Their self becomes a "project" displaying in "'stylistic self-consciousness' and 'aestheticisation of the body' which valorises inner feelings and emotions, yet demands outer expression and public exhibition" (135–6).

Gauthier and Martikainen found that in "consumer" and "consumption" society where the self functions as a commodity for social and cultural participation, self-presentation becomes crucial to any individual, and lifestyle becomes a way to identify (Gauthier and Martikainen 2013, 2–3). They describe a "commoditisation of more and more areas of life, the rise of lifestyles as loci for identity," and "the emergence of the consumer as an identity" (2). And talk of society as a setting where "self-presentation and the promotion of the self" become crucial for cultural and social participation (3), where the experience site of the practices is emphasized and gains in importance at the expense of belief (Gauthier 2017, 452). Religious practices have to compete to exist, and they thus offer "branded goods": "Branded goods are experiential and social commodities. What is sold is not an object but an experience that must appear authentic if it is to be meaningful" (Gauthier and Martikainen 2013, 13). This demand is answered by neo-spiritual practices like Gaga: "Many of the novel religious phenomena are putting emphasis on experience rather than belief and can be understood as expressions of this ethics of authenticity" (Gauthier 2017, 452). In this context, religion and religious practices are "operational," needing participation (Gauthier and Martikainen 2013, 15) as well as "more practical and experienced than represented and believed" (Gauthier 2017, 454).[4] They answer individual demands for identity creation or social values and goods such as "well-being," "healing" (Gauthier and Martikainen 2013, 15), and self-optimization (3). The demands are characteristics that Gaga also shares both in what it promises and in what it does.

Additionally, Dawson (2013) describes how in neoliberal consumer society individuals as commodified selves are deeply involved in a "prosumption" cycle. To participate in society, they do not only need to consume and be consumed at the same time, and their ability to do so represents their personal value (136–7). The "aestheticization" of one's own body and "the self's consumptive experience of itself as that which both produces and is produced" becomes motive for practicing "alternative religious repertoire" (141). Dawson adds, "It is this combination of self as agent (producer), beneficiary (product), and aesthete (consumer) which marks the alternative religious repertoire of the new middle class as a quintessentially prosumptive process" (142). According to Dawson, prosumptive practices are defined by the following particularities: The initiator of the effect of an individual experience in practice is always the individual themselves. In practice, the individual, by their own force, undergoes a transformation, "some form of direct (physical and emotional) or indirect (employment and living conditions) betterment to the spiritual prosumer" (138). The transformation happens within "the human body understood as an integrated psychophysical unit," which becomes the place for "self-betterment" to occur (138–9). The practice context typically allows for individuals to bring and apply their own background and experiences from other contexts, and it thus also enables them to switch between different practices and establish their very own "spiritual bricolage" (139). Practices allow for public image presentation (140). The common idea is that anybody has the potential to transform and to be successful. While hierarchy should not matter, climbing up a hierarchical ladder in a practice or gaining additional certifications of expertise in a specific practice is seen as something to be achieved (140).

In this social and cultural context, "well-being" and "health" are terms of particular importance and often represent the goal to be reached by the individual in practice. To Dominic Corrywright (2009, 2), well-being is a discursive concept related to "happiness, life satisfaction, quality of life, standard of living, measures and indices of economic stability and development that affect government policy and concepts that relate to the very notion of what it is to be human." Social success becomes measured by well-being, and "the pursuit of wellbeing then becomes a purpose of social action and an objective of social justice" (2). He further explains that in the same context "health is conceived as the ideal of what it is to be fully human which is achieved by attaining balance between mind, body and spirit" (14). When Jay Johnston (2013) describes "well-being spirituality," she takes it a step further, adding yet another characteristic: Well-being is to be seen as concerned with a "healing of self" but also of "other." She writes, "Emerging from this perspective is a worldview and practice that understands changes to the self (selfcare and responsibility) as intimately bound up with, and influential upon, the broader world and others within it (a care for and responsibility to Other)" (177). According to Johnston, well-being is linked to a perceived body topography and worldview: the interconnectedness of self and environment as "the expansive, energetic, subtle bodies of self" (177).

The particular effect of Israel's neoliberal consumer socio- and culturescape on contemporary Israeli religiosity and spirituality was noted by Israeli scholars. They described an increase in the neoliberally influenced secular middle class in demand for what they framed as "New Age" practices (see Kaplan and Werczberger 2017; Werczberger and Huss 2014). According to them, this Israeli "New Age" is a "multifaceted cultural phenomenon," including "lifestyle." These "New Age" practices are characterized by a "hope for personal transformation, which can be reached through body work, spiritual disciplines, natural diets, and renewed human relationships" (Ruah-Midbar 2013, 421–2). A valuable observation underlining the connection between Gaga and the social and cultural setting, if one talks of "New Age" in a debatable definition, broad and vague enough to include neo-spiritualities.

The social and cultural characteristics reflect in the aesthetic effect experienced and narrated by participants: Participants find transformation to be not only momentary transformation toward a better emotional-habitual state from sadness to euphoria but also transformation toward a different, healthy, and better body. Gaga apparently helps one to cope with difficult life situations and different forms of physical and emotional stress, or it is described as therapy and therapeutic. Gaga becomes something participants identify with, and especially the Gaga movement concept becomes something used as a possibility to represent the own identification with Gaga. In addition, participants take their experience (and the perceptual orders) from other practices, such as yoga, into Gaga class, and they allow it to shape their very individual Gaga experience. The Gaga experience thus remains individual. What participants value about Gaga is the diversity of people, the room for everybody, and the freedom of movement. Yet, contradictorily, they aim for an incorporation of the ideal Gaga movement concept, or they long for certification as a Gaga teacher as the culmination of their love for Gaga. Finally, participants acknowledge that the extent of the transformative effect of Gaga practice is partly their own responsibility. The social and cultural influence also reflects in the body topography in the third chapter.

The holistic human body as a site of self-transformation and self-optimization; self-awareness and especially sensory awareness of the own body as optimum bodily state; physical-psychological well-being and health as a state to be reached; well-being and health understood as dependent on the interrelation between mind and body; and individuals as self-responsible agents enacting, and being expected to enact a certain transformation—all of these characteristics of neo-spiritual practices stem from inherited historic body discourses. The aesthetics of these practices have their base in historic body practices that have been established in the context of body discourses discussed above. Neo-spiritual practices and the bodies they produce, but also the bodies that are subjects to neo-spirituality, are undeniable archives of historic discourses and, because of their performative character, reproduce historic discourse—sometimes willingly and consciously but in most of the cases unwillingly and unconsciously.

2

Ritual Environment Shaping Enactment

There are two main strands of Gaga classes called "Gaga/dancers" and "Gaga/people." Classes are nowadays, as a consequence of the Covid-19 pandemic, offered online,[1] as well as offline and in person in dance studios. With regard to the former, "Gaga/dancers classes are open to dancers and advanced dance students ages 16+. Classes [offline] last between an hour to an hour and fifteen minutes" (Gaga Movement Ltd. 2019b). Online classes are scheduled for forty-five minutes. In terms of the latter type of class, "Gaga/people classes are open to people ages 16+, regardless of their background in dance or movement. Classes [offline] last approximately one hour" (2019b). Online classes are scheduled for thirty minutes. In addition, Gaga Movement Ltd. offers Gagadim, which refers to Gaga classes for children—"Gagadim is open to children age 6–10 and accompanying adults" (2019b)—and Gagadol, classes for elders, adjusting to their physical abilities,[2] or for people with special needs, such as Parkinsonian patients (see Quinlan 2016, 187–8). In the course of the pandemic, the Gaga Movement Ltd. started to offer Gaga/seated classes online twice a week, scheduled for thirty minutes: "Gaga/seated class is available for a range of people who find it challenging to exercise while standing" (Gaga Movement Ltd. 2021). I conducted my research in the years prior to the pandemic's start in 2020, when ongoing Gaga/dancers and Gaga/people classes were offered in different Israeli cities and at different locations worldwide; the website listed ongoing classes in North America, Europe, and East Asia (Gaga Movement Ltd. 2019c). At the time of the research, the most extensive number of ongoing classes was to be found at the Suzanne Dellal Center in Tel Aviv, where participant observation was conducted. Apart from a regular schedule, Gaga classes have been offered in a workshop format worldwide, consisting of a weekend or an "intensive" week of more than one class per day. The non-Israeli classes I observed were often accompanied by Gaga/metodika classes or, in the case of Gaga/dancers, by the teaching of some of Naharin's choreographic material from Batsheva's repertoire.³ As a centralized organization, Gaga Movement Ltd. has guaranteed institutional similarity between the different classes. The company not only oversees all ongoing classes but also provides the only "certified" Gaga teacher training, which stipulates that Gaga teachers must return to the "home base" of Tel Aviv annually to update their Gaga knowledge. During the time of my research, professional dancers partaking in Gaga workshops, for example, had to sign an official form stating the following:

> I understand that this training does not license me as a teacher of Gaga ... I hereby declare that I will not call my teaching "Gaga," "based on Gaga," "Gaga inspired," "inspired by Gaga" or any other wording using the word "Gaga" ... I understand that I am free to incorporate what I learn in my dancing, choreographing, and teaching, yet under no circumstance I can declare that I teach Gaga, or use the word "Gaga" in regard to my teaching. If I incorporate what I learn in my teaching, I will encourage my students to experience Gaga for themselves with a certified Gaga teacher. I understand that breaking this commitment will be considered as offending the legal rights of Gaga. I understand that teaching Gaga requires special license given by Ohad Naharin.⁴

The specific organization of Gaga has been responsible for an aesthetical centralization of Gaga practice. In consequence, the research of aesthetics, body knowledge, and embodied experience in the context of classes held at Suzanne Dellal in Tel Aviv and its results can be understood as indicating as well as exemplifying a global phenomenon expanding beyond the classes in Israel to classes worldwide and, to a certain degree, to online classes.

As a next step in the aesthetic analysis of Gaga practice and its potentially aesthetically effective elements, I frame Gaga class, or rather Gaga classes, as ritual(s). At this point, I am talking of Gaga class as a ritual in the sense of a "minimal definition of ritual" provided by Ronald L. Grimes: "Ritual is embodied, condensed, and prescribed enactment" (2014, 195). It seems a favorable definition because, above all, it allows for the researching of aesthetic practices of "embodied, condensed, and prescribed enactment" in general, notwithstanding their classification as, for example, religious, political, and cultural, their classification by their social and cultural functionality, or their classification by fixed ritual characteristics, which a ritual should fulfill in order to be called ritual. Instead, Grimes' definition allows for a focus on the aesthetic work of rituals by including (1) the category of body and the embodied effect of rituals—"embodied"; (2) the notion of rituals as extraordinary aesthetic phenomena with complex working mechanisms that one needs to analyze in order to understand—"condensed"; and (3) the prescription, and thus repetitiveness, of rituals, as rituals not only implicitly shape behavior as inculturations or socializations do, but ritual techniques also explicitly prescribe what and how things have to be done—"prescribed." In addition, (4) the definition emphasizes that for ritual participants, rituals are not merely ordinary actions, but actions filled with particular intention and focus, where participants are totally involved in active participation—"enacted" (195-6). The definition thus allows one to research the transformation of body knowledge, looking at how bodies are involved in actions of repetitive patterns, and it enables a systemic analysis and definition of a practice-bound collective body knowledge. If ever, in the context of Aesthetics of Religion, talking of rituals becomes necessary, rituals seemingly need to be understood along Grimes' definition.

In *The Craft of Ritual Studies* (2014), Grimes' definition comes with a ritual theory, where he demands clarity about what defines ritual as it is used. According to Grimes, a ritual model should explain a ritual by analyzing "its static elements (using, e.g., mechanical metaphors)" alongside its "internal dynamics (using, e.g., narrative or dramatic metaphors)" and "interactions with their contexts (using, e.g., complex systems, cybernetic, ecological, or cognitive metaphors)" (183). It has to be comprehensive, consistent, and applicable in practice, and it should "provide orientation"—a definition of ritual, listing ritual elements, possible dynamics, and ritual functions, building the base for a subsequent interpretation (175). The ritual theory, in turn, comes with a practical concept for what to look at when describing a ritual: "elements of ritual" or "ritual elements" (231-93) and "dynamics of ritual" or "ritual dynamics" (294-337). Ritual elements are small "parts" that make up a ritual: "We imagine a ritual as constructed of, or deconstructable into, a set of elements that, by interacting, generate ritual processes" (294). Taking Grimes' ritual elements as a point of departure, I established the following categories as methodically relevant to my own research: (1) stage, covering Grimes' category "ritual places"; (2) actors and their roles, covering "ritual actors" and aspects of "ritual groups"; (3) script, covering "ritual actions" and "ritual times"; (4) language, covering "ritual language"; and (5) rules, covering the explicit ritual culture and "ritual institutions" discussed in different media of communication.

However, as Grimes succinctly puts it, "Listing a ritual's elements is no more (or less) enlightening than sorting a bucket of bolts, nuts, and washers into three piles" (2014, 294). Ritual elements are only the "nouns." To understand how rituals "work" or, in other words, "function" or "process," one must look at the "verbs": the ritual dynamics (294). Ritual effectivity stems from the integration of elements and dynamics within the ritual network. Ritual dynamics animate ritual elements and therefrom constitute rituals. This makes rituals relational, but also procedural—without animation, no ritual. Because ritual dynamics are linked to ritual participants performing them, describing a ritual by looking at its elements —as done in this chapter—needs the incorporation of ritual dynamics and an aspect of animation to define the ritual. Moreover, as the following will show, a ritual description can never be "fixed" in time and place and is always bound to the individual ritual participants embodying the ritual elements.

2.1 Stage

Stage is commonly understood as a "raised floor or platform, typically in a theatre, on which actors, entertainers, or speakers perform" (Lexico 2019). This seems to be an adequate definition from which to start in order to understand the ritual space in which a Gaga class is held: (1) The space is nonordinary—at least for the nonprofessional dancers taking part—and raised or elevated from daily life and routine; (2) it is the space where people enact Gaga, and the space is defined by the actions; and (3) it is also a space of "artistic" quality, a performance space, as Gaga participants connect the space to Batsheva and Batsheva dancers, with whom they share the space. A stage is not an unchangeable platform; there is technical equipment to change the stage, signifying a change of scenery, but nevertheless being a modification of the entity "stage." Actors have to adapt to the stage physically, as the way they act, sing, and dance will depend on what the stage looks like, its size, the other actors on stage, the material of the floor, and objects in space. However, behavioral adaptation will also occur. Actors will most likely act differently on stage than off stage. A stage also has immaterial features; it is immaterial as well as material. It has immaterial aesthetics, such as qualities and values, which influence the behavior and, consequently, the experience output of the one on stage. Moreover, stage changes will directly influence actors and their actions physically and psychologically as they adapt. A stage as a space thus functions in the sense of a "therapeutic landscape" (Lea 2008; Koch and Meissner 2015) with an embodied effect. Different stage or space features hold transformative power: the material characteristics on the first level, such as nature, and constructed places on the second level—in the sense of being symbolic, aside from immaterial characteristics such as social interaction in place and emotions created in place—with place remaining a relational process rather than something fixed (Koch and Meissner 2015; Lea 2008; see also Gesler 2003).

Furthermore, a stage denotes a ritual space: Rituals take place at a specific geographical place, which forms the *ritual setting* in which an artificial *ritual set* is constructed and in which the ritual is placed. Ritual space is limited—if not by the physical *boundaries* of human constructions, such as buildings, or natural or geographical features, then by the ritual actions themselves, creating the center, periphery, and outside of a ritual. In consequence, for some rituals, the physical space is defining, whereas in other rituals, it barely matters, and the *actions* creating the specific ritual set are important. Ritual participants behave differently when inside a ritual space, and a ritual space has specific *qualities and values*—space becomes an agent or, at least, a ritual experience-influencing factor. The peculiarity of a ritual space persists even when momentarily not used for rituals (Grimes 2014, 256–9).

Key questions now arise: What constitutes the stage or space of Gaga class? What are the material and immaterial aesthetics that the space provides to Gaga participants? How does space influence perception and experience? I turn to the following of Grimes' space features to answer these questions: The stage is constituted by the aesthetical categories *setting and set, boundaries, actions,* and *qualities and values*.

Setting and Set

To understand setting and set as aesthetics, it is necessary to paint an encompassing picture of the geographical surroundings the ritual is embedded in, including the particular local culture they come along with.

The setting of Gaga classes comprised the Suzanne Dellal Center in Neve Tzedek, Tel Aviv, in the building that housed the Batsheva Dance Company at that time. Compared to other Tel Avivian neighborhoods, Neve Tzedek is relatively calm. Buildings are not as high as elsewhere, streets are small, and no rush street passes through. It is a historical neighborhood dating back to the nineteenth century; from the 1980s, it came into the focus of gentrification and is now known to host artists and quite expensive artistry and fashion boutiques, cafés, and restaurants, as well as a large French community frequented by many tourists. Neve Tzedek lies on the outskirts of Jaffa, connecting it to the rest of Tel Aviv, separated from the seaside only by a large parking lot, a rush street, and some green. If no construction work was going on outside, then windows left open in the studio provided an incredibly quiet soundscape compared to the rest of the city, where the muezzins from Jaffa and sometimes music from other studios could occasionally be heard. Some windows provided a view to the sea. In addition to the soundscape and view that made it a specific Israeli setting, the setting's culture influenced the class schedule: No classes were held on the evening of Shabbat and on Shabbat, nor on the evening before Israeli-Jewish holidays—as Jewish holidays start at sundown the day before—and on holidays. The last classes before the weekend, Shabbat, or holidays were usually extraordinarily full of participants. When there was no possibility to hold the classes at the larger Studio Varda, due to company rehearsals, for example, presubscription was required, meaning that people wanting to participate had to sign up beforehand.

The so-called Studio Suzy (Figure 1) was the place in which Gaga classes were usually held. Studio Suzy was a dance studio located on the third and top floor

Figure 1 Studio Suzy after the first and before the second evening class on April 23, 2017.

of the Batsheva building. It was a square room with white walls and a gray dance floor of slightly roughened haptics, like hard plastic. On some days, there were especially slippery spots on the dance floor. The ceiling narrowed toward the center, as the room was located right under the pointed rooftop of the building. A huge ventilator hung from the ceiling, and there were openings for the air conditioner, which mainly blew on the floor area between the center of the room and wall, with the area close to the center and wall remaining rather unaffected. The studio also had large windows and a balcony door, facing the seaside and left open during ideal weather, and small windows in the shape of portholes facing east and south, usually tilted. The room was thus never fully closed off from outside the building. Furthermore, a large, visible analog clock had been installed. The dance floor was separated from the entrance area of the room not only by the floor material, plastic, and wood but also by the fact that it was not part of the square room, but a room with a low ceiling itself, connected to the square room by a pathway with one pillar in the middle. The doors of the entry area itself were not visible from the square room, nor were the wooden shelves where people could keep their shoes and bags. However, people also placed their belongings on the floor along the walls in the entrance area, visible from the dance floor. The sound system was located at the entrance pathway of the square room, and two loudspeakers were to be found in the two corners opposite the room.

 This rather fixed "landscape" of Studio Suzy was accompanied by a varying "soundscape," as well as a varying "lightscape" and "temperaturescape." The soundscape varied according to the teacher: Every teacher chose their own music for their Gaga class playlist, and as every teacher had different taste, the playlists turned out to be different, too. The music literally spanned all types of genres, from hip-hop and electronic music to folk, rock, and pop, both well known and unknown. Also, the playlists themselves contained slow and fast, happy and sad, and long and short tracks, and possibly tracks from different genres. The teacher adjusted the volume to their own voice, so the voice could be heard by all participants. Sometimes this adjustment took several attempts throughout the beginning of class. The teacher would also deliberately turn up the volume at some point. On some occasions, a teacher would even work without music. As mentioned above, the soundscape was also influenced by the outside: construction work and music from another dance studio, for example. Due to the prominent windows, the lightscape of the place in which the class was held varied with the time of the day, as well as with the weather. A special moment was the time of the evening class at sundown: The sky above the sea would turn bright pink, orange, and yellow, with the bright-colored sunlight shining in on the dance floor. The temperaturescape, on the other hand, varied with the time of the year and the weather. In the summer, when air conditioner and fan were switched on, for example, several spots in the room became "windy" and cold.

This space of Studio Suzy provided sensory stimuli and affordances, "opportunities for action in the environment that are perceived by the observer depending on her intentions" (Riener and Stefanucci 2014, 102), of different kinds: I could usually not resist watching the large clock to look at the time. I often found myself checking how much time we had left. This could have been due to the lack of flow I experienced, perhaps due to being a participant-observer, or due to my dislike of the structure of class and teaching mode of a specific teacher. It could have also been related to me being aware of my level of bodily exhaustion and estimating how much energy to put in at that very moment in order to "survive" class. Moreover, I did not enjoy standing in the stream of air coming from the air conditioner, so I tried avoiding it by choosing a place that was not affected for the beginning of class, continuing to avoid it especially when moving through the space. The air conditioner thus affected my individual movement range and space. On other days when many people were present, I would try to stay close to the windows all the time. Sometimes there were slippery spots on the floor, which I avoided in order not to slip and fall or which I moved across very carefully and being alert. I once witnessed a sunset over the sea with incredibly bright colors. Not only did it invoke emotions of beauty, awe, and gratefulness for being there to watch it, but the Gaga teacher also incorporated watching the sunset into her explicit instructions, thereby ensuring that it became a sensory stimulus to every participant following the instruction. In general, I experienced it as nice and relaxing to watch the sea through the windows, and on hot days, teachers would make us imagine running to the beach and jumping into the water to float. Finally, I could see the soundscape, as determined by the teacher's choice of music, influencing my experience. Here, following seemed to play a role: Did the music meet my mood of the day? Could the music raise my mood and energy level to an extent that I was animated to move and reach a state of flow?

Another dance studio at the Suzanne Dellal Center, where Gaga classes were held and which I consider worth mentioning, was Studio Varda (Figure 2) in the Batsheva building. Varda usually hosted the large Friday-morning classes and Gaga classes with Ohad Naharin. The studio was at least double the size of Studio Suzy, situated below Suzy on the second floor. The room had high ceilings and

Figure 2 Studio Varda before the evening class on April 24, 2017.

large windows on the two long sides, yet without Suzy's "far" sight. The dominant color in Varda was black, and one could tell that it was used for performance rehearsal as well as smaller performances. What made this class environment especially interesting was its "culturescape." The studio was clearly the dance and training studio of a dance company: Sometimes there were still performance requisites in the space when a Gaga class was held; or, when a class was held in Studio Suzy, Studio Varda's doors were closed, and one would pass by knowing that it was the Batsheva dancers training and rehearsing inside. Even foreigners would recognize the studio from watching the documentary *Mr. Gaga*.

Not only Studio Suzy and Studio Varda but also any studio and space in which Gaga classes were held shared one specific characteristic: Unlike the "usual" dance studio, the set excluded any mirrors. This space characteristic of absence is said to have a great impact on the embodied experience. The organizational idea behind it was put into words by Naharin: "We become more aware of our form since we never look at ourselves in a mirror; there are no mirrors" (Gaga Movement Ltd. 2017b). In the eyes of Gaga participants, the absence of mirrors played a significant part in making a Gaga class a space that was free of judgment: Ada, for example, believed that Gaga led to increased self-acceptance because the practicing space excluded mirrors.

Boundaries

In rituals, boundaries not only limit the ritual space but also function as both frontiers, which one must overcome to be able to participate, and walls of protection. Frontiers of rituals are formed by what I call "outer boundaries": These could be actions that must be enacted to be able to enter the ritual place, or they could be individual mindsets resulting in mental preconditions that participants must deal with on their way to class. The ritual space itself is denoted by "inner boundaries": material boundaries of the set, the room, and ritual actions setting and resetting immaterial boundaries to the space.

How far does the space of Gaga class expand? Where are the *outer boundaries*? Noam mentioned that, already on his way by foot from his parked car to the Suzanne Dellal Centre, he started raising his bodily awareness. When he saw his "good friend" arriving by bike, the following crossed his mind:

> And in a split second, putting all my thoughts aside, I became aware of all those small, medium, and big engines started to collaborate immaculately so my body carry my spirit to the hidden corner which maybe I will get the chance to hug and be hugged—and that will be a good starting point for Gaga class this morning. (Noam)

He further characterized this specific moment, as the moment from when he could "let go" and simply enjoy class. The experience-influencing and sensorially effective ritual space of Gaga classes thus expanded beyond the set of Studio Suzy. While these observations are helpful, outer ritual boundaries are difficult to be defined and generalized: Outer boundaries vary individually and remain of momentary character.

What can be examined, on the contrary, are the stages of "drawing closer" to the ritual space or frontiers, requiring participants to undertake actions to be able to enter the ritual space—in the case of Gaga: First, participants had to arrive at the Suzanne Dellal Center and the Batsheva building. Those who traveled by car had to park further away, while those who came by bike could at least enter the square and pedestrian area in which Suzanne Dellal was situated. Everyone had to walk the last meter. As demonstrated with Noam above, making one's way to the entrance could include mental and physical preparation for class. Second, at the entrance of the building, one passed by a desk, where an employee of Gaga Movement Ltd. would be seated. Every participant passed the employee, and this sometimes required waiting in line for a short time. If participants owned a "monthly pass," which guaranteed full access to all classes except special classes with Naharin by one payment of then 450 ILS per month, they could simply pass, telling the employee their name. If participants attended classes more often, they would be known to the employee and would not need to even provide their name; a simple exchange of greetings occurred. If participants were new or had to obtain a new "pass" of any kind, they would need some additional time to furnish their details, and either effect payment in cash or leave their credit card details. Anyhow, it meant a first physical-psychological contact with fellow Gaga participants. It also meant entering the "home" of the Batsheva Dance Company. Finally, it meant that one needed to be able to afford to pay for class, as one could not participate in class without paying. Third, participants could then proceed upstairs to the changing rooms and washrooms on the first floor, where they could get dressed for class or immediately head for the studio. One would meet more people on the way and start talking. The changing rooms consisted of one shared room with mirrors, where the professional dancers kept their belongings in lockers and changed in and out of their training clothes. Individuals would also meet people while filling up their water bottles, at the washroom, or waiting outside the studio for the doors to open. When meeting people one knew, conversation was sparked. Fourth, when one finally entered the studio, talking could continue. Participants would find a free space to leave their belongings, and they started searching for a place inside the studio where they would feel comfortable to start class. In summary, entering the space required physiological-psychological actions of movement effort, arriving, climbing up the stairs, changing clothes, and interpersonal communication. Potential additional frontiers to overcome were physiological-psychological preconditions: the love and admiration for Batsheva and Naharin, shyness, and thinking of oneself as not being a "good" dancer, as well as tiredness, a lack of motivation, and not wanting to meet people.

The *inner boundaries* of the ritual space were formed by the construction of setting and set. As already mentioned, the material of the floor marked the "dance floor." Entrance doors remained closed throughout class. In consequence, outside the doors was outside the ritual space. Still, these seemingly fixed material boundaries could be expanded by actions: On the one hand, the ritual space enlarged if participants, due to a high number in attendance, had to move on the "nondance floor" as well. Besides, the ritual space grew and shrank with the space used by the people for movement. Teachers could willingly influence the space by making people move through it and take up new or larger spaces or make space. On the other hand, the ritual space expanded beyond the material boundaries: Teachers made people connect to sensory audiovisual or even imaginary stimuli outside the dance studio, such as a specific sound or landscape viewed from the window or someone or something far away. Participants' awareness was directed outside the material space. The constant awareness required of the surroundings, other participants, the teacher's movement, and instructions was, alongside movement, the main tool for creating the ritual space and setting boundaries. In terms of ritual space, the "materiality" of the studio mattered less than actions.

Actions

As just observed, actions can expand and narrow ritual space. In addition, actions structure the space. Furthermore, actions form part of ritual institutions or ritual "culture." Meaning, even before actions structure the space, specific behavior and action guidelines structure it.

I was told by Gaga teacher Talia that, in addition to the absence of any mirrors, Gaga Movement Ltd. required at least $3m^2$ of room for each participant. Moreover, theoretically, people should not enter or leave the space throughout class. Apart from these theoretical requirements shaping the ritual space beforehand, this space was constantly updated, expanded, and narrowed throughout class itself by different ritual actions initiated through the teacher's instructions and movement. This shaping of space worked in two different ways: First, the teacher structured the space by where they placed themselves in the room and in connection to the group. Most of the teachers, though not all of them, chose to stand in the middle of the room and in the middle of the group throughout the main part of class. They would move through the room, however, if they required movement through the room and a change of place in their instructions. The ritual space was thus structured in the "teacher space" and the "participants' space." The latter space was further structured into different undercategories, depending on where participants placed themselves within the participants' space: My own preferred position, for example, was at the outer edge of the group, close to the space's material boundaries. I did not feel as much watched there as when dancing close to the teacher at the center of the group. I felt that I could express myself more authentically through my movement, and I also enjoyed having more space, only having to look out for people in one to three spatial directions, not multidimensionally. When standing close to the teachers, I felt as though I had to constantly interact with them—through smiling, for example, I also felt controlled on whether I was enacting the instructions correctly and thus constantly performing in the sense of overacting, alongside enacting and fearing being judged. Shira, for example, told me that this specific spatial situation—the distribution of teacher and participants in space—reminded her of a specific part of Israeli culture, namely, Israeli folk dance: To her, Gaga's ritual space became like the space Israeli folk dance rituals would take up. This similarity, for Shira, was not only provoked by the spatial distribution of ritual actors but also underlined and enforced by the different roles these actors took up in the space: teachers "activating" and "making participants dance."

In addition to the importance of where teachers placed themselves in terms of ritual space, the way the ritual space was structured by the teacher also influenced experience by influencing the distribution and communication of sensory information, as diagnosed by Dafna: "Surprisingly the teacher did not stand in the middle of the group, but rather on the side. This surprised me and made it hard to see her and hear her. A first challenge."

Second, participants' spatial awareness, and thus the range of relevant sensory stimuli perceived, was altered and directed, leading to a different experience of space and of the body in relation to the space and to a different experience in general by the incorporation of new sensory information. Instructions issued by teachers could sound as follows:

> *Imitate other people.*
> *Be aware of everything you sense, see, smell, hear, and let it become movement.*
> *Send your energy out.*
> *Show your generous skins (on your arms, armpit, chest, shoulders, back, lower back, stomach, pelvis) to someone faraway.*

Furthermore, the connection to audiovisual input, such as sound, the sunset over the sea, and the request to watch the ceiling carefully when lying on the floor or to observe the skin touching the floor or other material, formed part of this kind of instruction. By giving instructions and moving along, teachers provoked the movement of the people through space. They made people fill up empty spaces and use the room in the studio effectively. They also made participants change place, caused participants to digest sensory stimuli and adjust to the new position in space. This happened by instructions such as:

> *Spread better in the place.*
> *Walk/run in a circle.*
> *Walk and cross (each other's ways). Don't walk in a circle.*
> *Find yourself a new place.*

as well as *Shape the space around you* (fill all the space surrounding oneself with movement) and *Move tiny* (use less space than one could, decrease one's movement range) or, the contrary, *Stretch your skin. Move with a large skin.*

Other side-actions further structured the ritual space. There was the already mentioned resetting of spatial boundaries when people started using the nondance floor to move as well. Sometimes people even turned around the corner and out of sight, or they left the room to go to the lavatory and then rejoined. An additional influence on the ritual space was the number of people in the room. How movement actions could be carried out and what actions were chosen by the teacher to be carried out depended on the amount of room each person had to move. Noam wrote, "Class today was heavily crowded, which means a smaller territory to work on, which ultimately influenced the way I carried myself in space. I don't think I reached my maximum stretch—not physically nor emotionally."

In any case, as shown, participants experienced the ritual space individually to a certain degree: not only depending on where they were placed in relation to the group within the participants' space but also where they experienced and therefore actively set the spatial limits and defined the ritual space.

Qualities and Values

Set and setting, as well as the boundaries and actions providing a spatial structure, make the place unique and of particular value, and thus particularly effective as a ritual space. The qualities and values of a space manifest differently in the eyes of ritual actors. The Gaga space itself became extraordinary and different from other spaces in many ways. This does not mean that the Gaga space was always valued positively: For Ariel, classes at the Suzanne Dellal Centre were experienced as stricter and more serious, in a negative sense, compared to the classes taking place in Studio Naim, a commercial dance studio offering classes of many different styles to all kinds of people. Nevertheless, three qualities stood out. They were mentioned by several participants and were overall experienced as positive or producing a positive effect of practicing. The space was (a) *safe*, (b) *therapeutic*, and, above all, (c) *extraordinary*. These qualities, though attributes of one's physical presence in the ritual space of a Gaga class, were caused not only by space-related sensory stimuli but also mainly by the other ritual characteristics described in the following pages—actors, script, language, and rules. Space receives its quality by the ritual taking place in the space, by its animation.

"Safe," "therapeutic," and "extraordinary" are used here as endemic terms, derived from data. However, "safe" and "therapeutic space" are, especially in the field of geography, lively discussed concepts: The concept of a safe space emerged in the context of the women's movement at the end of the twentieth century (The Roestone Collective 2014, 1346). The discourse recognizes that the "perception of safety" of a space depends on "identity production and performance," space use and control, and, most importantly, the preconditions of the individual perceiving. It is neither "spatially" nor "temporally" determined (1349). From a materialist point of view, objects can define or create a safe place (1357). Furthermore, a safe space, as presented by The Roestone Collective (2014), is relational, and "because safe spaces are porous spaces, they can neither maintain separation entirely nor indefinitely" (1361). Geographer Wilbert Gesler, with his work on *Healing Places* (2003), is often introduced as one main initiator of the discussion on "therapeutic landscapes" (see Davidson and Parr 2007, 56; also Lea 2008, 90). He elaborated a "healing sense of place" (Gesler 2003, 2) depending on the nature of its environment—the interplay of its "natural," "built," symbolic," and "social" characteristics (8–16). However, researchers such as David Conradson (2005) have criticized the earlier approaches for their limited view: A particular space is said to own particular therapeutic features. They argue that not the landscape's qualities but the specific and individual interrelation of the landscape with the human experiencing the therapeutic is of importance: a relational understanding of therapeutic space influenced by a relational understanding of "self" (338, 340–1).

Safe Space

The space of a Gaga class became a safe space because participants felt that they were allowed to be whoever they wanted to be within that space. They felt they could move and behave freely. Many participants attributed this explicitly to the material absence of mirrors: "The fact that you are, you don't see yourself, which is the same like in yoga, it's wonderful because you are just within yourself ... you realize that nobody is giving a damn about you, everybody is in its own research, and it just is space, where it allow you to be" (Tamar). Furthermore, as Tamar already pointed out, a certain anonymity was part of the safety as well. As Eli said, it was a space quality "even before we're talking about the content of the class, the fact that nobody can watch you," alongside the age variety of participants and the absence of a "need to remember anything"—all this "removes the causes of frustration and judgement from the dance class." In addition, part of the anonymity, and thus the experienced safety of the space, stemmed from the fact that the community of Gaga ritual actors, especially Gaga participants, was limited and existed only within the space of the Gaga class. Some participants did not want people from other areas of their life entering this "sacred space" (Idan).

For some, such as Idan, accepting this freedom to be whoever and do whatever without self-judgment was a learning process:

> I'm embarrassed in that room too. I'm embarrassed for myself and I'm embarrassed for others. yea. I was like, this guy is like, it's like embarrassing, but then I'm like, you know at the end of it the what's more important is, he's allowed he's here, he's getting something out of it. He's allowed to embarrass himself. I'm allowed to embarrass myself.

Therapeutic Space

For most of the participants, a Gaga class also opened a therapeutic space. This was not only because it was a safe space but also because, on top of that, movement allowed for an experience of release due to ritual actions in combination with this safe space atmosphere. Tamar, for example, strongly emphasized the therapeutic effect of class and thus the ritual space. Arriving in the space in a "tired," "sad," "depressed" mood, Tamar left the place after class feeling "happy" and full of joy. She ascribed this to the space and the ritual transformative power. Tamar compared the space even to the space and possibilities established by drug consumption. The therapeutic effect of class depended on the individual emotional precondition with which one entered the space: "In a situation where I was in difficult spiritual places, the classes were even more meaningful" (Uri).

Extraordinary Space

What made Gaga an extraordinary space was that the experience could only be gained inside the space of a Gaga class. Class was a "different reality" (Dana) and, by this again, the space of class guaranteed safety for everybody to behave in an extraordinary way without being judged. The experience of Gaga was not repeatable outside the ritual space; it needed the space and was feeding from it: "The concentrated experience … heightened sensation of being in class and really being completely into the movement research experience of it … in the class you get a clean pure strong trip of having that experience" (Uri).

The Gaga space was also extraordinary because the community was extraordinary, as touched upon above: "It exists only within the studio, this family, it wasn't a basis for creation of something else, so far" (Uri). This extraordinary situation made the space not only safe but also therapeutic: "It's like therapy. Ya. It stays within Gaga [the community of people] and becomes like a world that you have, you know" (Sara). The community, and thus also the space, sometimes extended to talks outside the Suzanne Dellal Center before and after class, or at Café Dallal after class; however, there was rarely further personal interrelation and affiliation beyond. It mostly just did not happen, even if attempted. Sara added how the experience in the space depended on this special community, the connections and friendships, and the relations established with people in the ritual space. Uri expressed this by talking of his Gaga "family": "Some of the connections that I made in the classes, in this family, are very meaningful, I don't even know how to explain in what way." For him, as for Sara, for example, this "family" formed a key part of the space value:

> There is a connection that's made between people, happy connection, a sad connection, sometimes there are two sad people, sometimes are one who is really sad and someone else who picks that up. And without words or without an—most often it's the good energy, it's the people who come to you at the end of the class and they hug you, because of the positive energy that they received or—but, ya, there is something really, really, really special about the connections that where made there. (Uri)

In addition, the experience effect of the space and its value apparently varied with the setting and set of a class:

> I also, like, really feel the difference between the Gaga lessons in the different rooms. So, that's also, also has an effect. You know the like the big, the big one with big windows, of Batsheva, there must be some kind of energy there (smiling, slight laughter), you know, that also makes people get a little bit more crazy. (Sara)

For Sara, Studio Varda had a specific effect, which she somehow related to the fact that it was the main training studio of the Batsheva company. Moreover, Eli pointed out that the space probably had a greater effect on participants frequenting class as a leisure-time and thus extraordinary activity than it had on professional dancers of Batsheva for whom it formed part of the working space. That is also why he preferred taking Gaga/people classes in terms of experience, which was always related to the other participants.

In terms of what to take from talking about the "stage" of a Gaga class, the emphasis is that space must be viewed in its situational animated state. Gaga's ritual space was not a fixed space; and set and setting, apart from the absence of mirrors, were also not fixed; the sensational "scapes" varied with the time of the day, the season, the temperature, the number, and nature of people in the space, and all individual and collective ascriptions. Boundaries, too, were not fixed, as they depended on set and setting and because they consisted of individual as well as collective boundaries. What seemed quite fixed though was the spatial enactment through ritual institutions, such as the absence of mirrors and people watching; the not talking, not leaving the room throughout class, not coming in late, and keeping the teacher in sight; and ritual actions, which placed the teacher in the middle of the group and created a specific arrangement of the group around, leading to different experiences depending on one's place within the group. Some qualities and values were of a fixed character. However, their importance to individuals seemed to change with changes in individual preconditions, such as "the mood of the day," and changes in the space itself such as changes in set and setting, such as the room, and changes in the group of people participating.

2.2 Human Actors and Their Roles

When referring to a ritual actor, I primarily talk about a "ritualist: ritual participant, ritual actor, ritual insider, a person in ritual circumstance" (Grimes 2014, 251). First, all ritualists, independently from their roles, own ritual agency—even if due to their mere presence, they interfere in ritual. However, there are also ritual agents with stronger ritual agency, deciding the result and outcome of a ritual, but who do not have to be physically present as ritualists in the actual ritual (249–51). Ritual actors' influence on the ritual depends on the role each actor plays within the ritual: There are ritual leaders, who are "primary ritual actor[s]," and ritual followers, who are "secondary ritual actor[s]," and ritual actors often alternately take over both roles (249–50). Key roles are "ritual facilitator[s]," "facilitating agent[s]," without whom a ritual simply would not happen (251). Furthermore, ritual roles can represent the hierarchy of power within a ritual, or they can be of equal power. Important roles are usually officially named, and ritual actors' roles and agency can be defined and classified by whether the actors' actions are constitutive of a ritual and in what way. Ritual actors often act or take over ritual roles in groups (250–3). Moreover, actors entering a ritual always already belong to a certain social or cultural group, and social and cultural discourses, ideologies, and values consequently enter the ritual via actors. On the other side, these groups' infrastructures function as media to distribute "ritual know-how" (280).

To understand the particularities of ritual actors in a Gaga class, three main questions are posed and answered here: Who is present in the Gaga class—groups or individuals? What are the different roles in the class? Who possesses what kind of agency in the class?

Grouping Gaga Participants

In an average class, usually thirty to forty ritualists occupied the ritual space. Minimum numbers of ten to twenty ritualists were found in apprentice teachers' classes, where participation was free of charge and which took place after the morning class. Maximum numbers in regular classes were reached in Friday classes and classes held before holidays: over fifty people. Participation in classes with Naharin ranged from approximately eighty to hundred and even more people in the space.

While all ritualists entered a space with individual preconditions, they could also be classified into different groups of oppositional character (List 3). An individual ritualist would form part of a variety of groups, which characterized and influenced the way they enacted and experienced the ritual. The frontiers between the different groups of some of these theoretical categories are not to be taken definitively but rather as a continuum.

List 3 First Grouping of Participants

(1) The official role in the particular ritual: teacher—there is only one teacher—and participants
(2) The way they entered ritual space: nonpaying and paying
(3) Participants' relation to Batsheva and Gaga Movement Ltd.: affiliated through work as company dancers, part of management and staff, and Gaga teachers, or those not specifically affiliated—"just" customers
(4) Participants' dance "background": professionals and nonprofessionals
(5) Participants' cultural and language background: Israeli or international

---

For the output of the research, sorting ritualists into these different groups was of interest because of the following findings: (1) Being a teacher or a participant came with specific behavior requirements and thus determined the ritualist's enactment. (2) Nonpaying participants, accompanied by an affiliation with Batsheva or Gaga Movement Ltd., entered the ritual space without the additional frontier of payment. Paying participants were customers enlisting the services of Gaga Movement Ltd. as a service company. A Gaga class was a paid service, and this added additional value to the class—the value of money and the value of doing something extraordinary. It also put the service company and nonpaying ritualists in a position to guarantee a monetarily worthwhile experience. A "gray area" seemed to be the people who paid for a whole month's entry: It allowed them the freedom to decide how often to attend classes within a month without further worry about payment, or which classes to take and by which teachers. Interviewed participants with a monthly pass frequented classes five to six times a week or took three to four classes a week. Most of them showed up in class at least every second day, some even for morning and evening classes. "Customers" usually entered this circle by buying an inexpensive trial version of the monthly pass for their first time doing Gaga. (3) It made sense that for someone affiliated with Batsheva and Gaga through work, the ritual space and the ritual itself lost part of the "magic" they offered to others such as Uri, who was "admiring the people on stage and what they do and what they give" and for whom "it was always a fantasy to somehow one day find a way to know more or somehow ah BE there even." Furthermore, for others, working as a Gaga teacher or undertaking artistic projects with dance became something to be achieved: They not only became part of it throughout class, starting with Gaga, but also experienced the urge to make it their profession. (4) Having a professional or nonprofessional dance background seemed to influence the experience insofar as professional dancers took Gaga class as a training method to enhance their dance and performance skills—both consciously and unconsciously. Moreover, professionals, teachers, and participants brought along a movement repertoire, which they embodied throughout yearlong training such as "high legs," deep pliés, or a particular form and quality. As Eli observed, being a mere nonprofessional came with obvious "joy" and "nonexpectancy."

> And you could see also that people who come from abroad they really preferred the Gaga/people because it gives something out, it's shining, it's not people who train to be on stage some time and they need so beautiful and graceful, no they are people who're doing whatever they want. And this is real time, this is the real thing, there is no getting ready for something, okay?

(5) Throughout participant observation, I found that not being fluent in Modern Hebrew, I would miss small jokes made in class. I experienced people from Tel

Aviv in Gaga class as being close to the Gaga teachers and joking with them, as it seemed, not caring much about hierarchy, interpreting Gaga rules much more freely than people not at "home" in Tel Aviv Gaga culture, never behaving in a "shy" manner, and always "inside" the Gaga community. In addition, I reflected on how perhaps I could not grasp the "full" experience or understand the use of metaphors, such as "honey traveling the body," until discovering the important role honey plays in Jewish-Israeli holiday culture, or not knowing the reason for having to "take a cold shower" until having experienced the summer heat in Tel Aviv. When foreigners from the United States, Europe, and even Australia made up the bulk of participants, some teachers adjusted by not teaching in Hebrew but in English; others always only taught in English.

Ritualists could also be further distinguished (List 4).

List 4 Second Grouping of Participants

(1) Age
(2) Sex/gender
(3) Profession
(4) Time and amount of practicing
(5) Culture and language background
(6) The individual "body history" and individual body knowledge

(1) The age category correlated with the different life sections in which participants found themselves from the start of their professional career, when struggling to find a place, to having a family, having to deal with matrimonial problems such as divorce, or dealing with age-related physical problems. This mattered insofar as participants associated Gaga class with a physical-psychological transformative effect and betterment. (2) The sex/gender category could be potentially interesting in terms of comparing a Gaga class to other phenomena researched within religious studies. Participant observation revealed an average of two-thirds of people with "female" body characteristics and one-third with "male" body characteristics participating in class—however, I do not know about social and self-defined gender of participants other than my communication partners; they were a group of approximately three quarter women and one quarter men. (3) The professional background could be connected to the reasons people felt attracted to participating in Gaga: For participants with artistic backgrounds,

Gaga presented a new way of learning to express themselves and enhance their creativity or a new way in which to deal with a competitive work atmosphere. Some participants worked in the high-tech industry, and engaging with their bodies and increasing bodily awareness provided a welcome change to their work sphere. Other participants worked as yoga teachers or practitioners of different somatic body and movement therapies. For the psychologists, Gaga became an individual form of therapy and self-reflection needed. Other professions came with other reasons to practice Gaga. (4) As mentioned above, the interviewed participants usually practiced every second or third day and at least once a week, or every day and even twice a day. Some of them noted wanting to take part more often. Some of them were observed to prefer regular participation in morning classes, and others always attended one of the evening classes. Of those interviewed, some had been taking class for nearly a decade, and one only just started two months before. The amount of time spent practicing seemed to matter for the individual's emotional relationship to Gaga. (5) Depending on their individual background, some participants seemed to struggle with certain aspects of Israeli culture that they found incorporated into Gaga, like a "kibbutz arrogancy." Moreover, others were in some way inhibited from following their passion to dance because of their family culture: "I also come from a religious family and, you know, it [dance] wasn't the kind of thing to do, so I was not as connected" (Sara). Shira connected Gaga to Israeli folk dance. Others, not having grown up in Israel and not having had these experiences, did not connect Gaga to Israeli culture in any way, and even refused it, or did not feel justified to do so. (6) Depending on what implicit and explicit body knowledge they brought to Gaga class, participants interpreted and valued their perception and thus shaped their experience and the way they talk about it. Many had been or were practicing yoga; others, Ilan Lev, Feldenkrais, Alexander technique, contact improvisation, and conscious dance, such as 5rythms, Butoh, or ballet.

Identifying Ritual Roles

Aesthetically relevant in Gaga were a variety of ritual roles (List 5).

(1) The two most important "official" roles of ritualists in Gaga were the role of the teacher and that of participants. Together, they were ritual facilitators because, without them, Gaga class could not take place. Teachers were *ritual leaders*. They were supposed to start and end the class, choose the music for class, talk and give instructions to participants while moving along and deciding on which instructions to give. They were guiding participants' perception and movement,

establishing the ritual script and ritual space. Teachers were free to choose from a pool of possible Gaga movement and instruction repertoire—they had embodied Gaga classes taken with Naharin and others during teacher training—as long as they followed specific explicit guidelines concerning the script. The embodiment of Gaga instructions and movement guaranteed that teachers were following implicit guidelines. The teacher's role was restricted by Gaga Movement Ltd.: The company chose by whom and how often Gaga classes were taught in Tel Aviv. Teachers in Israel were required to attend company classes, mostly taught by Naharin, Naharin's monthly Gaga/people class, and classes by other teachers (Friedes Galili 2015, 375). Teachers working abroad advised the company about Gaga classes they were giving and paid a certain fee to the company—as far as I was told. They also returned to Israel every year "to continue their immersion and to update their knowledge of the evolving language" (375). In addition, senior teacher feedback from other teachers provided "a measure of quality control and encouraging dialogue" (375). Batsheva company dancers could be promoted as teachers, whereas outsiders had to apply to enter a teacher program. During in-field conversations, I learned that the application process was not easy and that a frequently asked requirement was that applying teachers had dance performance experience and were still actively performing. As Hannah told me, her teacher program was one year "of active time, it was nine month, three trimesters of three month each," where they studied every day. As emergent teachers, they took Gaga/dancers classes with the company, with the ensemble, or only as a small group, followed by studying Naharin's repertory—"which the idea was, and again not to learn it in order to perform it, to use it as another way of connecting to the language. There are parts and pieces that when you do them, you can understand better, what the terminology is" (Hannah). In so-called Metodika classes dedicated to explicitly exploring "techniques," they would invest much time in investigating a specific topic, movement, quality, or instruction by approaching it from different angles. They dealt with pedagogical issues and practiced teaching by teaching one another in small amounts of time first in "tool-box classes." Hannah added that the program changed from this fulltime program approach to a more open one, where emerging teachers still had classes to attend, but "they are in a sense on a much more independent track." "By the end we were working from nine ten in the morning until four five six in the evening every day five days a week. So, it's very intensive" (Hannah).

(2) Participants were ritual *followers* in the sense that they followed and consumed what was offered by the teacher. They did, however, possess agency on the output of the ritual. "Work instructions" by Gaga Movement Ltd., personal

instructions by the teacher given to people about to join their first Gaga class, and the teacher's instruction in class told participants how to behave. Participants were not allowed to stop moving, to talk throughout class, or to come late. They should "listen" to their bodies and be aware of their surroundings, the teacher, and other participants. Throughout Naharin's class in December 2016, for example, he reminded people to "watch your teacher every ten seconds!" and added: "I want to have a diagonal with everyone, so I can see everyone, everyone can see me." Following instructions in class, participants were guided to move in the space in a certain way and with a specific quality to perceive particularities by awareness guidance and to experience what the teacher offered.

Furthermore, ritualists enacted roles that did not necessarily enter official public discourse as such, but had a unique sensory impact: (3) the "(Batsheva) dancer" moving in an inspiring way, who can be copied or just admired by fellow ritualists; (4) fellow Gaga teachers or senior Gaga teachers offering feedback (as a participant, one could feel "watched" by them, although they were also a source of inspiration, and one recognized them as ritual specialists; sometimes one could tell the teacher was nervous or excited because of the other teachers' presence); (5) friends, whose mere presence enhanced experience; (6) people disturbing the ritual (they were stepping in and out of class, perhaps going to the washroom, looking at their phone, or even talking, and by doing so, they provided additional sensory information that other ritualists had then to deal with).

(7) Naharin's physical absence played a special role because it led to the *collective imagination of his authoritative presence*. Teachers would refer to him and present him as the source and inspiration for their ritual actions, for example, when introducing a new movement idea they gained in Naharin's class. Naharin's role of a teacher in classes taught by himself varied from that of other teachers because of the excessive authority he owned as the creator of Gaga. He could potentially introduce totally new movement ideas, and, following his own guidelines through yearlong embodiment and enactment of Gaga, he, differing from the other teachers, could potentially break free from them.

List 5 Aesthetically Effective Ritual Roles (Human)

(1) The leaders
(2) The followers
(3) The sources of inspiration/admiration

(4) The specialists as correctives, knowledge sources, authorities
(5) The "friends" as emotionally attached and empathetic
(6) The disturbers
(7) The (absent/imaginary present) "guru"

Identifying Ritual Agency

Teachers own agency because of their role as ritual leaders, guiding participants through verbal input and movement. Gaga teachers were officially recognized and certified by the company, and they used this to advertise themselves. Their names and short bios were found on the official Gaga website. Not everyone could become a teacher, which made it something desirable and aspirational to some participants. However, the teachers' individual agency varied according to their behavior, appearance, and mood, as perceived and interpreted by participants: A participant mentioned that she found it boring if all teachers just used what they heard and learned in Naharin's class. She preferred the teacher behaving as an "artist," combining "the basic principles of Gaga" with their own artistry. As Maya indicated in her diary, depending on the teacher, the class could either be successful in terms of a positive overall experience or fail in terms of a negative experience. On the one hand, a teacher who had "a very straight forward 'manly' approach," "interrupt[ed] the flow," and took himself too seriously was equally negative to Maya, as someone who was "too active and too 'on the surface,'" appeared "passive aggressive," or allowed the "energy" to become "stuck" and produced "a lot of breaks when she was explaining things and everybody was standing in place." Maya said she then had a hard time connecting to the teacher—the teacher did not possess much agency. On the other hand, Maya talked positively about a teacher with "charisma" and "beautiful movement that came from real knowledge and understanding of movement without any 'show off' just pure clean inspirational beauty that comes from within"—in this case an "inspirational" ensemble dancer. Another teacher owned the agency for producing a "spiritual experience":

> Really out of the ordinary teacher that creates deep, meaningful interesting, invigorating movement experiences. I was swept away by his energies and was eager to get more information and inspiration. The effort was meaningful and clear. The teacher's artistic background (in a variety of arts) and maturity went through and gave the feeling of being a part of a meaningful artistic research. (Maya)

Others mentioned similar experiences. Shira mentioned having left class because she could not stand a teacher's "harsh" energy and music, which she experienced as "awful." Participant observation also led me to the conclusion that the teacher's mood or choice of music, as well as the choice of ritual action, influenced the ritual output, and the teacher's agency thus depended on these parameters. As people knew beforehand who was going to teach, a teacher could even influence the decision of what class to attend.

Participants owned agency by the sensory input they provided to their fellow participants, but they owned agency to an even greater extent by the sensory input they provided to the teacher, who then took up the perceived for further ritual actions: Hannah noticed how teaching Gaga, as well as knowing what instructions to give, stemmed from "stay[ing] open to what's happening with the group" and "in the room." She would sometimes pick up something from a "particular individual"—sometimes going with the perceived, sometimes "countering" the perceived with her reaction.

Constant influence and a different kind of ritual agency was owned by Naharin. This seemed to be due not only to him being known as the creator of Gaga but also to his appearance in class when teaching: I observed him as always wearing his unique clothing, a long-sleeved t-shirt, stitched, and long "working pants" in modest colors such as blue, green, or gray. His appearance seemed intentional. Naharin seemed tall, and he had a special spatial presence. He had a deep, melodious voice, and he did not look his age at all. Giving class, Naharin seemed to be fully aware of himself performing the role of "Ohad Naharin," "Mr. Gaga." In terms of agency, it was interesting to consider what participants said about Naharin: Idan ascribed a "cultish" effect to Gaga—"It's more than just a movement class." He observed a "worshipping of Ohad," which he seemed to equally dislike and understand: "I mean, he's amazing." Tamar named Naharin "the greatest teacher of [her] life." He was the source of all "wisdom." The teachers were "his" and "channeling him." Sara thought of Gaga as something "genius," and the "genius" originated with Naharin because he created it. Eli, who in general seemed somewhat more critical of Gaga as an organization, nevertheless held Naharin in high regard when talking about him and called him "wise." Shira called Naharin "the master" and "guru" and said it was necessary "from time to time to have a class with the master." To her, his classes were special because he had "a very intense energy," "something unique," extraordinary agency, which he derived not only from his own aesthetical appearance but also from what participants ascribed to him by the way they behaved in his presence. Shira also considered Naharin's ability to oversee a room with many people and still see and note individual behavior or, at least, to appear to see and note it. She once felt being picked out by him and felt an instruction being directed to herself personally. Other teachers were only "mediators" through which she "receive[d] his teaching." In her interview, Ester told me about the "amazing," mind-blowing, overwhelming experience in Naharin's class. Quite contrary to other classes, she was "completely in it," as she let go and ended up "dripping wet"—she had not experienced this in public for a long time: "It's as though there is a motor that is ten times stronger. The engine is ten time's stronger, it's like: ouf! It blew my mind." Ester attributed Naharin's agency to a "combination of many things": "knowing that it's him," the number of ritualists, and the presence of great ex-Batsheva dancers and teachers—she was an admirer of Batsheva for a long time. However, as she said, "it's not just that": She believed that Naharin did things or behaved in a way that other teachers could never do, but he could, because people knew him as Ohad Naharin, the creator of Gaga. He owned authority over "philosophy and a method." According to Ester,

> Some of [the teachers] are superb, some of them excellent, ah—none of them are Ohad. Now when he does this, he's not, he's incorporating it all into his movement, he is not teaching the a-b-c of how to do it, that we have from our classes. He is taking us the one stage further of sort of flying with it. That's the way I understand it.

For Ester, "Ohad" was the only one who could dare to say "imitate me." Ester described her experience in Naharin's class as extraordinary and incomparable to other class experiences.

Similarly, to Uri, Naharin's (the "master's") classes were "different" from classes taught by others: "They have to be different because he is who he is." To Uri, some teachers owned a special agency, as they were his "idols for years," having "seen them on stage," and "to study with them it's like just that is an experience." However,

> So, with Ohad it's like that ten a hundred times, he' s the guy that created all of this and has done so much for the dance world and that I have seen so many of his works and admired his genius and then I'm there and he is teaching. And everything that I love about Gaga is this guy's creation. So, there is something special about going to a class with the master. This—regardless of what he ends up doing in the class. (Uri)

Uri also noticed how, in Naharin's classes, there was a specific ritual space characteristic: "There is no other class where the people are so ordered around the middle like in Ohad class, and where their gaze is focused on the teacher so strongly, as it is in Ohad's class. There is a magnetism space that is different than other classes, I think."

In addition, Naharin seemed to possess an extraordinary "personality" and "charisma." Participants described classes with Naharin as a heightened experience compared to classes with other teachers, not only due to who he is but also due to his aesthetical appearance. Vice versa, Gaga's popularity, the ritual effect, and the agency of the teacher seemed to profit from Naharin's agency.

2.3 Script

What defines a ritual as an enactment of a specific kind is the "script." Script, understood as the "written text of a stage play, screenplay, or broadcast" or "a plan of action" (*Merriam-Webster* 2019b), was chosen as the title to this next section, which focuses on the procedural, enactive, and "fleeting" character of ritual (see Grimes 2014, 263). Examining the script includes identifying what actions are happening throughout the course of a Gaga class. It is about "how class looks": Is there a specific timing and phrasing? What are the constitutive actions?

Script includes Grimes' categories *ritual action* and *ritual time*. Some aspects of ritual time, such as the "timing" in the sense of the time at which Gaga class takes place, as well as the "regularity" and the "frequency" of classes happening, have already been mentioned elsewhere, so they will only be briefly addressed here. For a script, the "duration," and especially the "phasing" of class, is now of interest. "Ritual phasing" is defined as the "temporal patterning ('rhythm') of a ritual," the "plot" of a ritual consisting of a "beginning, middle and end" (Grimes 2014, 262). A ritual consists of different ritual "phases" as "chronological subunits" of the whole ritual. Ritual phases can be explicit, in the sense of being recognized as such by all or some of the ritualists or because of distinct markers signifying the beginning of a new phase. However, ritual phases can also be implicit, only to be uncovered and made explicit through the eyes of a researcher. Each phase can be divided into smaller phases, smaller time units again, and sometimes phases are found to be repeated (266–7). Ritual and ritual phases are filled with and constitute the different ritual actions that are undertaken by ritualists in the context of the ritual. Ritualists are enacting the actions, and through their enactment, actions generate the ritual effect. Actions can also be the action of actively receiving and perceiving something and the action of actively avoiding action (246, also 243).

"Gaga/people" classes at the Suzanne Dellal Centre took place every workday. During my participant observation period, the classes were offered on Sundays, Mondays, Wednesdays, and Thursdays at 9 a.m., 7 p.m., and 8.15 p.m. On Tuesdays, only one regular class was held at 9 a.m. Once a month, "class with Ohad Naharin" was offered at 8 p.m. on a Tuesday evening. Friday evenings and the evenings of holidays were generally free of class. However, toward the end of my research, the center started to offer additional morning classes on Tuesdays and Thursdays. These classes were not planned to last a full hour as the other regular classes, but only fifty minutes from 8 to 8.50 a.m. The one hour of regular classes was occasionally shortened when class started some minutes late due to some "announcements" made about future classes and workshops, when the dance room was needed for company rehearsal afterwards, or on Yom HaShoah when, at 10 a.m. with the siren call, Israelis stood still to observe two minutes of silence. The sensory effect of a Gaga class was not bound to the one hour of class; the sensory atmosphere before and after class was equally important and effective, as was demonstrated earlier in the context of ritual space. The overall framing of ritual phasing consisted of the time before class, functioning as a prolog and phase of preparation; the time in class, which was the main part and experiential climax; and the time after class, functioning as an epilog and as time for reflection on the experience while leaving the ritual space and reentering "normality." These overall phases were explicit insofar as they were structured by the teacher who began and ended the class. Time before class was limited by the possibility to enter the building—usually not earlier than thirty minutes and not later than five minutes before class started. For newcomers, class started with a private instruction from the teacher regarding the "rules" of class. The general signal for the start of the class was the teacher starting the music, making their way to the middle of class, and starting to move. Only sometimes a "let's start" was required. Class ended with an individual "goodbye" from the teacher, usually accompanied by the lowering of the music volume and with applause from the participants. Time after class inside the classroom was limited if the room was needed for subsequent classes or rehearsals. If the room was not needed for company training or rehearsal, then people were free to stay and dance on, stretch, or talk. However, only a small percentage usually took advantage of the possibility, since many had to hurry and either head on to work in the mornings or go on dates in the evenings; some took it more slowly but left the room quite fast to go for a coffee. The phase of epilog usually continued throughout the changing room talks, the coffee talks, and on the way to the next appointment, and it faded out slowly.

In terms of whether there was a specific timing and ritual phasing to the time of class, the core "ritual," Gaga teachers as ritual leaders emphasized that teaching Gaga was significantly different from teaching other classes, as they did not need to prepare a schedule for class, including a particular set of actions, tasks, and instructions to give; they did not have to follow a fixed phasing: "With Gaga class, it's for me as teacher much more fluid and I don't know exactly what's going to happen" (Hannah). Hannah noted how, within the fixed phase of the "one hour time frame of the class," what was happening was structured by sensory input she experienced outside the class context such as body knowledge obtained in Gaga classes, body knowledge stemming from one's own physical-psychological constitution, or experiences inside the classroom observing other people in space. The phasing and content of class was thus variable and subject to daily change. Additional variety provided the simple fact that Gaga was a ritual still in evolution:

> Content has changed over time in a sense. Because Ohad is constantly researching, the research is constantly evolving; so, there are things that we do in class now, that we didn't do four years ago. There are things that we did four years ago, that we do far less now; there are tools that in a sense he has given us, that he didn't have to give three years ago; so, that has affected the teaching as well. (Hannah)

Hannah also mentioned that she had had problems with this open phasing and the lack of a "plan" at the beginning of teaching: "I will say, at the very beginning I was very, very nervous before (laughs) every class and now I am less so, I trust more in the process and in my body and my ability to be spontaneous and available and open to all of the dialogs happening at once."

However, other teachers hinted that phasing was not completely random and free: "We need to raise the heartbeat at least three times. If there's no speed, it's not a Gaga class … Well, it's not a rule, but it's at least: don't wait too long to have a moment of exaggeration or a moment of speed" (Ayala). Furthermore, some ritual followers noticed a specific phasing of Gaga classes. Idan, for example, pointed out the phase "at the end of class, where people just go wild," when the teacher turned up the music and let people "dance."

In opposition to the claimed freedom from a plan and structure, participant observation revealed an implicit "typical" structure and phasing that classes shared. Classes usually started with the action of "floating" (for more details on this and the following techniques, see Chapter 5). Sometimes there was no verbal instruction to float, but the teacher started moving in a way that was recognizable to participants as such. Instructions given at the beginning were usually about creating and raising awareness of the whole body and body state, "connecting to the body." In addition to awareness exercises, especially morning classes often contained a phase dedicated to stretching the muscles and mobilizing the joints. Not long after this, the teacher would work to raise the participants' body temperature by instructing them to increase movement speed, movement range, or movement effort or to move through the room. This would happen at least a second time during class, often in the form of an instruction to "run in place." While other phases after the beginning never followed in the same order, they were still fixed by actions provoked and passed on to participants as movements or instructions: There was a phase of movement in space, where ritualists moved through the room, changing place. There was a part where ritualists went down to the floor until lying down and started moving from there or went down and moved close to the floor. Many classes included set movement exercises such as bending, stretching, twisting the upper part of the body, such as "curving" and "looking under the table," or moving in set steps from right to left. Ritual leaders chose the rest of the ritual phases constituting actions from their own embodied explicit and implicit body knowledge. If actions and thus phases were repeated throughout different classes, it seemed most likely that an action had arisen in Naharin's or company classes. Toward the end of the ritual, teachers mostly included a phase of "free time to explore." Participants were told to recapitulate what they had heard, seen, and enacted in this specific class via movement. Some classes ended with what Idan called "going wild" to loud music. The instructions "find your own movement" and "don't take yourself too serious" could also be given in the context of the free exploration time. In addition, the body temperature and blood flow could be explicitly raised for a last time through movement such as "running," "taking a cold shower," or "drumming" with one's own hands on different parts of the body, all the while increasing the impact through counting. Often, however, participants were guided back to a state of bodily awareness at the very end of class: They were told to "listen" to the bodily aftermath of increased movement. Participants were left there to "listen to the echo" and "feel your new body" or "feel your body ready for the day." The last essential phase and action of a Gaga class seemed to be an applause aimed at the teacher after class in the form of clapping. The duration and intensity of the applause was found to correlate with the perceived "success" of class.

On the one hand, the ritual effect of a Gaga class primarily depended on the ritual actions of the teacher talking and moving, which together form the action of instructing and guiding participants and which provided the main sensory impact for participants (see Chapter 4). On the other hand, the effect needed the perceptive action of participants, the reception of visual and auditive input provided by the teachers, and the enactment of the instructions in the form of movement copying and performance of verbally requested movement. All of these actions were constitutive of a Gaga class and its effect. Alongside these actions, "side-actions" took place that influenced the individual effect by additional sensory input: Participants pulled up their sleeves, took off their clothes, or removed their socks; they chose and changed their place; and they smiled at one another, laughed, or even shed some tears as reactions to something perceived. Some left the room to go to the toilet and had a drink or looked at their phone, albeit rarely. A participant occasionally talked in reaction to the teacher. As experienced by myself, one could get "carried away" by one's own thoughts, starting to "day-dream." Participants also revealed to me that sometimes they would deliberately decide to not follow a task instructed, or they would go on with a movement, even though the teacher already requested a new one. Furthermore, the windows were opened, the air conditioner turned on or off, or the volume of music turned up or down.

2.4 Language

Language enters the description of a Gaga class as only one of many possible media providing aesthetic input, stimulating the senses, and shaping perception throughout class. Still, the aesthetical role of language, understood as words uttered, throughout class is central: Words throughout class "do" things (Grimes 2014, 276–7). Due to the nature of language perception, words are largely responsible for producing body knowledge actualizations. From an aesthetical point of view, especially words uttered by the teacher take up the position of "performative utterances" (276). Although, someone else talking could also provoke an embodied effect, for example, the emotional experience of annoyance or the experience of being disturbed. Therefore, not only "words of decorum," such as "instructions," "facilitating directives" and "announcements," and "incidental talk," but also words uttered outside the time frame of class, such as "commentary by participants" or "behind-the-scenes shoptalk among leaders," have a "performative" effect (276).

My research, observation, and analysis concentrated mainly on language of an English nature. This is because, first, during the month of participant observation, I only experienced one Gaga class held entirely in Hebrew and less than half of the other classes were taught equally in English and in Hebrew. English and Hebrew classes were taught by Gaga teachers with an Israeli cultural background, be it former or active Batsheva dancers or not. There was also sometimes a tendency to speak Hebrew, and other times English: Teachers would give the Hebrew version of an instruction first, count in Hebrew, and make affirmations and small talk in Hebrew, or the other way round. English-only classes were taught by Batsheva dancers with a foreign cultural background, by Israeli teachers who had taught abroad for a long time, or by foreigners who had immigrated to Israel. Having met at least one participant who did not speak English at all, it was only possible to guess that, perhaps to non-English speakers, the language lost part of its performative effect when they could not understand what was said.

The language used in the context of a Gaga class was not only of an English nature but also of a Gaga nature. I found a specific Gaga vocabulary entering spoken language. This language seemed to have existed from the beginning, when Naharin decided to connect particular words and imagery with specific movements and movement qualities:

> By the early 2000s, he had already articulated a significant physical and corresponding verbal vocabulary that may be considered the basis of Gaga. From this era, the dancers interviewed remember "floating," "curves and circles," "pulling the bones out of soft flesh," "thick" and "soft" textures, "letting go," "quaking" and "shaking," "other forces," "traveling movement" and "traveling balls" in the body, and finding "a good taste in your mouth." (Friedes Galili 2015, 370)

Gaga teachers usually did not come up with their own imagery to describe movement or body qualities to participants, but Gaga provided a pool of imagery in loosely fixed formulations, which teachers drew on. Part of Gaga's very own language is thus its imagery (Friedes Galili 2015, 372). Friedes Galili (370) mentions how an organized process of developing a Gaga language, a Gaga "lexicon," was enforced when Gaga became the main training method of Batsheva. Naharin would devise "new concepts and corresponding terms" "every few weeks," meaning that he coined particular names for his concepts, which were inspired by the Japanese language or by people who he knew possessed specific qualities that he wanted to name, such as the always available gardener (370–1). The terms became "shortcuts" for movements, movement qualities, and body parts: "Gaga's lexicon more broadly outlines a state, place in the body, or quality available for research, leaving the physical form relatively open" (371). However, with time, some of the Gaga vocabulary disappeared from use—"perhaps in response to the issue of accessibility," as Friedes Galili (371) suggests. The words were substituted by "common language" denotations such as "available" and "ready to snap," which substituted for the former used "dolfi," for example (371). The particular Gaga imagery remained as characteristic of the Gaga language. One part of the Gaga language vocabulary was dedicated to how to talk about the body: Gaga owned its own lexicon to talk about the different body parts, consisting of imagery alongside still-used Gaga-specific names, resulting in a Gaga body concept that teachers used as the base for talking about the body in class. Yet, the Gaga language was used not only by teachers during class but also by Gaga participants talking about Gaga: Participants spoke about their bodies consisting of the components of the Gaga body; the Gaga language even seemed to become the only way for participants to express their Gaga experiences and analyze them. Neither Gaga teachers nor Gaga participants cited the Gaga language from a written version or text; the taking-up of the language seemed to come naturally from partaking in class and listening to it.

Different forms of language with a possible performative effect could be found in a Gaga class (List 6): Most importantly, there were (1) the instructions given by the teacher. These performative utterances consisted of a variation of movement demands, which were variable in terms of both content and grammatical construction. Instructions often included imagery, metaphors, or descriptive parts. Due to the way they were designed and performed by teachers and the way they were perceived and enacted by participants, instructions unfolded a twofold performative effect: They became directly effective as aesthetics when participants listened to and understood them. They became performatively effective in a second step when they, first, caused ritual movement and, second, through it, caused an embodied effect. Hence instructions form a fundamental part of body knowledge transformation in Gaga, and they are treated in more detail in the further course of this book. Alongside instructions, the teacher's language included (2) affirmative utterances such as (in Hebrew) יפי "(slang) a beauty!" and יפה "Excellent! Well done! Bravo!" and טוב "good" or the English "nice" and "good." In addition, it consisted of (3) motivating and driving utterances to increase movement quality, such as "thicker"/"softer," "faster"/"slower," "further"/"tinier," or "bigger"/"smaller." Here, a specific format was (4) a countdown introduced by the teacher: counting down from ten to one in Hebrew or English while increasing a specific movement quality such as speed or strength to the maximum. Participants' language also came in here: Counting down was a collective language action performed by the teacher and participants together. Moreover, some teachers sometimes tended to make (5) "small talk": They shared with participants small personal stories, often funny or weird anecdotes, from their daily life. The performative effect of all teachers' language varied with their speed of talking, the number of words uttered, and their perceived agency. Finally, during class, not only language but also (6) the absence of language had a great performative potential: Participants were told not to talk during class. This meant that there was a sensory focus on the auditive input given by the teacher, and random utterances from participants, neglecting the ban, came to be experienced as disturbing. When the vocal contribution of participants was asked for in the action of counting down, the performative effect of language utterances was even greater: on the one hand, the sensory effect of hearing many saying a countdown and, on the other hand, the sensory effect of being physically involved through talking in the action of counting—not only enacting the transformation of the movement quality with the body but also connecting it to the voice. Furthermore, the basic absence of language from participants made it possible that their voice was used and addressed as a form of bodily movement, situating it along other media of bodily communication and expression. Teachers demanded its use as they demanded the movement of any other specific body part.

List 6 Aesthetically Effective Kinds of Language

(1) Instructions (performative utterances)
(2) Affirmative utterances
(3) Motivating and driving utterances
(4) Countdown
(5) Small talk
(6) Absence of language

Outside class but inside the Gaga context, language was a medium of communication and exchange not only between one participant and another but also between a participant and the teacher. In communication among participants, they exchanged small talk, yet they also reflected on their experience in Gaga, and by listening to others, they gained access to others' experiences, forming a new collective and shared discourse on the Gaga experience. Participants also exchanged greetings and friendly small talk with the teachers if they knew them personally, or they offered the teachers class-related verbal feedback mostly in the form of appreciation after a class they enjoyed; this sometimes turned into a more elaborate discussion about certain aspects.

2.5 Rules and Institutions

Gaga Movement Ltd. ensured that Gaga participants worldwide were provided with some kind of "rules" before their first class. Workshop participants received them via mail, whereas participants new to class were instructed orally by the teacher before class. Besides, they could be found on the official website: Gagapeople.com listed "work instructions" for people who wanted to join a Gaga class. They were already full of Gaga language. They underlined what Gaga Movement Ltd., as the author of the website, wanted the main behavioral guidelines and the rules for participation in class to be. By enabling future participants, or simply anyone frequenting the website, to read the rules and by teachers providing an obligatory oral version of the rules to every newcomer to class, not only a basic culture of ritual behavior but also a discourse on what Gaga's culture of ritual behavior looked like would be established.

Gaga's work instructions functioned as an explicit form of what Grimes calls "institutions": Individual ritualists entering a ritual establish ritual institutions. These institutions include all the necessary ritual know-how. It is because of these institutions that rituals can persist and be repeated throughout time, even if participating individuals change (Grimes 2014, 281). Ritual institutions can be written down, as is the case with Gaga's work instructions, but the written version does not necessarily coincide with the way in which the instructions are actually performed—even when the performance is claimed to follow the text (279).

The work instructions changed in terms of formulation, look, and structure from when participant observation started, in December 2016, to the summer of 2019, when this chapter was written. However, the main content (the general ideas) and the main character remained intact throughout the different versions. The evolution of the layout and content of the work instructions on the website demonstrated a unification in terms of both look and language. In addition, it reflected a professionalization of Gaga's ritual institutions. Gaga Movement Ltd. seemed to increasingly reflect on the effect particular written formulations could have on a potential reader, and the company thus shaped the work instructions in what was perceived as the optimal way to serve its aims. Throughout the years,

Gaga Movement Ltd. established a corporate language design and experienced a process of codification of ritual institutions, represented in the layout, content, and language of the instructions.

The main aspects of Gaga's ritual, its ritual institutions, and the rules conducted from the written versions of work instructions were as follows: (1) Ritualists should never stop their movement, though they were allowed to vary the intensity of movement, speed, and muscle tone. (2) Ritualists should think of the instructions as "layers of information." After enacting an instruction and the teacher offering a new instruction, the ritualists should possibly continue enacting—or at least aim to enact—the first one before enacting the next. (3) The basic bodily condition ritualists should create at the beginning of class and maintain throughout is the bodily awareness or holistic sensory awareness— "listening to the body." (4) Ritualists were told to experience "pleasure" through movement and especially during "effort," which could influence the experience output insofar as participants would most likely experience "pleasure." (5) On the other hand, ritualists were forbidden from experiencing "bad" pain; only "good" pain was allowed as "the burning sensation in our muscles." (6) An important rule of class was the ban on closing the eyes. (7) In addition, people were allowed to "copy" movement from others, that is, be "inspired" by others and "imitate" others. (8) However, participants were not allowed to talk unless the teacher demanded the use of voice are talking in an instruction. (9) It seemed to be especially important to remind participants to arrive on time while emphasizing that punctuality mattered as part of Gaga's ritual culture. The rule was that participants arriving late could not enter the ritual space or participate in class. (10) Finally, ritual participation was limited to people without shoes.

The oral versions of work instructions given by the teachers before and during class more or less reflected all of these rules, with emphasis placed on not stopping, bodily awareness, the enactment of different instructions at once, the difference between good pain and bad pain, and the possibility to copy others as another possibility to grasp the meaning of instruction. Participants were told not to feel forced to be creative. Regarding the rules of not speaking or coming late, for some teachers, these rules seemed highly important, and for others, less so. Furthermore, "pleasure within effort" is something participants were constantly reminded about throughout class, and the same holds for "layering." In addition to oral work instructions functioning as initial statements and reminders during class, their aspects were also constantly enacted, and thus embodied, during a Gaga class. For example, the teacher would issue many instructions during class with the aim of leading participants to a holistic awareness of their body and surroundings, creating "listening"—which is one among the basic rules. In this sense, not only were instructions given orally or in writing, but ritualists were also forced to enact them.

The discourse on Gaga's ritual institutions was not reflected solely in the work instructions. It was reflected in all aspects of the Gaga language discussed above. In addition to the work instructions, all information presented on the website, language- as well as content-wise, communicated a discourse on "Gaga" and thus Gaga culture: Gaga was presented as a "fundamentally physical" practice (Gaga Movement Ltd. 2019b). The "layering of information" was said to provide a "physical[ly] challenging experience." It was presented as a "workout that develops flexibility, stamina, agility, coordination, and efficiency of movement." It was "strengthening and invigorating the body." The workout effect of a Gaga class was created by an "exploration of form, speed, and effort" and an "investigation of soft and thick textures, delicacy and explosive power, and understatement and exaggeration" (Gaga Movement Ltd. 2019a). It seemed to be a characteristic of, as well as important for, Gaga practice to create and enhance its participants' physical fitness, which, from the website's point of view, meant becoming more flexible and agile, possessing more stamina, being able to better coordinate the movements, and using movement in an (energy-)efficient way. Gaga's aim was to "wake up" bodies not only by making them fitter but also by enabling people to "connect" to them through "deep listening," "awareness," and the "experience of physical sensations" (2019a). Not only bodily fitness but also bodily control, in the sense of an encompassing awareness of one's own body, was to be achieved. Fitness and awareness were highlighted in the sense of achievable physical constitution. On the other hand, Gaga was said to offer certain benefits exceeding mere physical betterment. Gaga offered a place where people could "refresh": "Gaga generates happiness and flow and increases the ability to cope with challenges" (2019a). Refreshing thus meant that Gaga provoked positive emotions and the ability to forget the reality outside class, established "flow," and helped one to deal with problematic situations. Gaga was said to create "pleasure" and enable participants to "enjoy the pleasure of movement in a welcoming, accepting atmosphere" (Gaga Movement Ltd. 2019b) and "to connect to … powerful emotions, and movement … in life" (2019a). Due to its "improvisational nature," Gaga practice was said to function individually, via a "deeply personal connection with Gaga" (Gaga Movement Ltd. 2019b). Gaga was presented as a practice that induced emotional-habitual transformation toward a better emotional-habitual state, and as a place where people could be "happy" and free from everyday life, free from prejudice, and free to experience emotions, being on a collective yet individual journey. In addition to highlighting Gaga's physical and psychological benefits, Gaga was displayed as a practice of ever-changing character: "Ohad Naharin continues to develop and research his movement language, and the classes evolve and vary accordingly" (Gaga Movement Ltd. 2019a).

Oral or written institutions do not always equal "reality" (the enacted culture), as Grimes emphasized, and the same is valid for Gaga. However, the oral and written know-how provides an imaginative behavioral guideline by which behavior is judged. Oral and written rules and culture directly affect the experience output, not only by the sensory restriction and sensory input they deliver but also by offering body schemes, worldviews, and experience schemata on how to judge the experienced.

The centralization of Gaga's aesthetics overseen by the Gaga Movement Ltd. guarantees the applicability of the observations in this chapter beyond the concrete ethnographic field of Gaga classes at Suzanne Dellal in Tel Aviv. However, as just shown, all environmental aesthetics are themselves highly relational and fluid. Small changes of "-scape," variation of actors and actions, the individual and contemporary and fleeting character of participants' emotional-habitual status, or alterations of the nature's sensory input—online formats, for example, come with sensory deprivation as well as with focusing on the audiovisual—are of significance to the experience output and, therefore, must be considered carefully. By this chapter I hope to have outlined some aesthetically important ritual categories to be considered in the analysis of ritualized practices in general, but most importantly, I hope for the reader to take away the knowledge about the relational nature of these categories.

3

Body Topography in Discussion

Gaga's "body topography"—a term borrowed from Susan Leigh Foster (1997, 238) and introduced to the research on Gaga by Friedes Galili (2015, 375)—denotes the explicit part of Gaga's aesthetics and body knowledge. This topography is observable as text communicated via various media or becomes explicit as movement. It is an explicit ideal that guides participants, while it also becomes something participants can self-identify with. Its explicitness makes it possible for participants to rely on it when perceiving their own bodies or when moving. The topography becomes an explicit perceptual order, which participants strive to incorporate. Leigh Foster's body topography represents a bodily compartment specific to what she calls a particular "dance technique" (1997, 238): the enactment of an ideal body knowledge. The body topography is animated in movement (238). The movement itself is crucial for the realization and transfer of a particular body topography, and thus is a characteristic part of it.

The body topography carries cultural and social historical discourses. These discourses are transferred to Gaga via the body history and body knowledge of Naharin. It is in body and movement that the embodiment of social and cultural discourses, historical and ideological body images, and movement conventions occurs. Some explicit discourses are embodied and experienced through cognitive mechanisms of semiotic understanding, while the implicit discourses are embodied through the enactment of a Gaga class. By taking on these culturally and socially shaped bodies and movement and participating with their transformed bodies in societies where they interact with other society members, Gaga participants themselves become media for the transfer of discourses.

To simplify the analysis of the body topography, I distinguish between the *Gaga body concept*, on the one hand, and the *Gaga movement style*, on the other. The *Gaga body concept* represents the Gaga body image understood from a "sociocultural" perspective: The Gaga body image consists of the "societal ideals" of how bodies function and should function; these ideals are discussed in different discourses within the Gaga "society" and are then "internalized by individuals" (Tiggemann 2012, 13), enabling them to successfully or unsuccessfully self-identify with Gaga's body image. The body image affects how participants experience their bodies and valuate and structure their experience. The explicit part of the body image, the "aesthetically ideal" body (Leigh Foster 1997, 237), is hidden and passed on in marketing language, instructions, and the aesthetic environment. It becomes both a "demonstrative" body (238), as enacted by the teacher, and a "perceived" body, when enacted by participants themselves (237). As Friedes Galili observes, "Over time, Gaga users can 'turn on their lena,' 'ignite many engines' throughout their body, 'cancel the box in their chest,' connect to the 'snake of their spine' and 'rope of their arms,' and so forth" (2015, 375–7).

Exploring *Gaga's movement style* means looking at Gaga's body topography in motion. Here also, one could talk of "aesthetically ideal," "demonstrative," and "perceived" movement (see Leigh Foster 1997, 237–8). Part of Gaga's movement is explicit, visible to an outside observer, though not textual, as carried out by the moving bodies; part of it remains implicit to the outside observer, only to be felt by the person enacting it themselves: "While the results of movement can be seen and heard, they are primarily received by the person doing the moving as felt experience, as kinesthesia" (Sklar 2000, 72). Following Judith Hamera (2007, 4–16), movement style is a technique producing collectively moving bodies and a common language shared within a community: "a lexicon, a grammar of/or affiliation—even a rhetoric—in motion. It facilitates interpersonal and social relations as it shapes bodies" (5). Movement style "govern[s] and standardize[s] dance practice" and "determine[s] how members of communities organized by technique analyze and understand their re-written bodies" (6). It also functions as an "archive" (6). Like the body concept, the movement style influences the embodied experience and the validation of experience by transforming individual movement techniques, movement qualities, and movement range when its movement "possibilities" are enacted. The movement style defines body scheme and perceptual order; it becomes a way of thinking.

Both body and movement united in the body topography hold the potential to affect what was introduced as body scheme, on the one hand, and embodied worldview, on the other. Body topography becomes embodied via the production of body knowledge in practice. Gaga participants are confronted with the sensory input of instructions and repeated tasks to enact, thereby communicating and stimulating the creation of the same body knowledge over and over again, until the topography is integrated and embodied.

3.1 Gaga Body Concept

The website of Gaga produces a discourse and collective know-how on Gaga, which includes offering a particular body image. Instructions complement the body image. Together, website and instructions have been functioning as dispositif for a Gaga body carrying the following characteristics:

The Gaga body is the subject and object of practice. It becomes the tool to gain "knowledge and self-awareness" (Gaga Movement Ltd. 2017c). On the one hand, physical sensations are valued over unembodied imagination and emotion (Gaga Movement Ltd. 2017b). On the other hand, there is no dichotomy between a self and a body: From the content of instructions, I understood that I am the body, and instructions are to be directly embodied by myself physically. "Sense," "spread," "float," and "smear yourself," for example, are instructions that address a holistic body concept, and their enactment needs the embodied self as the actor. Furthermore, in "Yawning," "making faces," and "becoming silly," for example, the body is intended to take on the physical part of the body knowledge of actions, which are connected to particular emotional states. No boundary remains between physical sensations and experienced emotions, though emotions are not explicitly addressed by the actions. Instead, Gaga techniques play with the physicality of emotional states as body knowledge transformations. Instructions such as "grab your bones" or "slide your bones out" show that, although the body should be viewed as a whole, there is a "you," a self, which remains in charge of the actions: It is "you" doing something with or to "your" body. Moreover, instructions such as "Being overwhelmed by movement," "Let the quake happen to you," and "Connect to far-away engines" imply that there is something within the body that somehow lies beyond the level of control of the aware self, something implicit. Nevertheless, the self can still willingly turn it on and off.

The Gaga body is always aware—in a constant state of focused attention and open monitoring of oneself and the surroundings. This awareness becomes the key to perceive one's "physical weaknesses" and eliminate them (Gaga Movement Ltd. 2017b, 2017c). The mode of attention is a "listening to the body" (Naharin in Gaga Movement Ltd. 2017c) and is seen as a baseline for everything else happening in class. Connected to the idea of awareness is the notion that there is a "flow of energy and information through our body in all directions" (Naharin in Gaga Movement Ltd. 2017b). Following class is said to increase awareness, as awareness is constantly trained by the instructions given (Gaga Movement Ltd. 2017b). The instructions train awareness by "sensing," which means perceiving sensations. Though teachers sometimes use the verb "feel" within the instructions, there is a clear distinction between "emotions" and sensations; only the latter is said to be of interest for Gaga practice. The "physicality" of sensations is emphasized. Instructions should become sensations, and sensations are to be created and observed. Instructions demand that participants pay attention to sensory input from the inside and outside of the body. In many cases, this sensory information is used for the creation of movement. Though instructions help bodies to sense collectively, they also include moments where participants are requested to sense individually—a "good taste in your mouth," a "happy memory," or "someone you love." The Gaga body is "calm and alert at once" (Naharin in Gaga Movement Ltd. 2017c) and "available" (Naharin in Gaga Movement Ltd. 2017b) to react. By listening to its senses with open "seeing" and never just "staring" eyes, the Gaga body never sleeps, shuts down, or drifts away and becomes unaware of what it is doing.

The Gaga body is a floating body. Floating is something the participants are steadily reminded of. Floating, the so-called default mode, the standby mode of the body, as teachers referred to it during class, provokes a body where everything is always active and controlled. Every part of the body should always be sensed and not "dropped into gravity." Again, the idea of floating is connected to the image that movement can travel through the body. The floating body is thus an interconnected body, where everything happening influences different areas of the body simultaneously. A floating body is also an aware body because every part of the body should be floating.

The Gaga body is a strong and flexible body with stamina and ideal posture. It is the body of "body builders with a soft spine" (Naharin in Gaga Movement Ltd. 2017b). It is able to move instinctively and like an animal (Gaga Movement Ltd. 2017c). The Gaga body is a "healthy" body with "ideal posture," measuring by the standards of popular and scientific medial discourse: Instructions increase the space between the chest and hips or pelvis, activate the pelvic floor muscles and the abdominal muscles, emphasize the importance of the movement of the lumbar spine and hip joints, and promote a free spine and shoulder blade movement. They ask for the head to float up and the knees to be slightly bent, aim at bringing the shoulder blades back, and clarify that only "good pain" is allowed. The Gaga body is also flexible in terms of movement quality: The body can become "spaghetti in boiling water"; it can be a body "standing in a cold shower" or "moving through" different textures, such as "honey," "Nutella," or "clay"; it can become "covered in (sticking feathers) feathers"; and it can become a "creature," an "animal," and move like one.

The Gaga body is a body in process, trying to be free of habits and working toward the ideal. This means constantly researching, trying to break patterns, and not repeating them. The ongoing research consists of "doing, listening, and understanding" at the same time. The Gaga body is always concerned with fighting its limits: "numb areas" and "physical fixations" (Gaga Movement Ltd. 2017c). The body possesses an "endlessness of possibilities" to move, which must be discovered and used (Naharin in Gaga Movement Ltd. 2017b, 2017c). The goal is to make movement more efficient based on the assumption that the body knows where to take the movement initiation from and does not waste its energy. The Gaga class is presented as the perfect workout toward an end: It includes exercises where both the heart rate is raised and muscles are trained, paired with moments of relaxation (Gaga Movement Ltd. 2017b). Moreover, coordination is practiced, and suboptimal movement habits are changed: "We change our movement habits by finding new ones" (Naharin in Gaga Movement Ltd. 2017c). A Gaga class is an embodiment of self-betterment, and a Gaga body is consequently a "better" body as a goal to be reached: "Do not return to the state your body was in before we started" (Gaga Movement Ltd. 2017a). Effort is positive, and "we learn to love our sweat" (Naharin in Gaga Movement Ltd. 2017b).

The Gaga body is a joyful body. It is enjoying itself. It "smiles," "grooves," "is silly," "enjoys the good taste in the mouth," "feels like it could go on forever," and, most importantly, "always finds pleasure within effort." The "burning sensation in our muscles" is interpreted as pleasure (Naharin in Gaga Movement Ltd. 2017b, 2017c). It is a body discovering, in a playful and childlike way, that "we are measuring and playing with the texture of our flesh and skin, we might be silly, we can laugh at ourselves" (Naharin in Gaga Movement Ltd. 2017b). It is a body that does not take itself too seriously or care about its looks. In class, "an experience of freedom and pleasure in a simple way" becomes possible through the body (Gaga Movement Ltd. 2017c), and the body is characterized by its "passion to move" (Naharin in Gaga Movement Ltd. 2017b).

It is simultaneously a highly individual and yet collective body. The body is aware of itself and "aware of people in the room" at the same time "and we realize that we are not in the center of it all" (Naharin in Gaga Movement Ltd. 2017b), meaning that "each person [is] with himself and others" (2017c). The Gaga body is a body that represents many of the participants' Gaga bodies at once, as the action of "copying" is emphasized to reach the movement and instruction aims. It is one body and many connected in movement.

In terms of an anatomical body image as the base for perception, Gaga instructions suggest that participants should view their own bodies as consisting of three layers—*skin, flesh*, and *bones*—each of which can be addressed separately for the creation of movement: "You know there are three layers: there is the skin, there is the flesh, which is everything in between your skin and your bones—muscles, tendons, intestines, the brain, your heart, and the bones" (field note 2017). This body image is a simplification of what is known about the anatomy of a human body and scientifically by medicine, biology, sport science, and others, and what is popularly discussed by books, blogs, magazines, sports teachers, and others. It already shows a characteristic of Gaga's body knowledge, which can be found articulated in different ways: an interconnectedness of everything happening within the body and a basic aim to maintain awareness of many different body parts at once.

The Gaga body encompasses a *suit of skin*, the *envelop of the skin*, in which everything else takes place. This idea is already present in popular discourses on the body connected to the discovery of fascia, which is the "superficial tissue lying just under the skin" (Haas 2018, 87). A body anatomically composed of skin, flesh, and bones is one where the pinky toe can be connected to the face by sharing either the same skin, which could be stretched or become too large, or the same flesh, which could be soft or thick. What is called fascia in popular discourse becomes something of a fluid nature in a Gaga class: The skin and flesh connection is "slippery"; the skin can "slide" on the flesh, and the flesh can move within the skin.

Gaga teacher Hannah reflected on *flesh* as follows:

> Flesh encompasses more than muscles. And I think the flesh is a soft tissue ... when I think about it, I'm really thinking about everything—regardless of what the anatomical term is—between the bones and the skin. And I remember at one point I had a conversation with Ohad about this and he said: it may be also including the skin ... I can zoom in more on a certain part of the body and deal just with say, the flesh in the hand or deal with—I mean, it could be that in a sense we're dealing with a specific muscle even though we're not naming it. Or I could just be very total.[1]

In addition, all the *bones* are thought to be disconnected and thus able to move freely within the flesh and the skin. The disconnected bones enable "endless movement possibilities." They can "float in the flesh" or "slide out of the flesh" like the bones in the flesh of "cooked chicken." Moreover, the imagined body shape, connected to the prosthetic perception of the body, is perceived as something fluid that can be constantly shaped: One could "become very fat or tiny," and the movement will change alike, or one could "paint the walls," "throw out," "give to others," or "keep movement for himself," in the sense of just moving or better listening to movement inside the body, not letting anybody see. The encompassing idea is transferred to the understanding of sensation: The "sensitive skin," the eyes with the gaze, the ears hearing, and even taste function as sensory systems. In Gaga, there is no "hierarchy of the senses"; all senses feed the same awareness and belong to the same information traveling the body. Eyes even come to be seen as part of the skin, which covers the whole body and is mostly addressed in its wholeness.

Apart from the embracing terms "skin," "flesh," and "bones," instructions address specific body parts. They draw attention to the body parts that usually, meaning throughout normal day-to-day life and other body practices, might not be verbally addressed or actively sensed or perceived as being engaged in movement: The *area behind the ears*, the *top of the mouth*, the *jaw*, the *moons* as the "pillows of the hands and feet" (Friedes Galili 2015, 387), and the *collarbones* are some areas of the body that are not usually an explicit part of sensory perception. Guiding participants' attention to these areas invokes an increased level of sensitivity toward incoming sensory information and movement in these areas. Negative space is often also addressed; the "space between" body parts inside and outside the body is also part of the Gaga body. Furthermore, body parts are sometimes addressed in their usual terms, but Naharin also devised specific denominations for areas of the body, which he believed to be crucial for his understanding of movement. He coined specific "images," which add a certain "typical" movement quality to specific areas (370–1). All of this is constantly repeated and used by the teachers in class as the image of a body to work with. The following were found to be the most repeated:

(1) *Pika*. "The place between the groin and rectum" (Friedes Galili 2015, 387) or, as they say in class, "the place between pipi and kaka [*sic!*]." During participant observation, I understood it as addressing the "pelvic floor," or better the "pelvic floor muscles," which was mentioned in other body or dance practices. Pika is "activated" using the muscles "holding in pee" or "sucking everything into the two (!) holes." It can be activated and dropped and does not necessarily have to be activated all the way

through class, though there is always an awareness of the possibility that it could.[2] A consequence of the activation of pika can be yoyo, which is described below.

(2) *Yoyo.* Yoyo stands for the action of "sucking your pika and lower abdomen toward each other" (387), an activation of the pelvic floor muscles joined by an activation of the lower abdominal muscles. Yoyo was also addressed as the "engine in the lower stomach" from which movement can be initiated.

(3) *Lena.*[3] Lena is addressed as "the most important engine": "the engine between the navel and groin" (387). "Lena is the sun always shining," activated with different levels of "intensity" or tension. It refers to the stomach area, as well as its counterpart on the back side—the lower core muscles. Lena, for me, became a synonym for a strong "center" or "core" requested by other body or dance practices, where it is also seen as central to movement, as the body part from which the force or the power to move initiates.[4] I also immediately connected lena to the "deeper" abdominal muscles, which are stored in my knowledge of the body as the most important ones, stabilizing and optimizing posture. In class, awareness about lena is trained; movements are done to activate lena and enable easier connection to it. Although exercises for the activation of the abdominal muscles are generally not directly attributed to their activation, they nevertheless emphasize the importance of this area. Lena is then used as a power source for movement: "Feel your lena, your big engine. Move from the engine." "Movement in Gaga initiates from the center and goes out."

(4) *Seaweed spine.* Another characteristic of Gaga is the seaweed spine, a "soft spine," where waves of "movement can travel through." It is also addressed as the *snake of the spine*. The seaweed spine, or snake of the spine, connects the "tail," the coccyx, to "a head floating on top of the spine." It can be looked at from the back, as well as from the front. Rather than connecting the idea of the seaweed spine to the four curves of the neutral human spine, the idea seems to be an endlessness of movement possibilities of a free spine, not hindered by tensed muscles. When enacting this, I imagined even more possibilities than the spine is anatomically able to do: "The spine is capable of flexion, extension, side bending, rotation, and various combinations of these movements" (Haas 2018, 42). The seaweed spine is something participants will be reminded to keep especially during exercises or when carrying out movement

instructions that require a great deal of effort. It is about "not getting stuck" in the spine, thus not risking a spine or back injury while tensing the muscles. It becomes observable from the outside as a wavy spine movement.

(5) *Rope of the arms.* This concept underlines the connection of arm movement to the chest area and specifically the shoulder blades, as well as the connection of movement from one arm to another through the chest. The rope of arms can "fold and unfold" and "slide in and out of the chest," and "movement can travel" similarly to how it travels the seaweed spine. Using the term "rope of the arms" instead of just "the arms" activates the use of muscle areas that seem to be highly efficient for the movement of arms or hands. Participants are even made aware of the differences in muscular efficiency: For example, the exercise of massaging the feet could be done from the "hand muscles" alone first, and then using the muscles from the shoulder blades, observing the different qualities of effort needed. Playing with the rope of the arms seems to involve the glenohumeral muscles "that connect the humerus bone to the trunk" and that "are responsible for the larger dynamic movements of your arms" (116) and the "arm muscles" at the same time.

(6) *Box of the chest.* The box of the chest is an image used for the upper body, including the rib cage. It can be isolated from the rest of the body, and it can become an engine for the rest of the body. It is also often "broken down" into smaller parts, from "collarbones moving in different direction[s]," making space between the ribs, to "breaking it in many boxes on [a] molecular level," thereby making movement, or at least the imagination thereof, possible in an atomically stiff part of the body. This seemed to help me to deal with muscle tension, which I often experienced in this area possibly due to "incorrect" posture and stress.

(7) *Home.* There is a different home for different parts of the body. It is the natural resting position, or, as with the home of the shoulder blades, the physically most optimal and efficient desired position. To the hands, home means slightly closed hands without pressure, "like the babies hold their hands in soft fists." The *home of the shoulder blades* is experienced by an action of lifting the shoulder blades and taking them back down. I also heard one teacher talking about the term "blabla," referring to the action of bringing the shoulder blades together in the back and pretending to hold a credit card between them, practically activating and stretching the home area by overemphasizing

the muscles' action in this position. The result is an erect posture with activated back muscles and an opening of the chest area in front.

(8) *Shoulder blades.* The shoulder blades are emphasized as being separated from the ribs and the spine. They can "caress" the ribs and spine and are free to move in every direction, asymmetrically, away from and closer to the spine, and away from each other. They are also connected to arm movements, or rather the arm movement is connected to them, in order to make it more efficient.

(9) *Pelvis.* The pelvic area is often addressed in Gaga. It is mostly not broken down into different bones, namely, the ilium, ischium, and pubic bones, or the sacrum, though sometimes an instruction might be given to "stretch your *pubic bones* away from each other" or to "separate your pubic bones." The pelvis can become an "engine for movement," similar to the box of the chest. Often, "sensing the free movement of the pelvis" and "playing with it" are requested. The ideal Gaga posture seems to be a "dropped pelvis," "dropped away from the chest," and thus an elongated spine between the chest and pelvis, increased space between the ribs and pelvis, while resting on slightly bent knees.[5]

(10) *Tail.* Instead of talking about the coccyx, Gaga teachers talk about the tail. This image implies that I imagine having a real tail, like the tail of an ape, which increases the connection to the peripersonal space around my coccyx and leads to the incorporation and enactment of my coccyx behaving like the tail of an animal. The instructions issued might be to "Stick your tail out," "Doodle with your tail," or "Initiate movement from your tail."

(11) *Ball joints.* In Gaga, all joints, even glide and hinge joints, are imagined as being ball joints with matching movement possibilities. Ball joints are not ball-and-socket joints, but rather imagined as two balls moving against and around each other. So, all joints are imagined as being able to rotate as well as to flex and extend. There is an action that one can "oil the joints," and there is an exercise of "tama," which I experienced as being an exercise to sense the ball movement possibilities by lifting an imagined ball in different directions with and within the hips and the chest.

(12) *Traveling stuff.* Perhaps the most important component of the Gaga body is *the traveling stuff*, which can be *traveling information* or just *traveling energy*. There are "four highways" of traveling energy and information in the body: "parallel and diagonal lines" called *mama*. The traveling stuff

can become a sensation when it becomes a traveling texture: *Magma*, with a thick texture and muscle tension, can travel inwards, for example, from the hands and feet to the center, while *lava*, or "energy," is traveling outwards from the center "towards the edges." One or more balls can be imagined to travel the body, "snakes" can slide through the body, and "honey is swallowed," in order to explore the traveling texture. Traveling stuff as a traveling texture creates a sensation; as traveling energy or information, it is tracing the perception of the sensory input. Teachers will allow participants to discover traveling energy as traveling information by imagination and sensing in a relaxed state. The "doors" should always be kept "open" for traveling information, meaning that one can constantly observe what is happening in different parts of the body and connect them with one another. It is similar to the idea of information from the sensual receptors reaching the brain, though, in the case of Gaga, the center of information seems to be the center of the body, not the brain itself.

(13) *Information.* Information is a sensory perception obtained by sensory reception. Gaga instructions are said to be information given to the body as well. There is thus an idea of the Gaga body providing and processing constant information from body-intern processes in interaction with information from the body-outside. Since no "hierarchy of the senses," or hierarchy of information, exists within the Gaga body, the information can become "layered." Information layers are built up, where previously obtained information can be kept and does not have to be lost when new information comes in. The Gaga body is something to be filled up with different layers of information throughout class. Teachers also acknowledge a possible information overload resulting in an action of "overthinking" or "overdoing." They then, for example, instruct a "shake" to "shake off all the information."

(14) *Inner groove.* The Gaga body owns its inner groove, an individual rhythm similar to a reaction to the rhythm of music, that participants can discover and connect to.

(15) *Voice.* The voice becomes a part of the Gaga body; it can be used in the same way as any other body part. "Let your voice" out is connected to letting the tension in the muscles go or "letting go within effort," as if the voice is a muscle and part of the flesh—which it could be. The voice is also connected to movement: It can accompany movement, and its quality can be transferred to the rest of the body, such as in "humming."

It is something that can be sensed in terms of having a sensational effect on the rest of the body. For instance, again using "hum," the vibration can be felt as an echo in other body parts. As with other body parts, the form of the voice is not important; only senseless sound is demanded, not talking.

3.2 Gaga Movement Style

The first step in conceptualizing a movement style is finding an adequate metalanguage to talk about movement. This is even more important in the case of Gaga, as most of the instructions only deal with movement qualities, and not with a particular movement form. Rather than prescribing concrete movement in space or body shapes, instructions are designed to modify force, impact, speed, and range of movement, as well as involved body parts. Sensations introduce modification of movement qualities and modes, which participants are told to imagine or recreate. A modification could also concern a modification of muscle tone, which will then affect movement force and impact in a second step. Or, instructions could primarily ask for the modification of awareness, which only possibly affects movement quality, as space is approached differently, for example. Enacted and perceived movement qualities are not necessarily observable from the outside: First, participants are not always able to embody the quality to the maximum degree or in a way that shows any visible change in movement quality taking place in their bodies at all. This could be for anatomical or physical reasons or because not every participant has the same "control" over their body and its movement. Second, some of the qualities are not designed to be observable from the outside, or, if they are, then the outcome is less precise in its actual look than the instructing input. A description of the Gaga movement style thus needs to cover both movement quality and movement modes, both of which need to be put into words.[6]

In such a context, the purpose of a metalanguage specifically is to make embodied movement, movement qualities, and movement modes, as well as the visible and invisible, visible on paper and understandable for an outside observer. The Gaga class itself offers a kind of metalanguage for movement and movement qualities. As movement is primarily initiated by the teacher's instructions, these instructions represent a way of verbalizing movement. A Gaga movement style is stored in the pool of instructions and in the demonstrative body of the teacher because the teacher's movement and spoken instructions are, at least ideally, directly connected and influence each other. Hence, to find a metalanguage of practical use, Gaga's own metalanguage, depicted by the instructional vocabulary, will be brought together with two different types of dance or better movement analysis systems: Laban Movement Analysis (LMA), useful to describe not only the historical, cultural, and social but also the perceptive-relevant particularities of movement; and the Language of Dance (LOD), which seems to be able to replenish LMA with a useful structuring method.

Dance notation and movement analysis systems like LMA and LOD were originally invented to script dance movement in a systematical way to preserve it and make it repeatable and analyzable. While the movement notation systems follow various approaches to documentation, they have in common their aim to capture the exact movement of a person—some only the explicit and visible, whereas others the implicit or, at least to the outside observer, invisible movement. The function of these systems changed with the use of videotaping. Dance notation nowadays has the function of a scientific analytical tool more than as a practical tool to capture and recreate.

LMA is not to be mistaken for the abstract symbol notation system Labanotation, also called Kinetography Laban. Choreographer and movement researcher Rudolf von Laban created both in the first half of the twentieth century. While Labanotation was developed further by Ann Hutchinson Guest (Abe et al. 2017, 330), LMA was evolved by Irmgard Bartenieff, Warren Lamb, and Lisa Ullman (332). Labanotation is a "structured description" (Guest 2005, 10) of movement with the aim of bringing down exact movement documentation on paper. The following are documented: "The body—the specific parts that move; Space—the specific direction, level, distance, or degree of motion; Time—meter and duration, such as the time value of a whole note, a quarter note, a sixteenth, etc.; also relative timing; Dynamics—the quality or 'texture' of the movement, whether it is strong, heavy, elastic, accented, emphasized, etc." (10).

On the other hand, LMA belongs to the "effort-shape description[s]" (Guest 2005, 9), which analyze movement "according to its energy content and use of: space ... time ... weight ... flow" (9–10). LMA is "concerned with the changing effort patterns that occur within the body," as well as with shape, "the expressiveness inherent in the spatial aspects contained in the movement." Hutchinson Guest valued LMA for its ability to describe movement "in terms of its quality and expression" and mentions that it could be of use for anthropological research (10).

LMA was developed from Laban's observation that every person moving has an Antrieb, an "inner attitude towards motion factors" (Bartenieff and

Lewis 2002, 51). The Antrieb thus relates to and depends on the motion factors, "Bewegungsfaktoren": space—"Raum," weight—"Kraft/Gewicht," time—"Zeit," and "Bewegungsfluss" (Klein, Barthel, and Wagner 2011). To not confound Laban's "Bewegungsfluss" with the body knowledge category of flow, I refer to Laban's fourth motion factor "Bewegungsfluss"—though commonly translated and established by Bartenieff and Dori Lewis as the English "flow"—with the word "flux." Laban's concept of *effort*, with its subcategories of *space*, *weight*, *time*, and *flux*, represents the Antrieb and the different movement qualities according to the motion factors. The movement qualities of the different effort subcategories are always defined in terms of two opposite qualities (Bartenieff and Lewis 2002, 51). The subcategories of effort refer to the quality of movements' performance and thus appear together and in different combinations according to specific movement qualities and the intention of a mover (53–62). To understand effort and the qualities of a certain movement, several questions can be asked, and certain answers can be given:

- Space: "In what manner do I approach the space?" (Bartenieff and Lewis 2002, 53)—direct, as in "zeroing in, pinpointing," or indirect, as in "encompassing focus, flexible" (55).
- Weight: "What is my impact?" (53)—strong, as in "impactful, vigorous, powerful," or light, as in "using fine touch, airy, delicate" (55).
- Time: "When do I need to complete the act?" (53)—sudden, as in "urgent, hasty," or sustained, as in "taking time, leisurely" (56).
- Flux: "How do I keep going?"—free, as in "easy flowing, streaming out, abandoned, ready to go," or bound, as in "controlling the flux, streaming inward, holding back, restrained, ready to stop" (53).

The idea of *shape* alongside effort is important insofar as, in Gaga, specific body parts require specific effort, and effort is accompanied by a certain movement in space—intended or unintended. Gaga is not only about effort but also about shape in connection with effort. Talking about shape includes talking about shape in connection to space, as every shape exists as movement performed in space. As no static shape is taken, no moment of stillness and absence of movement, shape is the interaction of the body with space. Laban named personal space "kinesphere," the space "within reach of the body" (Aristidou et al. 2015, 6–7). Kinesphere seems to be a "movement range" equivalent to peripersonal space, which includes the integration of the sensory systems creating a sense of body ownership in the space between the body and a perceived object. The environmental space is called "dynamosphere," "the space where the body's actions take place" (7).

LOD was found to be a complement to LMA and an alternative to Labanotation. In addition to LMA, LOD possesses the potential to provide a structure to an effort-based description:

> The Language of Dance®, like verbal language, has basic 'parts of speech.' There is a clearly constructed grammar that defines the relationship of the movement words to each other and their given function in the movement sentence. The basic element in the language of movement fall into the categories of nouns, verbs, and adverbs ... Movement means change and to produce change an action of some sort must occur. In the grammar of movement, these actions are the verbs. The parts of the body that move are the nouns. How the action is done the degree of change or the manner of performance is described by the adverb. (Guest 2005, 14)

LOD can be broken down into nouns, verbs, and adverbs, and movement is broken down and analyzed within these categories. To understand the movement, one could ask the following questions: What are the elements of movement; what moves in connection to what—which nouns? What kind of movement happens—which verb? And how does it happen timing-, dynamic-, space-, and performance-wise—which adverb (see Guest 2005, 14–15)? While naturally the effort of Gaga seems to be connected to the category of adverbs, all Gaga movement is creating effort. Thus, LOD can be understood as horizontal breaking down of movement within a Gaga class into sentences, a grammatical movement analysis. The effort functions as the vertical structure and semantics of every LOD sentence, exceeding the function of an adverb.

To make LMA and LOD fruitful as a metalanguage to the analysis of Gaga, ideas of LMA and LOD were combined and broken down to form the following notation and analysis system (List 7):

List 7 Metalanguage for Movement Description (LMA and LOD)

(1) Elements of movement: (a) body parts involved in movement and (b) parts of the environment that play a significant role in movement because sensory awareness or movement is directed toward them
(2) Action as the change of shape in space
(3) Movement quality and movement mode

This can be applied as a tool of analysis for movement in Gaga and finally takes us to what could be called the movement style of Gaga:

(1) *Elements of movement.* By nouns, Hutchinson quite generally addresses the total materiality of the space connected to the movement—in and outside the moving body (see Guest 2005, 14, 16). This is interesting insofar as it draws attention to the already discussed interconnection between a moving body and an aesthetic environment connected in their materiality. However, in terms of analysis, further distinction is required: (a) *Body parts.* The body itself as a physical-psychological body is subject to actions. It primarily does not appear as an element of instructions; instead, it is the not uttered "you" of the imperative within instructions. Many instructions, for example, begin with "be." In other cases, attention is drawn to certain body parts. However, it is mostly not "the" body parts as an object that one is dealing with, but "you" being "your" body parts moving: "stretch your skin," "float your bones out," or, at least, "let your bones float out." It leads to a heightened awareness of changes in the shape and space of these body parts, while the rest of the body remains involved in movement. If movement in Gaga is restricted to a certain area of the body, then the restricted movement is mostly used as an exercise to overcome exactly this restriction. The instruction might start with "thick flesh" in "the palm of your hand," while the rest of the body is "floating," and it might eventually turn to the whole body being "thick." (b) *Environment.* In instruction, components of the surroundings become addressed as objects toward which actions of movement can be directed. People can be told to connect to something they see, such as the sunset, the ceiling, or the other participants, through mere "connecting" or by making them addressees or initiators of action such as "sending to" or "taking from." By drawing attention toward the environment, environmental sensory stimuli form part of perception and the subsequent movement. Analyzing the elements of movement already reveals the concentration of perception on certain sensory input. Chosen elements of movement have an impact on body knowledge transformation. For example, if one concentrates on engaging a specific area of the stomach in movement, the abdominal muscles of the area will be activated, tense, and consequently become stronger, while one will be more aware of them at the same time. There is ergo more to identifying the elements of movements than just knowing about which body parts move or where movement is directed.

(2) *Action.* The "change of shape in space" is especially interesting in the sense of Hutchinson's "results of actions." They embrace the change of "relationship" to an element, the space, or their own body, as well as the change of visual

perceptible space (Guest 2005, 16). There are different kinds of actions in Gaga, and the actions form part of more than one kind at a time:

- Many actions in Gaga are connected to a certain quality, a specific effort. The actions are "result"-oriented. Some examples are as follows: "let your flesh melt" and "grab your flesh" or "become a bodybuilder"—here the weight significantly changes, "shake" and "quake" or "initiate movement" and "let the movement happen to you"—here, the approach to time changes, as does the approach to space and flux.
- Other actions are embodied metaphors, or "dancing metaphors" as Katan-Schmid (2017) calls them: "While dancing, dancers recall and invoke sensory-information and thereby bring the metaphor into current effect" (275), an embodied action, as she emphasizes (276–7). Metaphoric actions range from "floating," with the action of floating itself being an image to which the participant can connect, to a fully evolved image such as "becoming spaghetti in boiling water," "walking down a hill," "painting the room," "walls," "ceiling," or "floor."
- Another group of actions is connected to mechanical, anatomical movement possibilities, Hutchinson's (2005, 16) "flexion," "rotation," and "extension." Examples are as follows: "finding circles and curves," "rotating shoulders in and out," "bending knees and straightening them again," and "curving" the upper body.
- It is also interesting to point out that their action can be "active" or "passive" in terms of variations in time, space, and flux effort. "Letting circles and curves happen to you" or "being overwhelmed by circles and curves" implies a passive action happening to the body of the participants. This is naturally not possible, because, in either instance, the body will always be participating in it. Yet, the passivity of action affects effort: Space is only indirectly approached, while time seems to be endless, and flux is unbound. In contrast, "active" actions, such as the oppositional "initiating circles and curves," have at least in one effort component an extreme opposition to the "passive" action—here, for example, the direct space.
- Finally, a significant difference between actions is the space they occupy. This does not affect effort, but rather movement range—not only Laban's kinesphere but also peripersonal space as the space of sensory expansion and connection to surroundings. Some actions might consist of moving "on large scale" through the room such as "walking through the room." Others cover only a small environmental space such as "playing with the space

between different body parts." Furthermore, for certain actions, movements are limited to the space of the body itself such as "letting energy travel through the body," which is an action of perception in itself, and "letting thickness travel," which is an action still involving physicality, such as the control of muscle tone.

To conclude, endless possibilities of action combinations exist, as already mentioned. The groups are there only to provide an impression of the possible characteristics of actions in Gaga.

(3) *Movement quality and movement mode.* Movement qualities function as a visible movement underlying semantics, while movement modes denote often invisible body knowledge and inner emotional-habitual states in particular:

- Space effort is connected to a mode of attention. Gaga largely demands a total awareness, open monitoring, and indirect space effort of body and environment. Yet, sometimes, attention and actions are focused and directed on specific elements of the space, such as the aesthetics of the environment, including other people. Space is also approached directly and connected to a certain mode of proprioception and kinesthesia, including the knowledge about one's orientation in space as well as one's movement range—a mode of kinesphere when specific movement size or movement in space is indicated, such as "tiny" versus "big," "moving in space," or "crossing each other's path."
- Weight effort is related to the use of different amounts of muscle strength and tension and thus to another part of the mode of proprioception and kinesthesia in connection to the mode of muscle tone: Gaga plays with the variation between "soft" or "melted flesh" and "thick flesh." These metaphors indicate a variation of muscle tone and introduce a muscular contraction or release. Movement also varies between "delicate movement" and "airy movement" or imagined movement through different kinds of liquids of different thicknesses, until nearly no movement is any longer possible. Here, the weight is passively varied by giving different images to be embodied with a different weight impact.
- Concerning time effort, Gaga is the play with the "endlessness of time" versus "only ten seconds" to maximize the speed, strength, or energy input of an action. "Endless" movement is often also perceived as something with low weight impact, whereas the reduction of the action time span to ten seconds is mostly combined with an increase in force during the time span. Modification of time effort requires the mode of attention, as well as

the mode of proprioception and kinesthesia alongside a mode of decision (see Bartenieff and Lewis 2002, 53), building on priorly acquired body knowledge and body scheme. A variation of time effort also often comes with a variation of mode of thermoregulation.
- Flux effort, too, is related to the mode of proprioception and kinesthesia and the mode of attention. Most of the actions in Gaga encompass both extremes of flux: While movement is "easy flowing" and "streaming out" on the level of consciousness and awareness, it is always controlled, and participants should always be ready to react. Gaga demands that sensory input be not shut down; flux is controlled on psychological and sensory levels while giving in to free-flux movement. The bound flux only becomes visible if there is indeed an action binding it: a led exercise as well as an explicitly directed movement, such as "pulling the arms out to the side" or suddenly "exploding," in the sense of breaking the free flux with a sudden movement of bound flux.

A body topography, body concept as well as movement style, needs enactment to come alive implicitly and explicitly, perceived and demonstrative in the body of participants: By how they act and react in class, participants partake in its creation. Concentration and dedication, for example, make the instructions effective. Since rules and instructions during Gaga class tell the participants to concentrate on the embodiment of the instructions, participants compel themselves to do so. The awareness openly demanded creates a mode of attention where not following is not an option, but a command—a reciprocal system: Gaga's body topography itself works as a control mechanism. People will generally try to follow the instructions because they feel obliged. Through embodiment of the verbal and visual movement input, the Gaga body topography then comes to life.

Embodiment of the aesthetically ideal body topography seems to work. Gaga participants become collectively recognizable via their body topography. As a critical Gaga outsider mentioned in September 2017, "I don't like how people make Gaga their 'style': they move like Gaga—the very deep pliés of Batsheva—they dress in a very specific Gaga style like all the Batsheva dancers dress." However, while a body topography always shows collective tendencies, at the same time it always varies individually, as physical and psychological preconditions are individual: Different participants, for example, have different degrees of flexibility and mobility impacting their movement range. Stamina and strength vary. Additionally, some might admire the Batsheva dancers and the work of Naharin, and their emotions will shape their participation in class. They will see their bodies as a possibility to take part at Batsheva and try to embody the characteristic movement. They will copy not only the movement quality but also the shape and the aesthetics in terms of the sensation the movement provokes. They will try their best to look alike.

Understanding a neo-spiritual practice's body topography is crucial to understanding how aesthetics affect bodily behavior and embodied perception beyond the ritual frame. As neo-spiritual practices refrain from stating explicit philosophical worldviews or, at least, from declaring what they explicitly state as worldviews, the body topography becomes the explicit worldview, which is transferred to participants explicitly and implicitly via the body knowledge created audiovisually or in movement. Moreover, Gaga's characteristic worldview aka body topography allows to contextualize Gaga's aesthetics with other contemporary and potential neo-spiritual practices; it is neither a unique body concept nor movement style that Gaga practice advances. Therefore, understanding Gaga's body topography, in particular, can help to advance the understanding of neo-spiritual worldviews.

4

The Power of Instructions

Movement instructions in practices like Gaga are effective in different ways: On the one hand, they initiate external and internal movement intentionally performed by participants. This movement leads to a change in body knowledge and physical-psychological effect. On the other hand, images and semantics of instructions cause an embodied effect. Because of their aesthetical nature, instructions directly provoke a body knowledge transformation. Instruction perception and embodiment thus consist of different stages. First, participants hear and perceive instructions, and their bodies enact them in an implicit, unconscious way. Then, participants make an explicit and conscious effort to enact the perceived, trying to recreate the content of the heard and seen, with their bodies. Participants' embodied experience, the effect of the instructions on body knowledge, depends on how they perceive and embody the instructions. Understanding the nature of language perception, body knowledge transformation, and movement initiation through language, and the narrated experience stemming from these processes, is thus the base to unlock aesthetics.

The embodiment of language has been studied in various contexts. In "Excitable Speech" (1997), Butler investigated the potential of language to inflict wounds and the lasting effects on social self-identification. In "Excitable Speech," language is understood as performative, and Butler proposes John Langshaw Austin's theory on "speech acts" as a framework to understand how this can possibly happen. According to Butler, Austin highlighted the aesthetical context, the environment where an utterance was made, as crucial to a speech act's effect (1997, 2-3). Interestingly, Austin distinguished between "illocutionary speech acts," which have a direct embodied effect, "illocutionary speech acts produce effects" (17), and "perlocutionary speech acts." In the case of the latter, the effect is not produced by the utterance directly, but instead as a consequence of what was said and thus understood (3). The effect of an illocutionary speech act seems directly connected to the physical and psychological preconditions of the listener associated with an environment. Butler suggests that language can injure by catapulting the injured out of their known context (4). Moreover, if utterances are not made under "favorable" circumstances, including the right physical-psychological preconditions of an audience, for example, then there could also be no effect at all (16–17). Talking of illocutionary speech acts could aid in overcoming thinking about language as something with an effect. Language is effective in itself; it is action and consequences. As Butler observes, "The threat [of language] emerges precisely through the act that the body performs in the speaking the act" (11). In the sense of the following analysis, Gaga instructions carry both, illocutionary and perlocutionary agency and effect. This does not depend on what is said only, but rather on the agency of the teacher and the aesthetical context.

From speech acts to metaphors, dance philosopher and Gaga researcher Katan-Schmid (2017) explores the creation of movement in Gaga classes and dance in general as "dancing metaphors": "Dancing Metaphors designate the process of establishing a movement in terms of an imaginary case" (275). According to Katan-Schmid, dance movement is always produced via the assumption of "as-if." Given instructions function metaphorically. They ask dancers to enact body knowledge, which would usually not be established in the current situation or which would naturally not be established by a human body as a reaction to sensory information at all. Hence, they can only be imagined (276). Imagery initiates body knowledge (286). Moreover, it does not matter whether dance techniques include "intended metaphorical guidance"; dance's technical terms are metaphors, too (281). As Katan-Schmid further observes, "While dancing, dancers recall and invoke sensory-information and thereby bring the metaphor into current effect. This process … is enactive and involves a comprehensive engagement of body and mind" (275). Instruction comprehension and translation into movement is not cognitive but an embodied action (278–9). Existing body knowledge is brought "alive" by instructions (280). "The body doesn't follow a metaphorical instruction, but rather enacts and realizes its comprehensive possibilities within a full engagement of body and mind" (277). In this context, Katan-Schmid mentions George Lakoff and Mark Johnson's work on "Metaphors We Live By" (2003). In the context of "aesthetic experience," metaphors are presented as feeding from the physical and cultural reality of humans; that is how they are constructed and how they are possibly understood. The "imaginative rationality" allows one to draw on those physical and cultural concepts to grasp the meaning of metaphors: "It permits an understanding of one kind of experience in terms of another" (235). In an act of "artistry," real physical and cultural concepts are then applied to a new context, perhaps in a new look (235–6). As Katan-Schmid writes, "The metaphorical interplay of dancing brings about familiar movement patterns within a new assemblage" (2017, 277). However, in the context of this research, the focus of interest is slightly different than that of Katan-Schmid. The metaphorical movement's output as artistic performance consumable by an audience is not important; rather, the experience people gain when perceiving and enacting instructions becomes the most important and interesting part of the metaphor communication concept.

Let's remind ourselves in a next step that Gaga instructions are not a mere speech act, as the content of most of the instructions is accompanied by its enactment in the teachers' movement. They express bodily what they express in words—something neither Butler nor Katan-Schmidt tackled in significant detail, though they, surely, were well aware of. German scholars Lucia Traut and Annette Wilke propose a "critical term" to the study of religion that could be a useful concept for grasping this communicative act as a whole: "imagination" (Traut and Wilke 2014). As Traut and Wilke (22–3) write in their introduction to the German compendium on imagination, imagination denotes the human capacity to imagine, the action of imagination, and the contents and products of imagining action. Imagination is closely related to the concept of aesthetics. It is a cognitive act, producing embodied perceptual orders that influence sensory perception. Imagination can develop such a perceptual influence that the imagined becomes more "real" than reality. Therefore, imagination is of cultural and social relevance. It is an instrument for creating and implementing cultural and social values. The values then function as commonly shared perceptual orders and cognitive "filters" in collectives. The imagined can become the worldview of an individual or a group (21). In a group context, imagination holds a heightened transformative potential as different group members exchange imaginations and their embodied experiences, assuring one another of similarities, as well as creating similarities through exchange (21–2). The concept of imagination also seems of great use to explain why people sense what they are told even before they might enact it; how the imagined can influence experience beyond the context in which the imagined evolved; and how people come to express their experience recurring on the imagined.

The instruction design–perception–enactment process can be termed an action of imagination—at least in theory. Even Gaga teachers themselves are imagining and producing from imagination throughout class. The subunits of instruction design and perception and enactment can be analyzed as different steps of imagination. A closer look at every subunit traces how body knowledge transformation takes place during imagination. Yet, this split analysis in subunits remains but a work-around: In embodied reality and in body knowledge, instruction design, performance, perception, and enactment do not, of course, happen separate from one another.

4.1 Instruction Design

I begin the analysis of the instruction design by closely examining the "wording," the "lexicogrammatical level" (Halliday 1987, 144), of instructions. Linguist Michael Halliday (143) reflects on how the wording of language influences meaning-making. Exploring it could provide a "heightened understanding, because now we can see why the text meant, what it did" (143). Wording (List 8) seems of importance in terms of how instructions are perceived by participants:

List 8 (Wording) Categories for Instruction Design Analysis

(1) Verb forms used
(2) Verbs used
(3) Body involvement (how the body is mentioned)
(4) Imagery illustrating the required movement, movement quality, or movement mode
(5) Nonverbal component
(6) Agency of the teacher

The general *verb form* used in instructions is a hortative form. It could be "let's," substituting the imperative first-person plural, which means including the teacher as well as the participants addressed by the instructions, thereby potentially "foster[ing] an atmosphere of inclusion" (Friedes Galili 2015, 374), or it could be the second-person imperative. Gaga teacher Hannah mentioned that there was a tendency toward the usage of the latter, possibly because "at some point we need to cut it out and just be very direct." What Hannah observed was an instant reaction of her "tongue" to the circumstances. "The use of the imperative implies … it requests that the person receiving these words, will do that. Whether it's a physical action or whether it's the kind of action that listening is. So, it activates them, it should motivate and spark the kind of work that we're trying to do" (Hannah).

Either the *verb* used is one of movement, needing an action in space and the transformation of the physical body concerning muscle tone, posture, and thermoregulation, required as active or passive movement, or the teacher uses a verb indicating an action of sensory "observation," such as "feel," "sense," "connect to," potentially with an infinitive or gerund of a movement verb. Both forms imply a conscious and explicit activation of sensory receptors. However, the first form implies a direct activation into movement, whereas the second form seems to imply yet another step beforehand: the perception of sensory input. In such instruction, sensory awareness becomes the tool for initiation of the required movement.

Instructions mention *body* parts—sometimes "the" body parts, sometimes "your" body parts. The body is the subject as the embodied "you" acting, and it is the object as the intended target of all the actions demanded by instructions: "Let your body part do a movement." The body is addressed in a specific way: Common terms for limbs and organs are sometimes used; however, they are applied in a Gaga-specific, Gaga-body-centered way. Moreover, Gaga terms and imagery are sometimes used in reference to the body.

Gaga teachers use everyday *imagery*, which underlines the body knowledge. Most of the imagery seems to be "collective Gaga knowledge"—many teachers use similar imagery. A specific case is the imagery representing the Gaga concept, which is used as fixed vocabulary. Sometimes teachers seem to come up with personal imagery to underline movement. However, primarily if a new image is introduced, it might be introduced by many teachers at the same time, which makes it likely to have been featured during classes led by Naharin, which teachers frequent to obtain new ideas. The imagery is imagery originating in, or at least influenced by, a "Western" cultural hemisphere such as Nutella, spaghetti, glasses of wine. It also seems particularly bound to the social, cultural, and geographical contexts of Tel Aviv when many teachers adopt sea and water metaphors, or maybe even the use of "honey," as something consumed during Jewish holidays. Some imagery could be connected to contemporary popular discourses about contemporary spirituality, such as energy, outside forces, although this seems to be an unnecessary step, as this "contemporary spiritual" imagery also carries detached and "physical" Gaga-centered meaning. Various forms of nature imagery in Gaga classes have to do with volcanoes, magma, and lava, or earthquakes, shakes, and quakes, which are phenomena unlikely to have been witnessed by most of the participants. Nevertheless, this imagery is especially important, as it forms part of the Gaga language and Gaga movement repertoire. To enhance participants' imagination, it is thus often supported with additional imagery information: A quake is imagined as driving a car on a bumpy road, for example. Finally, instructions contain imagery based on form and space perception, such as circles and curves. All imagery used essentially consists of culturally shared metaphors. Thus, the metaphors alone are sure to have a collectively shared experience effect, as they are understood by most of the participants in the same way.

However, instructions are *not only language*; they are accompanied by the according movement. Most of the time, movement even comes before instructions: Teachers can be observed starting or trying out something new before they give the according instruction. This matches the teaching process, as Hannah described it: She teaches from an embodied situation of awareness of her own bodily sensations as well as sensory input from the environment such as the movement of other participants. This perception and enacting of sensory information come before verbalizing movement instructions to participants, even though she might consciously and unconsciously carry movement ideas from outside the specific class context in mind and body as explicit or implicit body knowledge and sensory input. Teachers' movements can only be of such effect because they are constantly highlighted as main sensory input. During participant observation, one Gaga teacher, who was giving class in Hebrew, even told the non-Hebrew-speaking participants to aim to understand the instructions just by watching.

Finally, the power of an instruction relies on the *agency of the speaker*: Perception of instructions varies according to the teacher uttering them. This seems to depend on participants' individual preconditions in combination with the aesthetics attached to a certain teacher: Can participants connect to the teacher through the language used and movement seen? Which place does the teacher occupy in the Gaga "hierarchy"—the "guru," the young Batsheva dancer, the former Batsheva dancer and long-experienced teacher, or the Gaga teacher who has never danced with Batsheva? In addition: How does the teacher utter the instruction; what is her appearance and performance?

4.2 Instruction Perception and Enactment

Participants report that they mainly experience what they are told to experience. Tamar mentioned how she would "feel everything the teacher tells [her] to imagine." To her, the instructions became physical sensations. Shira depicted it slightly differently. She also experienced a mechanism of direct embodiment of the instruction—to the extent that it was difficult to experience something else from what one was told. Shira said the instructions had so much "power" that she was not even enacting what they told her to enact or what she wanted to enact, but rather directly experiencing what they told her to experience. She thus clearly observed the illocutionary character of the instructions. Sara highlighted another aspect of direct perception: She said she no longer explicitly translated the instructions into movement. She was not "aware of the translation anymore," but her body directly performed the movement. For Sara, this did not depend on the general "power" of the instruction. Instead, it was because she had heard the wording and content of certain instructions and performed them often enough that instructions had become a language her body naturally "spoke." What all three of them reported was that instructions evoked some kind of direct and implicit embodied sensory effect as a result of their metaphorical power. This experience was difficult to withdraw from, and it became even more "direct" with more time spent practicing.

These observances tackle a transdisciplinary field of discourse on language perception, some of which were already introduced above, such as those of Butler (1997) or Lakoff and Johnson (2003). Language perception is also currently discussed in contemporary cognitive scientific and neuroscientific discourses, which highlight its embodied nature and which offer theoretical approaches to understanding the connection between language and experience. The embodied effect of language perception and successive comprehension is said to take place in the form of a "sensimotor simulation": "Embodied approaches to language comprehension hold that language is understood through the construction of sensorimotor simulations of the content of the linguistic input" (Kaschak et al. 2014, 120). Research showed that when people listen to movement vocabulary, parts of their neural systems responsible for planning and executing the movement are activated. The "wording," semantics, and grammar seem to play an important role in this embodied language comprehension (120; Scorolli 2014, 133). In addition, movement involving language seems to be processed fast when the according movement is attached to the language: when something moving in the environment can be visually observed as the movement mentioned (Kaschak et al. 2014, 121–2). The embodied processing seems to be even faster when another person moves and accompanies the movement with a first-person sentence describing the movement (Scorolli 2014, 133). The accompanying movement helps the person perceiving to comprehend the implicitly and explicitly "referential" and "semantic intentions" of the person moving. Furthermore, moving along while listening and comprehending supports the incorporation of "perceptual and motor information" (Alibali, Boncoddo, and Hostetter 2014, 155). However, the comprehension of language regarding movement is not solely related to the body: The comprehension of uttered emotions seems to depend on the ability to reproduce the implicit and explicit physical state of the emotions, the afferent emotions. The comprehension of "abstract" language concepts seems to be related to the body image and body scheme, especially the body's perceived spatial dimension (Kaschak et al. 2014, 122; see also Lakoff and Johnson 2003). Every language perception is thus embodied, only in a different way: "For instance, a large amount of imaging studies reported that the cognitive processing of words referring to actions activated motor structures of the brain … whereas words that refer to sensory information triggered activity in the brain regions involved in perceptual processing" (Coello and Fischer 2016, 2). As Claudia Scorolli (2014) emphasizes, embodied language comprehension also means that neither is language comprehension reducible to the physical brain area, nor can the body be reduced to the physical entity, as the body scheme influencing language comprehension is fluid and exceeding physical boundaries. Moreover, language perception and comprehension seems to depend not only on the perceiving individual but also on the interaction of their body with the environment (134). Language perception and its implicit and explicit comprehension can be described as a form of embodied simulation, which Vittorio Gallese (2018, 2017a, 2017b) has dedicated himself to researching. It is a "relational experience." Yet, when language does not occur alone, but in an environment and accompanied by movement, auditive input is mixed up with visual and other sensorimotor input, and the input together enables embodied simulation. "The embodied simulation of action likely provides the conditions allowing for the phenomenal quality of the experience of imagined or observed actions" (Gallese 2018, 73). In a framework such as this, collective language perception and enactment becomes possible due to collectively shared perceptual orders. However, again, it remains individual, as body knowledge is always individual, bound to the individual bodily preconditions.

What neuroscientists Peter Payne and Mardi A. Crane-Godreau (2013), researching the effect of mindful movement practices, summarize on the embodiment of imagery is of specific additional interest in the context of Gaga instructions' effect on participants: It has been reported that imagery repetitively used in movement practices has the potential to provoke physical sensation, "not an abstract mental picture, but an embodied 'felt sense' of interoceptive/

kinesthetic experience, usually with a clear hedonic component" (9). "Visual, interoceptive, and kinesthetic imagery" seems to provoke "actual changes in the physiology of the body and nervous system"—the following of which are especially interesting, for example: "a feeling of weightlessness in the limbs [see floating!] may indicate improved control of muscle tone via the reticular activating system in the brain stem" (9). The changes are observed as "significant, widespread, and lasting" (9):

> Motor imagery is known to activate areas of the brain responsible for generating internal sensations, such as the posterior parietal cortex and the pre-motor and supplementary motor areas ... Visualization can improve motor performance significantly ... and increase muscle strength ... Imagined movement activates many of the same areas of the brain as actual motion, although the patterns of activation are not identical ... The posterior parietal cortex, where the body image is constructed ... as well as the supplementary motor area, where motor plans are elaborated, are preferentially activated by imagined movement ... The effects of imagined movement extend to the autonomic system; cardio-vascular and skin resistance changes accompany imagined exertion ... and it is possible that other autonomic changes can be triggered as well, such as altered parasympathetic regulation of the heart ... improved autonomic regulation of the enteric nervous system, and increased capacity for social engagement through activation of the supra-diaphragmatic portion of the parasympathetic system—Porges' ventro-vagal system ... The positive effects of motor imagery can be predicted from the degree of autonomic responsiveness during the imagery. (Payne and Crane-Godreau 2013, 9)

In the case of Gaga, this could mean that not only a major part of the narrated Gaga effect, namely, the "hedonic" wow-moments, but also the positive body transformation is largely due to Gaga's effective use of imagery.

Apart from provoking an embodied effect, instructions also initiate an explicit reflection on the content of instructions, the awareness of one's own body, and the explicit initiation of movement. This reflection is a perlocutionary effect of the instructions, which, due to the illocutionary effect of language, seems to be not a possible but necessary reaction.

Due to the circumstances provoked by the instructions and the environment, participants become intensely "involved" and focused on the instruction—a perfect situation to experience flow, according to Mihaly Csikzentmihalyi (2014), as flow needs "intense and focused concentration" on a task (242). Instructions present a double task. First, they require attention on the auditive and visual sensory input given by instructions accompanied by movement. Second, the context of instructions conveys a movement task that participants are to enact. Shira said, the way the instructions were designed kept her concentrated: There was always an instruction, and sometimes even quite complex instructions were uttered and perceived, while the agent, teacher, and audience kept moving. She talked about how practicing Gaga asked a participant to be involved in an "intellectual way." It was about understanding the "complex" instructions while moving and listening to the teacher. Ester, too, reported a total concentration and involvement due to the constant input of verbal and visual instructions demanding movement, which she had to align with her own sensory perceived bodily state and with "what [she] feels is right for [her]." Uri mentioned how he would try to be aware of his mind wandering. He observed, rather than inhibited it. Mira, instead, saw forced concentration, in other words explicit self-control, as an obstacle to overcome on the way to experiencing the instructions: "During the class, I found some moments where I can let go and actually feel I'm getting much closer to the instructions then when I try hard and concentrate." This could be connected to the fact that reaching flow also includes giving up on part of the self-sense (137, 141). What is interesting is that both Ester and Shira talked about willingly maintaining a certain individual perspective: They stated that they would only follow the instructions to the extent that they could connect them to the state of their own body. They mentioned the option to individually choose what movements to enact—despite the instructions' illocutionary nature. In Ester's case, only in Naharin's class, she reported being able to let go of control and "fly" with it, and only here she stated having experienced a specific state of flow.

Participants also narrated a connection between instruction perception and interpretation, on the one hand, and their own worldview or embodied perceptual orders, on the other: Uri observed how prior knowledge and preconditions were explicitly and implicitly activated during instruction perception:

> If they just say floating then I've already got my, you know. It's at the stage where I bring in to it everything, or a lot of what's been said about floating, a lot of what I already researched in floating—they'll say floating and won't say water and I'll still think water. Or they'll say floating and I will think of my, ah you know, about in, smaller pieces of me, I wouldn't just think about the hands for example today, I wouldn't, when you say floating it goes immediately to the hands, the hands float. But my sit bones will float even if they don't say sit bones, okay, so that's one aspect of just doing this for a while now, okay. ... I think the body does it already. They say floating and something happens in my pelvis that doesn't need the mind to tell it to do something.

From what Uri spoke, the explicit and implicit effects of the instructions and their perception, comprehension, and enactment were difficult to separate. Uri also mentioned elsewhere that he would "enrich the images" with his own experiences.

During the interview, Dana gave me a detailed account of the process of instruction perception and enactment, though she found it, as she smilingly told me, "hard to describe." She said she would "try to imagine going all the way to the end, to the extreme of what he is saying," constantly asking herself whether she was embodying the given image, the given movement quality, or the given movement as much as possible. She revealed how she "forced" herself to dive deeper into experiencing the instructions with her body. Dana also stated that she would never try to portray the image given, but capture the idea, the movement quality, behind it, "trying to be as abstract as [she] can." This is interesting, as here Dana represented herself as having embodied the contemporary discourses of dance and art, where dance and art are said to be not about form but about quality. However, she also reflected the scientific discourses on the metaphoric effect of language: Dana tried to explicitly capture the embodied component of the images given. "I try to avoid thinking with images," she said. She described that if given an image-related instruction, she would initiate a reexperiencing of this image with her body. As with Uri, however, Dana realized that incorporating the images was not only her own work: "It's like there's is something of fluid moving inside of you and it's like could being affected by the words or by the ideas." The word "flesh," for example, is used in instructions, and Dana felt she was affected more by the sound than by the "meaning" of it: "Flesh is somethings that's, you know, it's kind of elastic and like, but it's like raw, I don't know."

To conclude, the embodied effect as a reaction to the instructions seems to be neither implicit nor explicit, but both at the same time. While instruction design and performance are important, they are only effective as they meet the participant who is open to perceive and enact them. In this constellation, instructions demonstrate the key role they play in embodied experience creation.

5

Transformation in Movement

I now turn my focus to the actual movement performance and the enactment of movement stimulated by the instructions in class. This might well come a bit late to those who assume that movement or body practices are primarily effective because of the movement they ask of their participants. If you followed this book so far, you will have understood by this point that a big part of Gaga's aesthetics, and neo-spiritual aesthetics in general, becomes effective even "before" participants start to consciously move their bodies during a ritual. Nevertheless, this does not make the actual movement itself less effective and less important: Bodies and body knowledge are characteristically transformed via movement.

Gaga classes employ a particular set of what I call here movement "techniques." "Gaga techniques" then stand for a variety of Gaga-specific and Gaga-characteristic movements being performed and enacted in the context of a Gaga class. They are initiated by the instructions and have explicit and implicit effects on the body of participants as well as on body knowledge transformation beyond the limits of the class. Gaga techniques are consequently found to be relevant in causing the experiences described by the participants. They are used by different teachers and in different classes to be repeatedly enacted by participants. The ongoing training in and exposure to the techniques lead to a continuous transformation of body knowledge. By enacting the techniques more often, the enactment of the body topography and thus the body knowledge becomes easier and more accessible, more implicit: "Gaga is like driving a car. At the beginning, you can hardly manage to drive, and later on, you can talk on the phone or drink a coffee while driving," a Gaga teacher mentioned in summer 2018. Gaga techniques and the body knowledge they create connect participants particularly to the cultural trends already reflected in Gaga's body topography, such as "awareness," constant "availability," and the neoliberal idea of self-responsibility for—always possible and aspirational—self-optimization and self-betterment.

5.1 Floating

Frequently throughout class, participants were reminded to keep "floating": "Floating is the 'default method' of the bodies," a Gaga teacher said in a class. "We are always floating, and then other instructions and actions happen on top."

Gaga's concept of floating builds on popular knowledge and common definitions of the action of floating: Floating incorporates a sensation of elevation and support, "not to sink," within the body, often accompanied by the instruction to "move easily through," referring both to the body moving through its surroundings and to the travel of movement through the body. The body is imagined as porous to movement: Floating is connected not only to the feeling of elevation but also to "letting movement travel through your whole body." This means that sensory input from movement or body knowledge transformation experienced in one body part could affect movement or body knowledge in another.

The action of floating conveys not only movement in space but also a certain quality of action. To clarify and provoke the aimed movement quality, imagery and metaphors are used. Floating is "spreading like oil on water or bread in milk," being "lifted up by balloons," or "being in water" while "being water." In most of the instructions, floating is connected to some form of liquid such as water or milk. One often heard, "Float your bones in soft flesh," the body being the liquid in which to float and the floating subject at once.

Sometimes floating can appear as an isolated movement brought to certain body parts. Participants were often reminded about floating their arms, the "rope of the arms," and not "dropping" their hands, "no dead hands." Floating can also become one partial task of a multitasking action, such as "Float in your upper body," or "Holding two glasses of wine" combined with the task of a shaking action in the pelvis; moving with "quick feet"; or any other movement in the lower body as opposed to the floating in the upper body.

The movement opposed to floating in terms of movement quality and sensation is "dropping into gravity" or "collapsing into gravity" or "being shaped by gravity"—body knowledge that can be used as movement to be enacted within an exercise, as counteraction and quality to floating, but that should generally be overcome. Instructions emphasized that floating meant using "as much effort as you need to hold your body parts up and to not let them drop into gravity." In addition, people were reminded that floating did not necessarily involve a large movement in space, but "availability" and "awareness." One can float while standing quasi-still but floating on the inside—something an outside observer could not necessarily see from the outside as an ongoing action.

In search for a definition of the body knowledge of floating, I came across what Payne and Crane-Godreau single out as a signature technique of somatic practices: "balanced tone," which is "a state of completely balanced tone, 'eutonis' ... in which every muscle is doing exactly what it should. This state is experienced as light, free, open, and effortless; but at the same time stable, powerful, and well-rooted" (2013, 4). This coincides with my observation: I experienced floating as a pleasurable state of my body; movement became light, easy, effortless. More, in floating, "attention is paid to correct postural alignment and to using the body as a whole" and as "muscles are being used in a well-coordinated and conscious way." This seems to lead to a "re-patterning [of] the motor nervous system." Participants might feel more grounded, and "self-efficacy, balance, and confidence" are enhanced, thereby "stabiliz[ing] mood swings and reduc[ing] depression and anxiety" (8).

Floating forms part of an explicit body topography incorporated as body knowledge: I could remind myself of the floating action while walking or doing other activities. Likewise, it is implicit: Sometimes I could just be floating without being aware of it, until I realized it. As with other Gaga actions, during the periods of extensive participatory observation in Tel Aviv, I found myself floating at my desk in front of my computer, especially when writing about floating. Some of my interview partners also mentioned finding themselves floating outside of class: on the street, while walking, in bed, and while doing yoga. As a likely result of the repetition of floating and the analysis of the sensation and kinesthetics of floating in every class, it eventually becomes a "habit" that the body can easily connect to on its own: Participants immediately started floating at the beginning of class or, rather, the teacher started to float without saying anything, and participants followed. For those who do Gaga regularly, floating does not necessarily have to be a reflected action anymore, though it can be brought into a conscious focus. Moreover, floating seems to have the potential to become an explicitly observable embodied movement style. However, as Eli reminded, floating as explicit and implicit body knowledge remains fleeting. Floating has to be continuously enacted to remain a part of the body knowledge.

Floating seems to be an example of instruction and movement in Gaga where implicit body knowledge grounded in the bodies of participants goes against the body knowledge explicitly verbalized, imagined, and simulated via the instructions: The body is, of course, not floating in water or zero gravity, but instead exposed to gravity and constantly tensing and stabilizing. There will naturally always be muscular effort due to the muscle tension involved when one's arms are stretched out to either side of the body, even though the body is said to be light and floating. Nevertheless, "floating them out" felt effortless compared to "holding" them. This is probably not only due to the embodied impact of imagery but also because floating involves a different kind of back muscles, alongside deep core muscles, to support the arms. The use of specific muscles, such as the deltoid or the trapezius, could make the holding action more efficient. Besides, depicting floating as an ongoing "action," involves movement, which makes the muscle effort felt as more supportable.

5.2 Sensory Awareness

Something that is very fundamental to Gaga is the listening to the body, ... we want to move, but from a place, where we're already listening to our body, right, that in a sense is the sort of primary action or first action, right, so it's not just: I'm moving and I'm not listening to my body at all, and then maybe at some point in the middle I start listening; ideally, we're already starting with this listening and this awareness. (Hannah)

As in other somatic practices, awareness in Gaga serves as "the function of isolating 'new' sensory-motor phenomena in order to learn to recognize and control them" (Hanna 1986). Awareness is a state of "attention" as well as a "becoming increasingly attentive to bodily sensations" and "includes the cultivation of interoceptive, proprioceptive, kinesthetic and spatial awareness" (Schmalzl, Powers, and Henje Blom 2015, 8). In somatic practices, awareness is introduced as the aimed embodied starting position for a successful practice experience as well as for the goal to be achieved.

Gaga techniques work with two types of awareness: "focused attention" and "open monitoring" of bodily sensations: "In short, FA [focused attention] techniques involve directing and sustaining attention on a single selected object (e.g., the sensation of the breath), whereas OM [open monitoring] techniques emphasize non-reactive metacognitive monitoring of perceived sensory, emotional or cognitive events that may arise from moment to moment during one's practice" (Schmalzl, Powers, and Henje Blom 2015, 8).

It is open monitoring (OM), which is connected to a successful Gaga class experience. To help people accomplish OM, instructions often train focused attention (FA) first by focusing awareness on a specific area of the body, which are not necessarily an anatomically recognizable body part, but part of the Gaga body concept such as "the area behind the ears," "under the armpits," "the soles of the feet," "the place between the shoulder blades," and "the sitting bones."

Objects of FA include (1) areas of the body on which one can visually focus; (2) body parts that at least cover or correspond to a certain area of the skin, but that remain out of sight due to physical incapacities; (3) body parts located "underneath the surface" of the skin, within the body itself; (4) and body parts or areas within the body that one could theoretically not sense, because there are either no, fewer, or nonmonitored sensory receptors, such as the instructions to sense "the collarbones floating in soft flesh" or "the box of the chest broken into small pieces," which introduce small-scale movement in the upper chest. Apart from FA on body areas, instructions might focus attention on the perception of one particular action or the interaction with one environmental object. Besides, even if not openly instructed, the body is in constant interaction with its surroundings by filling the space with its movement, or sensing space and people and reacting to them. The aesthetic facets of this connection range from just becoming aware of the information the surroundings have to offer, to using the "energy" and information stemming from the surroundings for movement, such as in "copying" or "connecting to." An additional level of awareness is required when instructions become more complex, demanding FA on different body areas, or movements and environmental objects at the same time. From there, FA could broaden into an OM. Instructions increase the integration of sensory systems, culminating in "being overwhelmed" with bodily sensations, movement, or information from outside the body.

By its techniques, Gaga practice trains various kinds of FA and creates corresponding body knowledge:

> *Alerting attention* is primarily recruited for tracking bodily sensations ... *Orienting attention* involves active scanning of the environment or an array of stimuli, and subsequent orientation toward, or selection of, a specific target for the execution of a behavior or task ... Orienting attention supports fine-tuning of neuromuscular feedback processing, and the consequent efficiency of muscle engagement for the execution of physical postures, movement sequences, and breathing techniques. *Executive attention* refers to the ability to selectively pay attention to relevant stimuli in our environment, while contemporarily inhibiting irrelevant information ... Executive functioning is used to maintain attention on present-moment physical and mental states, while simultaneously withholding attention from irrelevant distractions. (Schmalzl, Powers, and Henje Blom 2015, 8; italics added)

Awareness techniques increase, decrease, and adjust peripersonal space as well as body schemes, and train metacognitive awareness as a side-effect: Asking for inhibition of mind-wandering, connecting to a "good taste" or a "pleasant memory," and thinking of "someone you love" means that one monitors one's own emotions, thoughts, and experiences as well.

Gaga instructions initiate and create awareness via "listening," "feeling," "sensing," and "connecting to" sensory information. Classes often started with "listening" to one's own body, and throughout class, awareness was implicitly and explicitly drawn to the following integrated sensory systems:

(1) *Proprioception and kinesthesia.* Instructions train the isolated and "asymmetrical" movement of each body part. They allow participants to become aware of the space between different body parts, to vary and experience the distance between the body parts. They enable an awareness of all the joints' movement possibilities as well as of the interrelation between movement in the whole body and the muscle chains, which are different muscles partaking in a specific movement. Instructions vary movement quality. They enable participants to gain an overall idea of their movement possibilities and possibilities for movement control.

(2) *Skin.* Skin is addressed by just sensing or through touch, and an awareness is created from that experience.

(3) *Gaze.* The eyes, which participants must always keep open, form part of the skin and can be treated accordingly: One can "sense" with one's eyes. Vice versa, the awareness of the gaze is applied to other skin parts as well: One can "see" not only with the eyes but also with other areas of the body covered with skin—"eyes in hands, feet, knees, everywhere." Instructions try to overcome the dominance of vision, ensuring that information gained from the eyes does not become more important than that generated both in cutaneous receptors and within the muscle spindles of other parts of the body. Instructions produce a situation of OM including all the senses and remind participants to actively engage their eyes in perception. Observation showed that it is challenging to equalize all incoming sensory information, but it produces a feeling of presence and connectedness to the surrounding. Open eyes hindered mind-wandering. Occasionally teachers would give the instruction to close the eyes, acknowledging that closing one's eyes, shutting down visual sensual input, and focusing attention can amplify nonvisual sensation. Nevertheless, it is emphasized that this focusing of attention should be a deliberate decision and that the same quality of OM and FA should be equally maintained with open eyes.

(4) *Awareness of gravity.* The action of floating is connected to the idea of constantly "measuring gravity," knowing about the weight of the different body parts, and "just using enough effort to not collapse into gravity." Floating cultivates a combination of an awareness of kinesthesia, knowing about the position of the body part in space, and an awareness of exteroceptive information from the outside, perceiving the position of the body part within space. Sometimes the awareness of gravity is utilized to enhance sensation or relaxation. Lying on one's back on the floor, one can be told to "melt the flesh" until "lying in a puddle of your own flesh," or to "melt into the floor," acknowledging the sensation of being drawn toward the floor by gravity. From this mode of total relaxation, instructions might demand attention to traveling stuff or invite the body to start slightly moving again, shaking, or floating.

(5) *Traveling stuff.* From a physiological point of view, "movement happens when the nervous system sends electrical signals to and from relevant parts of the body" (Haas 2018, 15). The concept of traveling stuff seems to be designed to make participants aware of these electrical signals as so-called highways within the body, where information, energy, or movement can travel. Traveling stuff becomes a possibility to perform a body scan to create awareness: Instructions ask participants to trace the highways of information and energy with FA, or the highways of movement by sending movement or muscle tension in the form of "thick" or "soft flesh," both visualized as "balls," or even warmth through the body and focusing attention along the movement and muscular modes while maintaining an OM of proprioception.

(6) *Listening to the echo.* Participants are asked to perform a body-activating action that will raise the heartbeat or accelerate the blood flow or the body temperature in order to create the occurrence of an "echo" in nonmoving but floating body parts, or after a movement is suddenly halted. Awareness is raised toward these echoes and the body knowledge accompanying them. The sensation connected to echo is "amplified" by active movement and is used for movement creation in the quality of what was observed.

(7) *Covert imitation.* Some instructions, such as "copy me" or "kagami," include explicit FA on teachers' movements. However, knowing what movement and what movement quality to enact requires constant implicit FA on the moving teacher.

There is also a kind of instruction where awareness is not demanded but necessary to complete the task itself. Awareness becomes the starting point as well as the result of an action. Some movements such as floating seem to be impossible to enact without awareness, because reaching a balanced tone includes a certain level of awareness and asks for its maintenance.

Three final observations remain. First, awareness also appears to be the base to be able to teach Gaga. Teachers, as Hannah revealed, teach according to what sensory information they receive from their bodies and what their bodies "tell" them to do, while they use and react to incoming environmental information from participants or the setting. Second, with ongoing training, being aware becomes implicit and explicit body knowledge. On the one hand, participants will keep reminding themselves to be aware. On the other hand, they will realize an increased level of awareness—which, as they also realize, vanishes as easily as it appeared. Third, Gaga discourse acknowledges the possibility that there is a difference between people in terms of how or at what level they can become aware of things. The advice given to participants, in case of obstacles they cannot overcome is, "Fake it, until you make it!"

5.3 Availability

> Dolfi—the famous availability in Gaga,

a Gaga teacher put it in a class in 2018. Where floating appears to be a signature movement instruction and awareness is the most effective part of techniques with influence on body knowledge, "availability" or "dolfi" seems to be a signature movement quality or movement mode demanded by the instructions. I witnessed "available" inscribed on promotional products such as t-shirts that participants bought from Gaga Movement Ltd.

Teachers constantly required participants to maintain a physical state of availability throughout class—the embodied quality of "being ready to snap into movement," where the body is ready to shift to enacting visible instant and quick movement. Availability requires OM awareness and total proprioceptive control. As in floating and its state of balanced tone, muscles need to be neither too tensed nor too relaxed. The posture must allow for quick postural changes. Availability in Gaga seems to be a state of "alert attention":

> Sustained attention, vigilance and alertness vaguely define the ability to increase and maintain response readiness in preparation for an impending stimulus.

Specified as phasic alertness (task specific), which is distinguishable from intrinsic alertness (a general cognitive control of arousal), this capacity can be thought of as a foundational form of attention on which other attentional functions rest. (Raz and Buhle 2006, 371)

Being available is a direct consequence of being aware of what is happening on the level of the body in combination with a constant exteroceptive awareness, always being awake and present, and being able to process information coming in from the environment. In addition, it is also an embodied effect of awareness or certain movement, such as floating.

Being available seems to have a practical movement effect: A joint that can bend at any time or a muscle that is loose does not get injured when caught by a sudden movement; a fall or a contact with the floor will not provoke an injury such as a broken bone. Besides, loose muscles allow for quicker movement and faster reaction. Being available also requires a connection to the sources of strength, the "main engines," within the body: Techniques often create an embodied posture of bent knees and a dropped pelvis. Bent knees and the pelvis as the center of gravity provide a source of stability and enable fast reaction by a push into the floor from a stable place. Furthermore, movement trains awareness, strength, and control of abdominal, especially core muscles, and intrinsic muscles, which is crucial for instant reaction, for not losing balance, and for finding strength to quickly react while the rest of the body is relaxed.

The other way round, techniques train availability by the enactment of fast and sudden and strong movement from a state of relaxation and listening to the body. The observation revealed the difficulty in initiating such sudden movement, because as soon as one decided to initiate the movement, it lost its "surprise moment" and suddenness—also to an outside observer. It seemed easier, however, when instructions asked to imagine and enact "punching" or "exploding." Fast reaction also became more effective from a place of muscular relaxation and OM. The most effective availability training I experienced was when teachers instructed participants to lie down on the floor, be available, and then instantly react to an auditory clue such as clapping. The demanded reaction could be sitting or standing up immediately as a reaction to the cue. The cue then had to not be self-responsibly imagined but was imposed as a stimulus from the outside. Specific imagery was also helpful in this regard: An image, for example, to improve fast reaction appeared to be "animalistic power." The image of an "animal"—imagined as a wild predator—really helped to connect to availability, alertness, and fast reaction. Interestingly, from the semantics of the situation, it did not come to mind that I could have embodied a harmless, peaceful animal. Depending on what movement quality the teacher wanted to emphasize, a fast reaction could be demanded in a muscle tensed mode—muscle contraction. However, a fast reaction could also be asked to be done in a "soft" way, with "soft muscles." Both types of fast reactions were hence based on an embodied state of keeping a "soft spine."

Via a direct connection not only to a state of heightened awareness but also to fast reaction, availability influences proprioception and peripersonal space, and has a side-effect on muscular tension and posture, as well as on stamina, strength, and thermoregulation. Besides, availability appears to be, at least to an extent, body knowledge visible from the outside: Those available and alert seemed separable from the daydreaming by look only.

5.4 Overcoming Physical and Psychological Preconditions

> Yes, changing habits. I think Gaga is also a lot about: having the choice … In Gaga it's not about the shape, it's about the possibilities, the movement possibilities, the availability to move in any direction I wish to, with safe sense of my body. So … I want to un-restrict myself in that sense, like undo blockades … in my head as well as in my body. (Talia)

As with availability, there are instructions demanding "breaking" of "patterns" and "continuous research," while naturally all instructions are in fact recreating a new form of "patterns" via body knowledge. "Patterns" are likewise addressed as movement "habits," and instructions ask for "changing habits." The Gaga body concept to be created is a body that is flexible with "endless movement possibilities," constantly aware and floating, neglecting gravity, finding "pleasure within effort," and never searching for form, but for physical movement quality. The undesired movement habits are consequently the opposite of these characteristics. "Changing the habits" implies that there are embodied "habits" not good for the body in a way. In addition, given as guidance, it implies that there must be constant change: Even habits created by Gaga are to be renewed.

If not simply requiring "change," then Gaga techniques work to overcome preconditions by the enactment of following instructions:

(1) "Stopping movement" is such a central habit to be broken that it is even included in the "work instructions" for class: "Never stop moving."

(2) "Don't collapse into gravity," teachers would say. Participants are asked to avoid a total relaxation and maintain a balanced tone needed for a healthy posture or to be able to fast-react to a certain input.

(3) An action of common body knowledge is to close the eyes during concentration. Likewise, it is common that thoughts wander to other concerns outside of class. Both actions are to be avoided in the Gaga class context, as they are framed as inhibiting total awareness. Participants are constantly reminded before or throughout class not to close their eyes and to stay focused.

(4) Gaga instructions work by constantly updating, changing, and increasing the movement range via actions or imagery. They include movements where participants can try out movement possibilities and movement ranges of joints and different modes of muscle tone. Instructions train the mobilization of joints and introduce tissue stretching. Participants are encouraged, and sometimes forced, to leave their comfort zone of a personal movement range and expand it. Instructions also communicate the idea that there is no end to a movement: The knees become ball joints, even though they are not. Instructions thus build on and increase the small rotation ability of the knee joints.

(5) Instructions change postural habits framed as suboptimal. They remind participants that the head is related to spine movement and moves along. The spine is to be kept "flexible" during whatever movement. By imagining and enacting a "soft" and flexible spine, muscular stiffness in the back appears to be loosened, and postural habits are therefore transformed. Experimentation with movement of the shoulder blades, such as "bringing them together" in the back or far apart, seems to fulfill a similar purpose. Back muscles are trained and stretched.

(6) Instructions also address symmetrical movement of the right and left body sides as a poor habit. They explicitly train the integration of asymmetrical movement by "finding asymmetrical movement" in the left and right sides, for example.

(7) By the variation of effort, instructions break the movement quality patterns of each participant, the individual "predilections for particular Effort elements" (Bartenieff and Lewis 2002, 53). Intended variation of effort leads to a mover's movement being shaped by the instruction given and by FA, rather than by an implicit body scheme, intentions, or an emotional state. Within the instructions, Gaga covers the effort people would not encounter or embody outside of class. Thus, by embodying the effort, participants expand their movement quality range.

(8) Instructions are also designed to not allow people to stay in their comfort zone of "effort" in the sense of body knowledge perceived as hard work. Physical effort and muscle work are associated with "pleasure." Hard work is reframed as

positive. Counting down from ten to one while increasing the effort and "let's do it again" or even "piece of cake," in the sense that the instruction is not difficult to accomplish, trick people into performing effort they would not usually endure or do not believe they can endure.

(9) Furthermore, participants are forced into actions that seem "inadequate" for adults: "Sticking the tongue out," "being an animal," "making faces," "laughing," and other instructions require participants to overcome inhibiting preconditions and readjust values.

All the different actions of "breaking" physical-psychological body knowledge most possibly lead to an update of the individual body scheme and transformation of self-perception.

5.5 Movement Control

A basic characteristic of Gaga instructions is that they initiate movement of two different kinds of control: "self-willed movement" and "spontaneous movement that is not controlled voluntarily" (Schmalzl, Crane-Godreau, and Payne 2014, 2). In the context of other somatic practices, researchers found this characteristic to have an effect on self-sense and agency (2). What I experienced myself is that the self-willed movement was often more difficult to enact and to maintain. Movement initiated via instructions that suggested a passive role of myself as the mover felt easier to enact, as if less strength was needed. This was especially the case with movements of the following character:

Self-willed: Grab your bones out. / Pull your bones out. / Shake.
Not controlled: Let your bones slide out. / Feel like someone is pulling your arms out. / Quake.

But also:

Self-willed: Move.
Not controlled: Let the outside forces move you. / Connect to your engines.

Instructions commanding noncontrolled movement put me in the role of an observer: My focus was on the sensory perception of a movement, rather than on the conscious enactment. Letting go of movement control also seemed to help me to expand my movement range beyond what I would normally do; I let myself "be overwhelmed."

As the instructions show, the difference between self-controlled and noncontrolled movement lies only in the chosen wording, depending on whether the mover is addressed as the subject and movement actor, or as the object and movement receiver. The initiator of noncontrolled movement could be anonymous, "be moved," or it could be specific body parts or sensory information from the environment, "far-away engines," or just the movement itself, "let the movement travel." The wording has the potential to affect self-sense and sense of movement agency.

Instructions also quite practically train movement control when asking participants to change between an actively or passively introduced relaxation and contraction, for example, in the movement pair of "collapse" and "float."

5.6 Skin Sensory System

In Gaga, the skin is assigned the role of a main sensory system. The skin becomes the interface for the reception of sensory information of body state and movement as well as of surroundings, which in turn becomes a point of departure for movement enactment—a body knowledge manipulation via the skin addressed by Koch's concept of "tattooing" (2017, 396). Tattooing in Gaga works mainly by imagery and, occasionally, self-touch and physical contact with environmental stimuli. Instructions draw attention to specific skin areas or to the envelop of the skin as a whole. To change movement quality, instructions initiate a particular skin-centered body knowledge via movement or imagination.

The skin is an encompassing outside frontier of the Gaga body, including eyes and the inside of the mouth. When drawing attention to the skin as a sensory organ, imagery often also involves attention to the space surrounding the skin, such as "evaporate," or under the skin, such as "the tickling sensation under the skin." In the Gaga body concept, flesh and bones can move around freely within the skin, as can bones within flesh. The skin is seen as an entity separate and separable from the flesh, though occasionally both can be "glued" together again. The connection between skin and flesh can be "slippery" like "soap." The Gaga skin seems to include epidermis, dermis, and eventually the fascia. Instructions do not differentiate between sensation on top or underneath the skin. From a participant's point of view, it is difficult to locate the exact place of the skin sense as on top or underneath the skin; the information remains unprecise. Still, sensual input seems to become easily accessible if the outside of the skin is somehow involved—be it because of an outside stimulus, touch with something or self-touch imposed, or an inside movement causing the skin to move as well. In many situations, the "skin" will not be directly addressed as a sensory organ; nevertheless, it is involved in the sensation and, through the sensation, in action. Skin then functions as an implicit sensory organ.

Skin awareness is demanded and trained (1) via FA by "listening to" and trying to capture a particular sensory input, a special case being the use of touch, or by imagining a sensory input, or (2) via OM. Attention can be guided toward skin tension, "feel the stretch of your skin," or toward "fine touch" and pressure, "feel touch of the skin with air/clothes/floor/…" Sometimes participants are told to place their own hand on a body part and pay attention to what they sense with their hand when the body moves. The skin of the hand becomes the perceiving organ, and the hand also becomes an outside sensory stimulus to increase skin sensation. Afterwards, participants are often asked to recreate the same skin sensation without the sensory "help" of the hand. The objects of FA are often specific areas of the skin, such as "the skin behind the ears," "the skin under your armpits," "the skin between the shoulder blades," and others; some are experienced as easier, others as more difficult to access sensory-wise. Sometimes the skin is not specifically named, but the context reveals that skin sensation is involved: "sense the back of your neck" or "feel the area between your shoulder blades." In the process, participants are learning to localize sensations within their bodies, while focusing on a sensory input heightens the awareness of the environment. Using the skin, sensation trains and expands prosthetic perception by "sensing the people behind you with your back" and alters the peripersonal space. It seems as if, in Gaga, a great part of the skin sense's transformative potential depends on the fact that the outside is not only observed but also literally incorporated into movement via imagination, as one "evaporates" into the environment or "gives" and "receives" from the environment. Imagination leads to one's understanding of the sensory connection to the environment as a communication channel working both ways. Instructions ask for the observation of what an environmental stimulus, such as touch, provokes within one's body: How is the way I touch the floor, the sensory information received from the skin sense, related to the body knowledge as a whole? If I touch the floor "gently," like a "good friend," I can "receive it" and will not get hurt when falling. If I push the floor, I can use it as an "excess force," an "engine" to move. The perceptive space seems to be in constant construction; sensation is constantly revised.

As already mentioned, not only is skin sensation actively observed as such in class, but a (re)action can also stem from a certain skin sensation. Skin sensation is always connected to moving with a certain quality: Participants are told to look for a certain sensation such as the sensing of the "stretch of the skin." To sense stretched skin, one needs to cause their skin to stretch and thus perform a certain action. Depending on the skin sensation, the action will vary. Within class, participants are sometimes told to look for a certain skin sensation that they can recreate by drawing on priorly gained body knowledge only, such as "take a cold shower." Some instructions can be given differently, highlighting the perception of (imagined) sensory information, or highlighting the recreation of sensory information: "feel your delicate skin" versus "let your skin become delicate," "feel your generous skin" versus "become generous," and "feel your tight skin" or "become tight" versus "let your skin become tight." Sometimes it is an action that creates a skin sensation like "yawn." Yet, from a movement quality and movement mode point of view, the output seems to be the same. Variations of skin sensation, of whatever origin, also create change in posture, strength, stamina, and flexibility. Varying the "space between the shoulder blades," for example, leads to a mobilization of the shoulder blades, upper back, and chest area.

5.7 Effective Strength Sources

The Gaga body concept includes "engines," also known as "motors": different areas usually inside but also outside the participant's body. These areas can become (imaginary) sources of movement. Instructions tell participants to "ignite" them or "initiate" movement with them. First option, one makes the addressed engine the source of movement by contracting the muscles attached. Second option, one experiments with moving the engine and then let the movement of the rest of the body be initiated from this movement input. Third option, attention focuses on the engine, and movement is created by using the sensory input provided by it. The term "energy" is discussed in the same context: If a body part, an area of the body, or a part of the environment functions as the "source of energy," then it seems to function like an "engine." Yet, talking of the "source of energy" seems to be rather about keeping an OM of the possible movement impact of the addressed bodily or environmental stimulus.

I observed that basically any body part could become a source of movement, as in "initiate movement from your hands," yet instructions appeared to constantly draw attention to particular areas of the body: the center of the body, the lena, the pika, "the area between ribcage and pelvis," and the ribcage or chest and pelvis. "Igniting" the engine lena involves activating the core muscles—a general activation in the middle of the body without thinking about what the core muscles actually look like or how they function. Yoyo, on the other hand, involves the activation of the pelvic floor muscles, the pika, joined by an activation of the lower abdominal muscles. Both the engines, lena and yoyo, are felt as muscle contraction in said areas, supporting movement in terms of quality, strength, and postural support. I observed that, involving lena and yoyo as well as pika, I could move faster and more precisely, and it inhibited pain in the lower back. Using the box of the chest and the pelvis as an engine, on the other hand, felt like mobilizing a certain anatomical area of the body, both imagined as having a box-like shape, and allowing this area to become more important within movement generation. The rest of the body, with its movement, seemed to react to the movement of chest and pelvis. In general, testing engines appeared to be about exploring which body areas and corresponding muscles were the most effective and efficient to use to accomplish an action, exploring movement possibilities and movement qualities.

A specific case is the use of "far-away engines." From what I witnessed during class, far-away engines could be either a body part on the opposite side of the body—opposite in terms of the longest distance when traveling along the body surface or through the body's interior—or a stimulus presented by the environment. Using far-away engines then means either an increase in encompassing proprioception or exteroception. "Engaging" far-away engines seemed to require less use of strength to accomplish movement. The connection to such engines in the environment becomes effective in terms of peripersonal space. The own action is set in interaction with an object visually perceived as far away, demanding an opening-up of the perceptive space and prosthetic perception, while the object becomes effective for movement creation.

5.8 Movement Qualities

Let's do Kagami. Mirror me. But rather than copying my movements, copy my quality.

In Gaga, there is no set form that participants are told to embody; in its origin as a technique to improve performance on stage, it is the movement qualities—or the effort, to say it with Labans Movement Analysis (LMA)—that instructions shape. With its instructions Gaga covers a broad range of different movement qualities or efforts. As a choreographer, Naharin filled his choreographies with those different qualities and Gaga has functioned as a language for expressing the choreographies. Within Gaga classes, though, the different efforts first enable people to experience a variety of body knowledge. Instructions are designed to create a variation of effort, especially within one of LMA's four effort elements: direct to indirect space, strong to light weight, sudden to sustained time, and free to bound flux. Effort elements always occur in different "combinations." There is never only a single effort involved in a single movement instruction. The range of effort combinations reflects the effort range and thus the movement style that Gaga covers. Sometimes instructions pertain to two efforts only, producing Laban's "Inner States: Incomplete Effort, Inner Attitudes": when the mostly used free flux does not play an explicit part but only an implicit part in an action (Bartenieff and Lewis 2002, 58–60).

Central to instructions in Gaga class seems to be the constant (re)introduction of effort combinations. Instructions modify a momentary combination, or the introduction of a totally new one. First, effort could be transformed—one effort becomes the "layer" of another. Second, effort could be "faded out" into another. Third, effort could be transformed in a direct way by commanding the "switch" from one effort combination to the other. The action of "layering" is an action of changing one of the effort elements—though instructions require participants to keep the memory of effort from before. In the action of "switching," effort elements will be changed for good:

- *Layering.* The action of "moving in clay" could be added to "circles and curves," and the weight is changed; by "instead of doing them, let them happen to you," the flux becomes free instead of bound; or by "feel like you can do it forever," "feel like you can do it for one hour," and "feel like you can do it for ten seconds," the effort element of time is adjusted.
- *Switching.* One could switch from moving with "soft flesh" to moving with "thick flesh," changing only weight, while the other effort elements remain the same. In contrast, from "floating," one could also "snap into movement," requiring a sudden change in all effort elements at once.

In terms of effort variation, the most significant effort states are probably "floating" and its counteraction, "snapping into movement," or slight variations of both, as they occur in the instructions. Floating as a state of awareness and availability with no approach to space, weight, and time is characterized by a "neutral" flux effort. Though, as soon as instructions and imagery are added, the actions carried out resembles Laban's Basic Effort Action: "float." "Letting movement travel through" creates an indirect approach to space. "Measuring weight," "only using the effort needed to resist gravity," and "being uplifted on a molecular level" create a light approach to weight. "Feel like you have plenty of time" creates a sustained approach to time. Also, the effort of floating seems inseparable from its inversion: "snapping into movement," or "exploding." "Snapping" is Laban's punch with direct space, strong weight, and sudden time. The action could be modified by emphasizing the "softness" within the body while punching (a dab with light weight), or the action becomes spaceless (when space does not matter) or weightless (when weight is not emphasized). However, the central element, sudden time, remains.

Instructions Playing with Space

As already mentioned, instructions play with both FA and OM, and this affects space effort. Instructions in Gaga generally require an encompassing focus and a flexible attitude toward space, created via instructions such as "seeing," "listening to," and "sensing the space"—there is no intended direction to an action—and they lead to an open mode of attention. In addition, there are also actions with a direct space effort: "walking through the room," not slowly or walking fast, and "changing direction very often"; "connecting to the horizon," "connecting," and "giving movement" to a certain person and then switching the focus to another person; going up and down from the floor; or stretching the back with bent knees in different directions. The emphasized isolated movement of body parts may also involve a direct approach to space, as it is a specific body part that is addressed. Some instructions seem to shape only the mode of attention, yet shape space effort as well: Becoming "big" or becoming tiny, moving into a "too large skin" or a "very tight skin," and stepping into a "diving suit" or "under a blanket" create a sensitivity toward space and the movement range, ranging from making small movements close to the body center to stretching out the limbs and reaching far. Space has an even greater impact on "giving to" and "receiving from." The instruction will provoke a postural "opening up" of the body toward space, such as open arms, and a change of movement range, such as wide movements. The "opening up" usually happens from the place that instructions indicate as the center of the movement such as "give from your heart" or "receive through your hands."

Instructions Playing with Weight

In Gaga classes, visible and invisible variations of weight and variations of muscle mode are continuously happening. Weight is addressed in many ways: through the tension of flesh, by different engines, and through images of specific action. A varying weight can be singled out as the central quality defining the movement in "switching" between thick and soft flesh, and between tensed and released muscles. Thick flesh is connected to a strong weight effort; movement with thick flesh has an impact. Soft flesh is connected to light effort; movement with soft flesh has a "delicate" quality. Instructions can initiate a strong weight in one body part, and light weight in another. When "thick flesh is engaged" to move faster, meaning with more power and impact, the effort becomes strong. Other instructions also have an impact on weight. There is a strong "bodybuilder"—though with a "soft spine." There is light "delicate" movement, "bony movement," "feeling the air traveling through your body," and "feeling being carried by water." "Thickness" can also ask to "travel" the body from one body part to another, or "thickness" can switch places, having one body part moving in a strong way, while the rest of the body is light.

Weight is also not always "hundred percent" strong or light. In Gaga classes, the different possibilities of weight are addressed as different "levels of thickness" or "effort," for example. Instructions can demand a "moving through" liquid of different consistencies, indirectly provoking a variation in weight. Instructions can also ask for different percentages of thickness: "ten percent" of thickness or effort, "thirty percent," "seventy percent," "ninety percent," or "hundred percent," and the other way around. In either instance, there is an acceleration or variation of weight from one extreme to the other.

Instructions Playing with Time

It seems as if most of the movements throughout class are of a sustained time effort: People are "taking their time," moving leisurely, and able to "go on forever." This does not say anything about speed: Sustained effort could be accompanying either a slow or a fast speed movement. Sustained effort is broken by sudden "moments of 'exaggeration,'" where the time starts to matter, where movement must be completed within a certain timeframe. This can become significant in terms of the quality of a certain movement. Teachers will emphasize the suddenness and immediateness of a "punch" or "explosion," demanding the movement again and again until they are satisfied by the visible time effort. In addition, the sustained effort is changed by actions such as counting down from ten to one while exaggerating what is done. The movement quality—apart from an exaggeration of other qualities or effort—becomes "hasty" and "urgent." Time can also be addressed otherwise: Teachers would, for example, give the instruction "feel like you could keep going forever," "for one day," "for one hour," "for ten minutes," "for one minute," or "for ten seconds." Here, time is only modified by the instruction—from "sustained," as in "taking time, leisurely" to "sudden," as in "urgent, hasty" (Bartenieff and Lewis 2002, 56).

Instructions Playing with Flux

Variations of flux effort in Gaga classes appear mostly as changes in perceived movement initiation, a movement mode invisible to the outside. Participants are told to either "let a movement happen to them" or "engage themselves into the movement" and actually "move their body parts," adjusting the inner flux by adjusting attention as well as proprioception and kinesthesia. "Letting movement happen to oneself" creates free flux, which is connected to OM. The cumulation of free flux is perhaps when one is told to be "overwhelmed by movement." In contrast to free flux, bound flux requires FA on movement. Teachers might create a certain movement with free flux and then break it by bound flux, such as "floating" broken by "snapping into movement" or "exploding." In terms of posture, for example, they might emphasize the free flux of hip joint movement and then demand the bound flux of "grabbing a body part into movement." Transformation of flux effort is also involved in enacting "pushing the floor" and then "letting go into the floor" or "sinking into the floor." A prime example of flux variation might be "shake," the active "shaking" of body parts, in contrast to "quake," "feel like an earthquake is happening" "in you" or "underneath you," or the "bumpy road" feeling. Even though both seem to be of the same quality in terms of being an uncontrolled shaking action of the body, they vary in how they are perceived. A teacher once introduced the image of a "flipper machine" in the pelvis, with the ball moving around in the machine creating the action: "quaking," in which one would feel like the static machine being moved by and moving along with the ball within, or "shaking," in which the machine becomes alive sending the ball around.

Teachers are free in the imagery they use to "play with" space, weight, time, and flux. However, it is characteristic of Gaga classes that many of the possibilities are covered throughout classes, exploring the broad variety that exists for the body to move. A certain set of instructions is also found to be repeated: In Gaga, most of the efforts are created through specific images given in instructions; therefore, the efforts are both repetitive and key elements to Gaga classes and Gaga's body topography, especially the Gaga movement style.

5.9 Muscle Contraction and Relaxation

Gaga works with different types of muscle contractions: static contraction as well as concentric and eccentric dynamic contraction (see Haas 2018, 5). Even static contraction does not mean stopping a movement and contracting the muscles, although the contraction becomes a requested action in itself like in "becoming a bodybuilder with a soft spine": It includes monitoring how one could contract every muscle in the body—apart from the ones surrounding the spine—in the form of a static contraction, yet not letting the static contraction stop oneself from being able to move. Introducing muscle contraction via "moving through clay" appears to create similar body knowledge with a slightly different mode: In an imaginary manner, one must contract muscled to be able to "move through a very thick texture"; the contraction results from an imaginary situation. Instructions also demand the embodiment of a "thick texture" that can "travel the body" as "lava," "magma," or "honey." The static contraction is then "traveling the body" in a sense that oneself will try to "thicken" (contract) one area of the body after the other, depending on where the "thickness" is "traveling." Apart from static contraction, Gaga is full of moments of dynamic contraction initiated by instructions: The "engines" are used to move; muscles are "engaged into movement"; bones are "grabbed out" or "pulled out" by muscles.

It is important to mention that instructions will not include an action named "muscle contraction"; instead, they will say, "activate the flesh," "get thick," "move through something thick," "connect to thick flesh," "wear thick flesh," "let your flesh become thick," "grab your bones," or "be a bodybuilder." Sometimes muscle contraction is an active action, as, for example, in the case of "wear thick flesh." Sometimes it does not become directly addressed in the instruction as action, but it is very obviously the only active content of the action initiated, such as "move through thick liquid." At other times, muscle contraction is passive in the sense that it is an effect of something else, such as "yawning" or "taking a cold shower." Furthermore, instructions do not address specific muscles separately, but rather address specific areas of the body and thus the muscles that are attached to those areas. One can "activate the flesh" of any specific area, resulting only implicitly, but not explicitly, in different muscles attached to this area contracting with different intensity.

In the context of a Gaga class, muscle contraction comes up in different contexts and thus has different functions. Gaga techniques work by constantly changing between muscle contraction and relaxation. (1) On the one hand, instructions in class often initiate muscle contraction or tension and then release the tension and relax the muscles, and vice versa. (2) On the other hand, contraction and relaxation are required at the same time but in different body parts; or a sudden and fast muscle contraction out of the relaxed state is demanded. (3) More, instructions train a balanced tone, a certain ideal contraction in-between contraction and relaxation, as well as increase proprioceptive control.

Changing between Tension and Relaxation

The variation of "thick and soft flesh," or tensed and released, contracted and relaxed muscles, is a central theme to Gaga classes. It turns up in the form of manifold instructions. Apart from "thick flesh" and "soft flesh," different imagery, metaphors, and actions are used with the same effect of contracting or tensing muscles and then releasing the tension and relaxing again: Participants are told to move through a liquid with low density, "soft feathers," "air," a liquid with higher density, "water," a liquid with medium density, "Nutella," "honey," a liquid with high density, and "clay." There is an instruction to "grab your bones" in opposition to "let your bones slide out." Ideal images used in instructions for contraction are also "squeezing like an orange or a lemon" and "becoming juicy" or "juicy flesh." Contraction and relaxation can also stem from activating the skin sense and using touch—be it with the hands in "push the floor" or "touch the floor as someone you love; the feet in "knead the floor like dough," "receive the floor," or "give into the floor"; other body parts; or the whole body in "push against the floor" or "use the push against the floor" and "melt into the floor." Teachers sometimes initiate contraction, then relaxation, then contraction again, and so on. The time span given between instructions to allow participants to accomplish a task often becomes shorter. So, in the end, teachers ask for a quick change between contracting and releasing the muscles. In addition, there are periods of intense muscular work, followed by periods of total relaxation: For example, "let go," "relax into the floor," or "float" follows "spaghetti in boiling water" or other moments of "exaggeration." The state of relaxation is used for monitoring the embodied state as a result of the muscular work before. I observed that during these periods of relaxation, I could perceive excessive "lightness" as well as increased sensitivity to the sensory information of the previously contracted muscles. It seemed much easier to relax after contraction than without it. The relaxation appeared to be physical as well as psychological. Sometimes participants were asked to keep enacting a movement while varying the weight effort—from muscular contraction to relaxation: "Find circles and curves with soft flesh now. Listen to the difference." I then perceived a significant difference in body knowledge: Performing an action with relaxed muscles, after tensing them, felt much easier than when muscles were explicitly contracted.

In addition to creating muscular relaxation via contraction, instructions introduce relaxation via the "drumming on the body," demanding that participants "drum with soft hands" on the body, legs, arms, head, or back, except on the torso from legs to chest, increasing the intensity with a countdown. Already while beating, I observed a release of tensed muscles—a somehow painful yet pleasant sensation, which made me want to hit especially the tensed areas more often. I even felt as though I did not have enough force to hit as hard as I would like. This problem was solved in Gaga/dancers' classes, where participants could pair up, and one would hit the other. It seemed to have the effect of a massage; muscles relaxed. Actions such as these also create increased blood flow and a higher body temperature, which I perceived as a "tickling sensation" in the whole body. What seems to be crucial to a positively experienced outcome of "drumming" is that teachers instruct people to relax in order to receive while the hands, which one uses to beat, should also be relaxed. An alternative, second way to release and relax the muscles is the action of shaking or quaking, such as in "shake off your flesh," or the instruction "Separate the flesh from the bones." The muscles seem to loosen and relax due to the quick action without tension. Indeed, they seemed to have to be relaxed to achieve the "right" shaking action, which requires free movement of the joints in all possible directions. Throughout the action, I could really feel my flesh wobble like pudding. I could also feel the "tickling" effect of the drumming, shaking, and quaking, which presumably increased the blood flow. Shaking is often used as an instruction to relax after periods of high muscular effort or high tension.

Training Isolated and Fast Contraction

Gaga trains one's ability to control the muscles, their contraction, and their relaxation via instructions like "swallowing honey through your hands in your whole body." After "swallowing," the honey could be guided to "travel" to a specific part of the body. The teacher might even name all the body parts that the honey is "passing through," making participants aware of any body part on the way. I observed "swallowing honey" as an active action of muscle contraction. I contracted the muscles of the body part where I imagined the honey to be. Imagining the contraction as a liquid traveling my body, I created an unbroken chain of isolated contractions. After the honey "passed," the attaching muscles of a body part had to be released. The exercise thus presented a training of contracting specific muscles isolated from others and practicing actively releasing those muscles afterwards. The honey or contraction is usually imagined to "travel in" from the outer parts of the body, the hands and feet, toward the center, the torso and the navel area. Later, the action is reversed, imagined as initiating now in the center of the body and "traveling out" toward the "edges," to the hands and feet. In a last step, the traveling stuff should then travel out and in at the same time. Sometimes the traveling stuff is not asked to travel in a particular direction, but just from one to another place within the body. This seemed to require an additional letting go of symmetric and controlled muscle contraction while still maintaining the focused control and the ability to contract specific areas. Other than a liquid such as honey, further imagery used for traveling stuff could be "balls traveling your body." The different image appeared to cause an even more specific and localizable contraction.

In addition to the training of isolated contractions, other instructions train the fast reaction of muscles. "Snapping into movement" or "exploding" are examples. Both movements are mostly initiated from a balanced tone. From this state, participants are made to evoke direct muscle contractions, often with an emphasis on the lower stomach and the stomach area as the center of the "explosion." In the "explosions," the isolated contraction of the abdominals "echoes" in the rest of the body. "Snapping," contrary to "exploding," seemed to require rather an instant overall contraction of the muscles. The image that comes to my mind to describe the sensation I observed is being like an animal waiting patiently and then leaping forward to capture the pray.

Training Balanced Tone, Ideal Contraction, and Proprioceptive Control

In accordance with Gaga's body topography, participants are asked to keep on open-monitoring the mode of muscle tone and to maintain a balanced tone as a base to movement. Muscles remain activated in the sense of maintaining proprioceptive control. During observation, I felt randomly in a state of total relaxation beyond the balanced tone, and when I did, it was only for a short amount of time, and I would, still, not let go of monitoring and induce total mental relaxation or allow an emptiness of mind. Additionally, muscles are trained to be contracted in a dynamic way to not "block" joint movement. Instructions demand a "letting go" within muscle tension to increase movement range. Furthermore, they provide ongoing exercises that train muscle contraction while elongating instead of shortening the muscles. An often-practiced exercise involves standing in an erect position with both arms stretching out in a sideward direction at shoulder level—"float up your arms." Stretching is introduced either by "feel like someone is pulling your arms out" and "let your bones slide out of your flesh" or by "pull your arms out" and "grab your arms out even further." While the former is experienced slightly differently than the latter, both lead to a dynamic contraction with long muscles, nonetheless. Finally, the training of isolated contractions comes with an increased feeling of proprioceptive awareness, understanding, and control. I observed that I learned not only how I had to release specific muscles to gain and keep freedom of the joints but also which muscles I needed to perform quick and goal-oriented movement. I could then keep moving effectively and efficiently while keeping a broad movement range.

5.10 Stamina, Strength, Flexibility, and Posture

Gaga becomes especially effective in the way participants' (1) stamina, (2) muscular strength, (3) flexibility, and (4) posture are transformed during practice. With ongoing practice, I experienced an increase of stamina alongside proprioceptive control, which enhanced my ability to use my strength efficiently. More, I witnessed my posture transform lastingly: My tendency to round my upper back disappeared, possibly also to the increased flexibility and force in the muscles of my chest and shoulder area. Other participants affirmed me that their postural flexibility increased, joints mobilized, and movement range expanded. Along with all of this, participants felt a decrease especially in pain, and they experienced an improvement in physical well-being due to afferent emotions possibly related to psychological well-being. We can conclude that in the context of Gaga, an individually perceived as well as outwardly visible body transformation takes place. This transformed body carries not only body knowledge connected to broader historical cultural and social discourses but also the apparently typical Gaga body concept and movement style, such as the always flexible spine available to movement, the animalistic way to move, the bent knees, and the dropped pelvis.

Stamina

Gaga demands and therefore trains both aerobic, highlighting the consumption of oxygen during stages of effort, and anaerobic stamina, exercising with oxygen shortage (see Haas 2018, 12–13). Above all, aerobic stamina is created by a Gaga class, being one hour of constant movement without stopping. Participants need and learn to manage their stamina and strength. Aerobic stamina is also cultivated when participants are told to imagine and enact what potentially moving "forever" could look like and how much energy is needed to fulfill an action for a long period of time without getting exhausted. Ongoing aerobic movement is accompanied by moments of anaerobic movement: Instructions initiate short periods of exaggerated movement, "moments of exaggeration." These "moments of exaggeration" could include not only the exaggeration of strength used but also, as important in the case of aerobic stamina, the exaggeration of speed, adjusting time and flow effort.

Typical movement actions to "raise the heartbeat," as Ayala called it, are "running in place," "shaking" or "quaking," "being overwhelmed with movement," "moving through space" in a fast way, "happy feet" and "tap dancing" feet, or the sensation of "the floor is becoming very hot." "Running in place" is the action of jogging on the spot. The speed can be increased by the running legs or by the arms, which are moving along, bent, at the sides of the body. Legs or arms are enacted as the "motor" for the rest of the body. Teachers often point out that relaxed muscles attached to the joints are required in order to allow the movement to become as fast as possible. With a countdown from ten to one, the speed increases.

In the context of Gaga class, even anaerobic movement seemed comparatively easy to bear. Given the nature of the imagery, there was always an element of fun involved, and I could enjoy exhaustion. It felt as if Gaga instructions were "tricking" me into training stamina.

Strength

The creation of strength is directly connected to the muscles' contraction and relaxation, as strength is built up through muscle work (see Haas 2018, 13–14). Like sports and body and movement practices in general, Gaga especially addresses the various abdominal muscles, the muscles of the legs and arms, the muscles along the spine, and the muscles in the upper back. However, because of the holistic anatomical concept of the Gaga body, instructions never refer to muscles; instead, they address the flesh or skin in different body areas, not necessarily identical to muscle allocation. As mentioned above, instructions also do not mention muscle contraction: Flesh can be "grabbed" or used to "grab" the bones, or it can become "thick" and of a "thick texture." The skin can become "narrow" or "tight," or it can be "stretched," likewise modifying muscular tension.

Gaga techniques put an emphasis on strength creation in core muscles. The always soft spine, such as the head-to-tail coccyx connection, causes activation, contraction, relaxation of the muscles along the spine, as well as other core muscles. The combination of the soft spine and the free movement of the shoulder blade, and the chest leads to an activation of the muscles all over the torso, particularly those of the upper back attached to the shoulder joints. Instructions focus on the "distance between the ribcage and the pelvis" and its variation and likewise affect different core muscles. By asking participants to keep all their posture-stabilizing muscles involved while working other muscles, like in the instruction "bodybuilder with a soft spine," instructions practice the maintenance of an activated core in combination with muscular flexibility during "moments of effort." Strength is created in a dynamic way.

The core muscles become explicitly addressed by pika and lena. Pika, the pelvic floor muscles, are activated by yoyo, which is described as a "sucking in" of the pelvic floor muscles, similar to "having to pee but not being able to." Lena, the "big engine" in the center, underneath the navel, is "activated" as the "sun shining" and "origin of movement." Participants will be told to "lift the pika" and "drop it" or "move from the lena." Teachers might introduce a time span during class when participants maintain the contraction of lena or yoyo while performing other movements. Some teachers would tell participants to try to keep lena or yoyo throughout class; others would tell participants to release the tension again.

Most classes include at least one of several exercises to train the core area and generate awareness of core muscles. There are, for example, exercises similar to what is known as sit-ups: moving from lying on the floor to a sitting position and then to lying down again. The form is usually free; it could mean coming up straight or rather coming up via the side of the body. The legs are either resting on the floor or lifted in the air, while the whole body is to be kept floating. Sometimes the action speeds up due to a countdown. Another exercise works simply by lifting and moving the legs, arms, head, and upper torso in the air while sitting on the floor. The "mermaid" exercise not only trains core muscles but also leg muscles: keeping the legs tightly held together and moving them around through the air like a mermaid tail while resting the upper body on the elbows or optionally floating it. Quite similarly, teachers might introduce the action of "creating waves" with the body while lying on the side. When standing, core muscles are engaged without body weight by "pressing out the juice of a lemon in the stomach," or "making faces with the stomach." Often after exercises involving a great deal of strength, instructions introduce a moment of relaxation, for example, lying on the floor.

Arm muscles are strengthened while standing, during instructions and actions such as "float your arms up," felt as requiring less arm strength, maybe more back strength; "let the bones slide out of your flesh," felt as the relevant muscles contracting in an elongated way; "take your arms out to the side"; or "grab your arms out to the side," felt as a stronger direct contraction of muscles attached to the arm area. Depending on the image applied to introduce the holding action, different muscles felt involved; the goal, it seems, is to create muscular efficiency while supporting the arms. In addition, arm strength and upper back strength are trained in push-up–like exercises. After placing the hands in front of the feet, an increasing amount of weight would be transferred from the feet to the hands. Hands slowly get placed further and further away from the body, with the spine and the rest of the body "kept alive" until the body position is that of a so-called plank or push-up position. Teachers will tell participants to move closer to the floor and further away, "bring your body closer to the floor and further away again" and "go in and out of the floor," resulting in a bending of the elbows. Participants are also told to "play with the distance" of pelvis and floor. Here also a period of contraction often follows a period of relaxation on the floor. Another more active exercise is the action of "crawling," where people build similar strength to that in push-ups while moving through the room on hands and feet. Crawling includes the creation of arm and leg strength as well as core strength. Movement quality and movement mode variations finetune muscular tone range and possibilities as well as proprioception: the body weight "collapsing" on the arm; the body "giving in into the floor"; the hand "receiving the floor" or "touching the floor like someone you love" or, contrarily, "pushing the floor."

Leg strength is required and created in nearly all instructions, yet some seem to focus specifically on it. There is the "standing on one leg," balancing on one leg, with the other leg in the air or on the floor not carrying any weight. The standing leg can "drill" into the floor, kept straight or bent, experimenting with how balance can be best kept, sensing the contact with the floor through the foot. The other leg can "float" up, experimenting with "what muscles can be engaged to lift the leg when the leg is moved around through the air." Instructions lead participants to become aware of how leg movement could be initiated in connection to or separated from the pelvic area. There is the action of bending the knees, standing in a parallel position with feet apart. The bending is usually accompanied by the curving, bending, arching, or twisting of the torso, involving a strengthening as well as a stretch of the upper body. There is also an exercise where legs are taken further apart, in a dance second position, feet parallel or turned out. The legs are bent, and the pelvis is brought as deep as possible toward the floor, training flexibility while strengthening at the same time. Finally, the muscles of the feet are worked in different ways using their contact zone with the floor. "Kneading the floor like dough" with the feet, for example, uses the floor as a counterpart to which different feet muscles can apply pressure to become stronger. The foot is not trained as a whole, rather participants are encouraged to use different parts of the foot. A particular part of the foot addressed are the moons or the "pillows of the feet," which are parallel to the moons of the hands.

Given that participants are told to "find pleasure with effort," in Gaga, the action of creating strength is discussed and introduced as something pleasant and achievable. Not only by "finding pleasure" but also by applying playful and colorful vocabulary and images, as with stamina, people are somehow "tricked" into enduring great muscular effort. Strength creation often appears as a side-effect of imagery or movement, although some exercises are especially designed for it.

Flexibility

The creation of flexibility in Gaga classes integrates (1) the elongation of muscles, providing movement efficiency and preventing injuries; (2) the creation of "free joint movement" by mobilizing the joint area, muscles, tendons, and other fibers attached; and the (3) "undoing" of restrictions in movement range due to shortened muscles.

The elongation of the muscles during action has already been mentioned in several contexts above: The more passively perceived elongation of "sliding out of the bones" and the active elongation of "grabbing out" are effectively used imagery. However, stretching as an action of elongating muscles is sometimes addressed by itself. A stretching action might be introduced via the sensory system skin: "stretching the skin," imagining the skin as a "blanket" and "stretching the blanket," "yawning," "making faces with the whole body," and others. Teachers demand "finding stretch in many small places." They also emphasize that a stretch in a Gaga class should never become static but should always involve movement and thus be dynamic.

Instructions train "free joint movement" by directly addressing the joints or by letting the joints indirectly participate in movement. The concept of joints that Gaga's instructions transmit is an image of joints with limitless movement range. Instead of naming different types of joints, all joints become addressed as ball joints. In one instruction, participants are told to imagine "two balls moving around each other" in each of the joints and are asked to "move the balls around each other," observing the sensation. In another instruction, joints are mobilized by "oiling"—for me, this seemed to be a literal, rather than metaphorical, image, as synovial fluid is produced by joint movement. The image and action of embodying "circles and curves" in different body parts has a similar output. The system of "tama" appeared as a specific action to mobilize the joints: Tama involves lifting the chest, for example, over a "wool ball," imagining "wrapping the wool around a wool ball with the chest." It means lifting the body part in different directions and then dropping it and lifting it again from the opposite direction, describing a vertical circular movement with the chest in different directions, which can later become asymmetrical or transferred to different body parts. Special attention is paid to the mobilization of the hip joints as well as the chest area, or the shoulder blades by "stretch the skin between your shoulder blades," "bring your shoulder blades close to each other and away from each other," "find asymmetrical movement in the shoulder blades." There is also always attention toward the vertebrae of the spine in the form of free spine movement, with emphasis on the area between the shoulder blades and the sacrum. This is important as many people acknowledge to suffer from back pain and tension because of "poor" posture, which they find is relieved with Gaga practice. "Sliding the shoulder blades" and "letting the pelvis become slippery like soap," for example, are actions that caused me to feel tensional release in both areas. Some exercises combine different mobilizations, such as running in place, which requires "free movement" of the shoulder blades as well as the hips, and all mobilization of joints seems to include a release of tension in the fibers attached to the joints through movement.

Furthermore, exercises such as bending forward, taking the head to the floor and touching the floor with the hands, or sitting with straight legs, sometimes slightly opened, reintroduce participants to movements they might once have been able to do, yet are no longer able to perform, because their muscles shortened due to their everyday activities. Those kinds of exercises slowly broaden participants' movement range.

Posture

Posture is the result of flexibility and strength. Gaga instructions address the different skeletal movement possibilities and exaggerate the imagination of what is possible, creating the image of an endlessly flexible posture and limitless movement range. Even though some movements might not be anatomically possible, imagination helps participants to move beyond a movement range they are accustomed to. The perceived limits of physical restrictions embodied as body scheme are adjusted with practice. Instructions train the constant activation of core muscles, effectively supporting an erect posture, by instructions such as "floating" and "never dropping into gravity." They also train balance and fast reactions in case of a loss of postural balance: "If you fall, you fall." There is also an emphasis on monitoring the contact with the floor—grounding the posture.

Physiologically, the ideal Gaga posture is what comes with a balanced tone. The jaw is dropped. The shoulder blades are brought "home." The pelvis and chest can move freely. "The head is floating up." The head is moved in elongation with the spine; it is seen as part of the spine. The spine is a seaweed spine. The torso is erect, and the pelvis is dropped away from the ribs. The knees are bent. Body parts and especially the right and left sides of the body move asymmetrically. The bodies' strength, flexibility, and posture are "animalistic."

5.11 Covert Imitation and Collective Enactment

In Gaga, participants partake in collective body knowledge in an individual way: There is the teacher providing collectively perceivable auditive and visual input, yet the way in which participants enact and embody the input depends on their individual body scheme and body knowledge precondition. The collective tendencies of body knowledge transformed in class become transparent in the collective movement style of Gaga class participants, rendering them recognizable. Additionally, the perceived effect of Gaga class narrated as experience as well as the way the experience is articulated show collective tendencies of Gaga's aesthetics.

The collective effect seems to be enforced by certain techniques of covert imitation and collective movement enactment: A Gaga class happens in a setting that forces participants to connect to the teacher and other participants; since there is no mirror to check on one's own look, one has to communicate with others. By only looking at the teacher and the other participants, in combination with one's own sensation, one can discover how the instruction could be embodied. It is an intense sensory communication with the environment and the body at the same time, a back and forth of communicating, perceiving outside aesthetics, sensing the outside, and translating it into one's own sensation and adjusting one's own body. Teachers emphasize that there is a correct movement quality connected to an instruction, and this quality is provided by the teacher in the middle. The teacher moves while the participants are told to copy the "quality of the movement" rather than the "form" or "shape." Teachers talk about how their demonstrative body becomes the carrier of an aesthetical-ideal body image. They encourage participants to imitate their bodies and movements in moments they feel participants failing in accomplishing a task. The effect is enforced by the teacher standing in the center of participants. Due to this specific setting, covert imitation is experienced strongly. There appears to be no way to avoid it. Teachers might sometimes also directly correct a particular person verbally. They give them individual guidance on how to execute their movement "correctly." Other times, the correction is not directed toward an individual, but to the group. Teachers might modify the instructions, go back to a previous instruction, or add additional imagery to clarify what they want participants to enact. The use of repeatedly and culturally and socially shared imagery or specific exercises with a strong verbal as well as form and shape guidance by the teacher also guarantees a collective body knowledge creation. Actions like counting down together, shouting out the numbers collectively, and meanwhile exaggerating movement create a strong shared emotional state and collectively shared exhaustion afterwards. The auditive perceivable sound of other voices, one's emotional state, and the exhaustion it transmits create an aesthetic community. Furthermore, "copying movement" is not restricted to "copy the teacher." Instructions also demand covert imitation of other participants. Teachers command participants to "look at the other people," "see them," "try to capture their movement quality," and "copy them." Participants are told to focus attention on the other and embody what they perceive as new movement. The music that the teacher utilizes to accompany the movement plays a key part in creating body knowledge, too. People would react to the sensory atmosphere created by the music: the beat, the key, and the music "quality."

In-field conversations suggested that during Gaga classes, a somehow unique level of connecting with other people's bodies is reached. Participants mentioned "becoming the other" person, reaching a level of total sensory identification. Moreover, participants like Shira experienced it as impossible to not follow the instructions or not embody the demonstrative body image or movement style, because "the power of the group is quite strong!" resulting from "all the people doing ... more or less the same thing." This was not only implicit by moving along collectively in an unaware mode; Shira also felt an explicit obligation to follow along. The setting provokes an aesthetic context that allows the instructions to become sensorially effective.

5.12 "Fake It Until You Make it!"

While covert imitation in all its variations is a central method of guidance, a Gaga class also offers other techniques to align and support the embodiment of Gaga's body topography. "Fake it until you make it!" is used as general advice on what to do when feeling lost or unable to fulfill the aim of an instruction. Participants are told to just pretend enacting the instruction. The idea behind it, as a teacher in class mentioned, is that one could start off with a minimum amount of sensory information on how an action or movement quality feels. As soon as this information is captured, one could copy the sensation on a larger scale, "increase the volume." "Fake it until you make it!" not only seems to allow participants to let go of negative emotional states, such as frustration, but also encourages a participant's reflection on whether they really completed the task given, preparing an additional level of conscious body knowledge embodiment. Furthermore, a focus on actual incoming sensory information from the touch of the skin with air, cloth, floor, or visual and auditory input (and not only imagery) helps to accomplish a demanded movement quality. However, instructions seem to be designed in such a way that it is impossible to accomplish the full action the instructions are aiming at. Though requested to be aware of everything at one time, I observed that I never accomplished a way to actually do this. It seemed a constant process, a constant trying. Teachers articulated this topic during class. They confessed how difficult or impossible the accomplishment of certain actions was from their own perspective. This design appeared to work: One seemed to never get bored, because the final goal was never accomplished. As a participant, the more difficult a task seemed to be, the harder I would try to achieve it.

The "layering of information" accomplishes the task of embodiment in yet another way: Participants are asked to continue with the instructed movement or movement quality during the enactment of a new instruction or task. As an example, "do circles and curves" could be followed by "shake." "Circles and curves" should then be continued while enacting the shake. Teachers present the idea that the first enacted movement, here "circles and curves," becomes the base "layer" to the second, here "shake." Theoretically, an indefinite number of layers could be added on. "Layering the information" appears to imply that body knowledge is memorized in a lasting way, quite like when teachers ask for a "recapitulation" of what was done during class. Instructions usually initiate recapitulation as an action in the last minutes of class. Participants are given a time span of usually one song to "go over" and "recapitulate" the instructions given and enacted during class. Participants are also told to focus on what they take personal interest in. Both actions, layering and recapitulating, require the capacity of an individual to memorize implicit and explicit body knowledge experienced during class, as well as a high reflexivity of one's own action and embodied awareness. Participants train to be fully aware throughout class. Both are actions of repetition, and that is how they become effective in body knowledge creation. Repetition is not only demanded by participants, but it is also a tool used by teachers. During the same class, instructions are repeated using the same or different wording, and during the course of different classes, main ideas are constantly repeated. Instructions initiate all forms of effort over and over again, and different teachers use the same imagery and similar wording. Koch mentions (2018, 6) that repetition of movement is a specific way of practicing particular body schemata in "neuronal modularization." As the amount of repetition increases, the activation of this new schemata, the reenactment of the already enacted body concept or movement style, and body knowledge become easier and more intuitive (6).

Probably because of the techniques to align and support embodiment, I observed that the more I did Gaga, the more I could connect to its body knowledge implicitly and explicitly outside of class, the more I felt able to write about it and contemplate Gaga's body knowledge, and the more I could immediately and consciously enact the movement style—inside as well as outside of Gaga class.

5.13 Discovery, Play, and Recreation

"What other place do you know, where people can move so freely and play?" a Gaga class participant asked me in 2018. During my observations and research, I figured there are three aspects that lead participants to experience Gaga class as such a recreational atmosphere: (1) The used imagery creates an atmosphere of "playfulness"; (2) movements create "playfulness"; and (3) the context creates "playfulness."

Playful Imagery

Imagery includes semantics and metaphors connected to pleasurable experiences. In addition, it reflects "playfulness" in the sense of being "nonordinary." First, images given in instructions often include sweet treats; for example, "Taste something sweet in your mouth," "Taste chocolate in your mouth," "Taste chocolate" in other body parts, "Swallow honey," and "Move through Nutella." Most participants likely connect "something sweet" to positive emotional states and enjoyable experiences. Furthermore, as chocolate, honey, and Nutella are not the healthiest foods, perhaps embodying sensations connected to their taste could be perceived as doing something unusual or even forbidden. They are foods, some might not allow themselves to taste, except on extraordinary occasions. This imagery could also possibly function as connecting participants to pleasurable memories, maybe childhood memories, when one indulged in sweets or was covered in chocolate when eating it. Second, there are images, such as a "cold shower," that could be experienced as pleasurable in the context of an Israeli Gaga class during summer, or after having sweated a lot. Moreover, perceiving a sudden cold sensation appears to be connected to an emotional state of excitement. Third, "silliness," demanded as a movement quality, seems to function as playful imagery. "Silliness" appears to be connected to "unnormal" adult behavior: "Being silly" is commonly understood as being "foolish," "insane," a "lunatic," "senseless," "simpleminded," and not "sensible" or "wise" (Merriam-Webster 2019c). However, in the context of a Gaga class, "silly" seems to refer to more of a childish silliness and to be of a positive nature. The output of instructed "silliness" is usually that participants are asked to free themselves from wanting to look a certain way or to accomplish a particular form: "Connect to your silliest self" or "Find your silly dance." Participants are commanded to move regardless of what the movement looks like—it is even better if the movement does look really "silly." Fourth, imagery also alters the serious context of a dance class with adults because it introduces the movement qualities of nonhuman beings, such as in "Overcooked spaghetti in boiling water," "Imagine an earthquake" in your pelvis or underneath your feet, and "Be a car on a bumpy road." Embodying these images becomes a game. I personally associated a strong emotion of "playfulness" with the image of becoming an "animal" and "moving like an animal." I experienced it as taking on another identity with the attributed characteristics and movement possibilities. I had fun embodying the image, and I felt free from classical movement and behavior conventions.

Playful Movement

Not only the perception and enactment of imagery but also enacted movements as such create a playful space. Practicing Gaga offers participants a space where they are required to perform nonordinary movement. Gaga techniques, for example, include movements on the lower room level and the floor. This is a level not included in most everyday movement. Just to be on the floor and move there is something extraordinary. Getting onto the floor and up again in a fast way becomes like a game played when younger. Then there is the action of crawling on all fours, hands and feet, without lifting the pelvis, introduced as crawling like an "animal" or the "animal walk." Though highly exhausting, it generates a playful atmosphere when seeing all these adults crawling around through the room, sometimes bumping into one another. There is also embodying the sensation of "overcooked spaghetti" on the floor, allowing one's body to become wobbly and bouncy, and one's movement fast but meaningless. Sometimes teachers command participants to "stick the tongue out" during movement, "yawn" openly, or "make funny faces"—and it is indeed funny to watch a whole group of adults doing so. However, because the emphasis lies on the physical sensation, which is often afterwards translated to other body parts, even though the situation is comical and hilarious, I mostly did not experience an urge to laugh. A Gaga class provides the context to allow the extraordinary to become normal. Another action to which I would attribute a playful character is the use of the voice in Gaga. Sometimes the voice is just "let out" in a loud sigh, or the voice is used to accompany movement, a sensation of the voice just flowing out in a high or low tone, whatever a movement is perceived to require, and of letting go of controlling one's voice. Physical and psychological conventions are broken, leading to an experience of freedom. Another movement with a playful component is "bouncy movement" as bounce seems to belong to children's movements. There are actions creating experiences of playfulness and freedom by rearranging the physical movement range: Not only "shaking" and "quaking" but also other movements cause participants to "break movement patterns." These movements also fit the category of playfulness and freedom: "Shaking," for example, is often connected to the image of "shaking things off" or "shaking thoughts off." In addition, throughout class, participants are constantly discovering new sensations and new movement possibilities; class becomes a "journey" and an adventure. There is also explicit space open to movement free of all the conventions of instructions: With "connect to your own movement" and "find your passion to move," participants are free to move however they like and which makes them feel good. Moreover, the image of passion already implies a quality of exaggeration and playfulness. Finally, there is the action of "laughing" or "smiling," first as usual and then with the whole body. I observed that when laughing was demanded by the teacher, I first had to force myself to laugh, but in the process, it became easier, also because everybody laughed. I experienced it as somehow self-sustaining: I then really had to laugh and experienced an emotional state of happiness. The same occurred when "smiling": In the end, I would really feel, not only sense, the "smiling."

Playful Context

By including all these instructions and imagery, teachers define the space of a Gaga class as an area open to "research" and experimentation with movement, where any movement is possible. It becomes a space free of judgment because all participants participate and must participate in the movement. The individual is never left alone or individual in such a situation, so the freedom exists to perform playful movements full-out, without feeling awkward. A Gaga class thus becomes a playground. Furthermore, one is not able to judge or criticize oneself, as there are no mirrors: Many Gaga participants I talked with believed that Gaga led to self-acceptance because of the absence of mirrors. Apart from this, teachers even make a request to "Connect to your weaknesses." Then, the Gaga class is a space where "pleasure" is the main goal to be found, and even "effort" is pleasurable. If teachers think participants take a task too seriously, and if they see that a task is difficult for participants to accomplish, they could use the phrase "piece of cake," in Hebrew קטן עלי, katan alay, meaning "small on me." "Piece of cake" became famous in popular Gaga discourse.[1] However, I found participants telling me that whereas they really liked teachers saying "piece of cake," the Hebrew "קטן עלי" did not have the same effect. Here might ultimately help the teachers' "Don't take yourself too serious!"

Gaga's aesthetics unfold as body knowledge via the embodiment of body topography and instructions, the performance of techniques in relation to the aesthetics of the ritual setting, and in interdependence with socially and culturally shaped individual as well as collective preconditions. This makes Gaga's aesthetics, as the following chapters will show, individually yet also collectively effective. It also makes Gaga's aesthetics a fixed object to study yet highly relational and variable in its nature, depending on an assemblage of varying and continuously developing aesthetical relevant factors. The analysis of aesthetics can only be a snapshot, still it remains valuable beyond the snapshot and can be fixed in written form. Techniques and body topography are not unique to Gaga, come with a history, and will prevail in a future even without Gaga if social and cultural circumstances will not change drastically. Therefore, aesthetics and the aesthetic effect and the possibility to research and capture it will equally prevail.

The exemplary analysis of body knowledge affecting aesthetics, undertaken in this and the preceding chapters, is valuable beyond its exemplary function; it is a guideline of what aesthetics to look for in order to define neo-spiritual practices. For the following part of this book, let's remember: Aesthetics become aesthetics by affecting. Thus, aesthetic effect plays an equally important role as sensory input, or, rather, for the rest of this book, the experience output is at least as important to look at as the aesthetics just analyzed.

Part 2

Gaga Participants: Aesthetics Perceived

6

Narrating Body Knowledge

This next significant part of the book examines the effect and aesthetics of Gaga as they were narrated by Gaga participants. This is ergo the part of body knowledge that was shared in situations of communication as experience. It is the following that finally offers insights into the relations between body knowledge and an explicit individual yet collective worldview, "between sensory, cognitive and socio-cultural aspects of world-construction, and the role of [Gaga practice] within this dynamic" (Grieser and Johnston 2017b, 2). To cite Lakoff and Johnson:

> But our conceptual system is not something we are normally aware of. In most of the little things we do every day, we simply think and act more or less automatically along certain lines. Just what these lines are is by no means obvious. One way to find out is by looking at language. Since communication is based on the same conceptual system that we use in thinking and acting, language is an important source of evidence for what that system is like. (2003, 4)

If we presume that an individual "conceptual system"—correspondingly perceptual order, but also worldview, body scheme, event schema, or experience filter—materializes in language, language is the place where collective and individual body knowledge can become fully explicit beyond the limits of the individual.

This is what was found in Gaga participants' conversations, interviews, and experience diaries: Gaga participants provided "experience narratives" as data to be interpreted. These experience narratives can, citing Ann Taves and Egil Asprem (2016), be understood as particular "experience events" stored in "event models." They have been singled out from an ongoing "flow of experience" generated by "episodic," "semantic," and "procedural memory" by the individual's internalized "working model": individual preconditions meeting the actual body knowledge actualization caused by environmental or body-intern stimuli. A working model determines the limits of an experience event and, thus, what enters the narration as relevant experience. Coming back to Lakoff and Johnson: Narrated experience tells us about not only the collective aesthetics of practices and collectively effective stimuli but also the individually relevant aesthetics. It tells us about individual embodied preconditions, which reflect in a conceptual system, and what of the collective aesthetics, according to preconditions or conceptual system, are thought to be of individual importance (Taves and Asprem 2016, 47–54).

In this overall context, the first aim is to show the connection between language and experience in narration and the individual and collective character of this connection. The way in which participants verbalize their experienced body knowledge is not random.

6.1 How to Verbalize Extraordinary Experience

Implicit "mental models" of experiences, experienced body knowledge, become explicit to an individual in "factual and episodic records of past experiences and events" (Menon 2014, 76). However, another level of explicitness is reached when people articulate their experience to others in the communicative situations in which they find themselves. Some situations require the utterance of a so-called short-lived and thus short-term memory (Menon 2014, 77); the conversational exchange directly after class might be such. Other situations lead to a reflection on experience and thus more thoughtfully constructed experience narratives, such as the form of a scheduled interview. One might tend to say that the first one, the short-lived experience impressions, is of specific interest to experience-centered or even more to phenomenological research. However, all short-term memories eventually become woven into larger narratives. By repeating and reflecting on them with focused attention, they come to form an explicit part of "autobiographical memory" and the "self-narrative" (Menon 2014, 76–7). With constant "reproduction" and "reinterpretation" of what has happened in the form of explicit narration, for example, this explicit memory becomes effective as body knowledge. From this point of view, explicit narrations only constitute a different step and different level of body knowledge (Menon 2014, 80).

To further understand how participants of a practice like Gaga reproduce, reinterpret, and thus transform their own experienced body knowledge, (1) oral and (2) written experience have to be closely examined:

Oral Experience Reproduction

In contrast to other parts of the interview where the interviewed participant constructs narratives concerning Gaga, thereby affording Gaga a certain space in autobiographical memory and self-narrative, the description of actual experience seems to be a rough draft, a first version of reproducing what was experienced. The reproduction of experience happens in a climatic structure, where the goal and focus of the narration becomes a reviving of the experienced in verbalization. Using short sentence rows, repeating the same word, playing with intonation and volume of the voice, using adjectives to emphasize the sensational and emotional effect of an experience, and using exclamations and interjections—it appears that the participant is talking while developing thoughts at the same time. The participant seems to build up a climax to make the listening interviewer understand the extraordinary sensational and emotional effect of an embodied experience.[1]

Example 1: Tamar

And and I feel this energetical field ve very strongly that I'm—an and this is aMAzing, because you realize the the strength of your brain and of your mind. so ah ... so ya. (slight laugh)

The interview with Tamar is special because it was held right after class, spontaneously, with her still sweating and still "high"—happy, energized, literally radiating. Due to the situation, she is enthusiastic about Gaga and the experience she had, and she has much to say in a short time—she also could not stay long. Repetitions such as "and and" are abundant, and the talking and thinking process seem to amalgamate. Furthermore, her "and and I feel this energetical field ve very strongly that I'm—an and this is aMAzing" is a prime example of how participants tend to get lost in experience descriptions during interviews. They then suddenly seem to remember the interview situation, returning to the encompassing narrative or interpretation of the experience. Like Tamar, who laughs at this point, participants express their emotions connected with a certain experience not only through words such as "aMAzing" but also through intonation and volume variation or mimics, facial expressions, and other nonverbal modes.

Example 2: Uri

But: one of the first NEW sensations I had going to Gaga classes was ahm the opportunity to be a child. To be a child. To be happy and carefree and to move around like a child without inhibition to be silly—I love the silly word. I think it's a fanTAstic metaphor. He's a genius it's really so much about being silly, and let yourself be silly, and enJOY the silliness. Ahm and and and it's it's in the spirit, it's not a the silly movement, it's the silly senSAtion, it's the silly MINDset, not to be serious. Ahm so ya I I I experienced a lot of things that are completely in the spirit in the mentality in in the area of of of feelings and that all there that's completely not physical, ahm and it happens in the class. and you asked about taking away and, ya, it goes with me, it goes ya you don't need, you need you need—it's not that you need—but there is an opportunity to be silly in other ways, in life, and not to take things to seriously in life and and to take pleasure in simple things like movement and and andso ya I take, I think I take more balance with me.

Uri starts off with a narrative, sharing one of his favorite experiences throughout class: "One of the first NEW sensations I had ... was ... the opportunity ... to be a child." He then clarifies what he meant by being "silly." "Silly" seems to function as an emotional trigger. Uri gets carried away in describing "silly," its positive emotional effect, and the embodied experience: "I love the silly word. I think it's a fanTAstic metaphor. He's a genius. ahm and and and it's it's in the spirit, it's not a the silly movement, it's the silly senSAtion, it's the silly MINDset, not to be serious." In these lines, various characteristics of experience description can be found: repetition, short sentence rows, and emphasizing. It is a reproduction of the silly experience as well as an act of finding out what the important part of the experience is to the individual, an interpretation, while talking. As Tamar, Uri uses "(ahm) so ya"' to exit the reproduction of his experience and to come back to the overall narrative structure, although he still keeps the mode of reflected talk: the mode of talking while thinking, and thinking while talking. The narrative structure is broken once more when Uri drifts away from the narrative arc, the reaction to a primary posed question, to describe the experience he had in this context: Starting with "and you asked about taking away and, ya, it goes with me," he appears to get carried away again: "It goes ya you don't need, you need you need—it's not that you need." Regarding the experience, Uri observes, "But there is an opportunity to be silly in other ways, in life, and not to take things to seriously in life and and to take pleasure in simple things like movement and and and." He finally turns back to the narrative again: "So ya I take, I think I take more balance with me."

Example 3: Ester

I I was overwhelmed. it was the Only time—usually I do Gaga, for a whole hour, I do it completely, I'm in it completely, I don't stop, you know, but I don't perspire, I don't sweat. I went, because I trust Ohad, and I kept telling myself: but remember, you have to decide how far you can do it. It was as though there were just an engine, an engine that is ten times stronger. And I said to him at the end, I was I was dripping wet I was dripping WET at the end of that hour and I was overJOYed, I haven't perspired, I haven't sweated like that in a very long time, certainly not in public, okay? I was completely wet and I went to him and I said: look, you know I love the Gaga and the teachers are all great, but for SOme reason when YOU do it, it's as though there is a motor that is ten times stronger. The engine is TEN time's stronger, it's like OUF! It blew my mind. I'm going to go to every single class that I can, if I'm not busy, that he teaches.

Here, Ester describes her "overwhelming" experience during Naharin's Gaga class. There is an underlying experience narrative here: Ester had a unique experience during Ohad's class, and she told him this after class. From the beginning on, she builds up what she says as a narrative climax illustrating the unique experience. For example, she talks about an opposite experience first. Ester finally breaks the underlying narrative to talk about the unique experience itself: "And I said to him at the end, I was I was dripping wet ... I was completely wet and I went to him and I said." She adds descriptive and illustrative passages: "It's as though there is a motor that is ten times stronger ... it blew my mind." Yet, everything in her reproduction of the experience seems rather constructed, already interpreted, and thought-through, a narrative with descriptive passages for narrative reasons. Ester illustrates, verbalizes, and emphasizes the great emotional impact of her experience by different stylistic means. In her talking, she thoroughly—and in a sophisticated way—elaborates the experience reproductions other interviewed participants showed further: (1) repetition—"I was dripping wet I was dripping WET at the end of that hour," (2) asyndeton—"it's ... it," (3) emphasis—"ten times stronger ... TEN times," (4) interjection (or exclamation)—"OUF!," (5) hyperbole—"dripping wet," (6) accumulation and tautology—"I haven't perspired, I haven't sweated," (7) climax—"it's as though there is a motor that is ten times stronger. The engine is TEN times stronger, it's like OUF! It blew my mind."

Looking at these interview excerpts of experience reproductions in context, even without additional data from the experience diaries, it is possible to figure out the continuum between emotional and sensational impressions, experience reproduction as a rather spontaneous output, and elaborated accounts when experience has already been reflected on in some way: from how Tamar verbalizes her experience, on the one hand, to how Ester verbalizes hers on the other. The more elaborated versions include accounts of chronological experience as the outlining structure to experience descriptions. In general, interviews conducted right after class seem different from those held outside of the class context: Right after class, many of the experienced emotions and sensations were still present, and some participants gave more impressions on experienced body knowledge than constructed experience narratives. Contrarily, if the verbalization occurred outside of the class context, participants would not find it easy to talk about experienced body knowledge throughout class, but they definitely could talk about the place of this Gaga experience as body knowledge in their life. Their experience verbalization seemed to be more reflected upon thinking while talking, instead of talking while thinking. Overall, it is interesting that all people interviewed got carried away within and by the experience descriptions they gave—sometimes unwillingly, sometimes willingly. In addition, while talking about a physical sensational experience and describing the body knowledge connected to Gaga, all interviewees would always move while talking. They accompanied what they expressed verbally by the Gaga movement style, mostly with the movement of their upper body. This seems a common characteristic of physical experience reproduction: "People often produce gestures when talking about bodily actions that they have performed" (Alibali, Boncoddo, and Hostetter 2014, 152). Thoughts on body knowledge and body knowledge itself are aligned in embodied memory or "embodied remembering": "The recall of personally experienced events even in more typical contexts often has a kinesthetic component" (Sutton and Williamson 2014, 318).

Written Experience Reproduction

Due to the medium of written language, the experience diaries lack the interview possibilities to express experiences in a "lively" manner, using voice, mimics, and gesture to reperform the embodied experience to the interviewer. Therefore, writers have to reproduce them differently.[2]

Example 1: Maya

Lesson 1: Today it took me a while to connect to the class—The teacher has a very straight forward "manly" approach and sometimes it makes it hard to open up and interrupts the flow. Like many teachers, he said not to take things too seriously but he him self looks totally serious throughout the class There was a turning point for me once he started the "Kagami" as there was a scene of humour there and it made me laugh and relax.

Lesson 2: I really didn't connect to the class, I've been with this teacher in the past and there wasn't a connection back then as well. I decided to give it another try and it was the same. The feeling was that we where doing a lot without an obvious reason or meaning it was too active and too "on the surface" there was a "passive aggressive" feel to it.

Lesson 3: I really enjoyed class Today. The teacher was a dancer from the ensemble and was very inspirational. She had a lot of charisma & beautiful movement that comes from real knowledge and understanding of movement without any "show off" just pure clan inspirational beauty that comes from within.

Lesson 4: This class was a spiritual experience! Really out of the ordinary teacher that creates deep, meaningful interesting, invigorating movenent experiences. I was swapped away by his energies and was eager to get more information and inspiration. The effort was meaningful and clear. The teacher's artistic background (in a veriaty of arts) and maturity went through and gave the feeling of being a part of a meaningful artistic reaserch.

Lesson 5: The techer in this class was an intern. You could really feel her lack of experience (I've been to a few classes with intrens before, who where natural teachers and had real good flow) The energy was kinda "stuck" there where a lot of breaks when she was explaining things and everybody was standing in place. It felt a bit like the opposite of gaga to me.

When Maya sent me her experience diary, she defined it as "very raw, just whatever came out after classes without editing." This means seeing her diary as a spontaneous experience output, albeit different from the spoken spontaneous outputs. Maya does not go into details, and past tense is her preferred verb form. She starts most of her diary entries by summing up the overall experience she had during class, valued in terms of emotions: (1) very positive—expressed by the exclamation, "This class was a spiritual experience!"; (2) positive—"I really enjoyed class Today"; (3) negative (with a positive ending)—"Today it took me a while to connect to the class"; and (4) very negative—"I really didn't connect to the class." Maya then proceeds to a closer reflection and analysis of the reasons for that emotional-habitual state provoked by class. She elaborates on possibly supporting arguments to the thesis she posed. Interestingly, Maya's argumentation is always bound to the teacher's action—an observation that will be of further importance. The actions of the teachers, or simply the teachers' characteristics, cause different "feelings," positive or negative. Maya illustrates her "feelings" by (1) mentioning body knowledge—"laugh and relax," (2) using metaphors and imagery—"too 'on the surface' there was a 'passive aggressive' feel to it," and (3) highlighting the metaphors with quotation marks as though emphasizing the symbolical function. Words carrying positive semantic values reveal the positivity of the experience: "Just pure clean inspirational beauty that comes from within" and "meaningful and clear." They also show experience filters: Maya finds positivity in "inspiration" and "clarity."

Example 2: Noam

> The quite soft music that was playing in the background and the slow motion movement of the teacher immediately swept everybody down to a parallel universe that exists only when you calm everything down—from the tip of the head to through my uncontrollable flow of thoughts keeping down through my rib cage and all over my internal organ, pelvis, thighs, all the way down to my pinky's nail—trying to listen the connections of all those parts that structure the body—"my body." trying to capture the ever continues flow of life inside out and outside in, using my awareness to the law of nature (that deeply influences any human been from the second thar birth takes place till death arrives)—gravity. weighing all my organs trying to develop the understanding of how much energy i need in order to just stand up and do nothing and maybe' with that understanding, i'll will use this infinite force for my benefits and begin to use the exact amount of energy for each tusk i need to do—not more not less!

Noam offers as a diary entry what the interview with Ester offers as an oral account: an elaborated experience account with (1) a chronological, narrative introduction and (2) an experience description of sensations and their individual interpretation. (1) The narrative tells about the environment and atmosphere in the past continuous tense and the action going on in the past tense. Hence, the action is already full of evaluating and interpreting imagery: "swept down," "parallel universe." (2) The sensations are described using the present participle without "be": "keeping," "trying," "using," and "weighing." The ellipses appear to revive the sensations in a similar way to oral experience descriptions, creating immediateness.[3] What Noam describes as experienced sensations—body knowledge—seem to be Gaga instructions individually interpreted and assigned meaning. He presents an account of how he constructs a perception of sensations, rather than emotions; he makes general instructions given by the teacher his own, through interpretation:

> Trying to listen the connections of all those parts that structure the body [instruction]—'my body' [interpretation]. Trying to capture the ever continues flow [instruction] of life [interpretation] inside out and outside in [instruction], using my awareness [instruction] to the law of nature (that deeply influences any human been from the second that birth takes place till death arrives) [interpretation]—gravity [instruction].

The way Noam writes about his experience makes it possible for Gaga "insiders" to filter out what was going on in class, for Gaga "outsiders" it remains an individual experience narrative.

There are clear differences within Gaga diary entries. The majority of diary entries look like Maya's: the paper medium seemed to restrict people from giving a rather "rough" experience of body knowledge in the form of the emotions and sensations during class, eventually only pointing out extraordinary body knowledge, wow-moments, but not elaborating them further. Noam's diary, in contrast, reveals perceptive structures rather than emotions. It seems as if his writing is quite close to his actual experience during class: Noam follows the instructions and makes them his own; he adjusts them according to his individual body scheme. Interestingly, my field notes show similar tendencies: the ones on paper are much shorter than the ones I kept on my computer, and both are short compared to the ones I audio-taped and only made a transcription from later on. Yet, what all of my notes lack are stylistic forms—this demonstrates the influence of knowing about having a listener or reader when drafting.

Conclusion

To conclude, first, the situation and medium of verbalization and communication influences the verbalized output, the reproduction. The spoken experience descriptions provided by participants in the interviews differ from the written experience descriptions scripted in diaries. On the one hand, descriptions in an oral context seem to mirror the emotions and sensations of the experienced, as well as the embodied effect of body knowledge itself. The given description becomes an act of reinterpreting. Written descriptions, on the other hand, seem more "neutral," put into a refined narrative form, because they were written down. Written descriptions seem to be the result of a thought-through process of reinterpretation, not the act of remembering an experience itself. An oral description is a description of extraordinary body knowledge, a revival of the body knowledge, whereas a written description is the body knowledge already passed, interpreted, and stored. Furthermore, the time participants have to reflect on certain experiences seems to play an important role. While the path from emotion and sensation impressions to a refined narrative, and from an oral output to a written output, is to be understood as a continuum, most descriptions are to be found in between or consisting of parts of both kinds.

Second, all narrated experiences are somehow colored by emotions and thus show that they have been already interpreted to different degrees. During the interviews, the interpretation seems to happen by and during the act of talking. Third, by using certain grammatical structures and stylistic forms, especially metaphors and illustrating imagery, the verbalizing people try to illustrate and retell what they experienced in a "lively" way. The narrative structure of retelling the experience that people had during a Gaga class is (1) a chronological narrative, a narrative arc or frame of contextualizing and evaluating function, told in the past tense, optional to the interviews, sometimes only an introductory phrase; and (2) an illustrative description full of stylistic forms, told in the present-like present tense, the present continuous, using present participles. The sensational and emotional experience description usually breaks a narrative arc, where experience is recounted chronologically. The structure reflects a "climacto-telic structure," which Christopher Rühlemann (2013) observes in his work on English conversation and storytelling when narrators want to dramatize. Rühlemann mentions how narrators would start from (1) an author-like description of the setting, the frame, and move toward a situation (2) where experience is "immediatized," meaning that it is made immediately experienceable to the listener or reader by providing the aesthetics needed and reducing the distance between the narrator and the recipient of the narration (Rühlemann 2013, 170–2): "The sequence climax turns the recipients into witnesses: recipients gain direct access" (170). This structure also seems to reflect different levels of remembering experience: (1) remembering actions and (2) remembering sensations and emotions during those actions.

6.2 Experience Expressed in Gaga Language

Apart from the abovementioned mechanisms of verbalization, there is another interesting aspect that reveals much about the experiencing and the embodiment of body knowledge: People take up the "Gaga language," vocabulary, words, and phrases used in the context of Gaga class, to formulate explicit experiences. The Gaga language, the body topography it communicates, and, due to its inseparability from language, Gaga-related body knowledge become part of the self-narrative and autobiographical memory of participants by building a base for the formulation of the experience memory. Some people really appear to experience an embodied Gaga framework already. They cannot help but talk about Gaga in Gaga language. For others, the Gaga language becomes a deliberately used system or metalanguage to describe the nature of experience.

When experience is created in verbalization and is later stored in its verbalized version, both forms of Gaga language usage affect and influence body knowledge perception and interpretation itself. So, how does Gaga language enter experience talk?

The Gaga's Body Topography Incorporated

Participants talk about their bodies consisting of the components of the Gaga body concept. When participants discuss embodied experience and their bodies transforming in the context of a Gaga class, they describe their bodies with bodily characteristics, transmitted by the language of the Gaga class. A central characteristic by which participants describe themselves and their bodies is *availability*: "I always had availability, Gaga allows me to tune and hunt and expand my availability" (Uri). Availability becomes used in building self-identity processes. Another characteristic transferred to participants' talking is *gravity* and the possibility "to be pulled down by gravity": "Well obviously you feel more optimistic, you feel like gravity isn't pulling you down as much" (Ester). "Being pulled down by gravity" is the "opposite to being available," to what Ester calls "this inner activity, mental or physical." Alongside being an embodied characteristic, "not being pulled down by gravity" becomes an embodied metaphor for experiencing one's life. A fully incorporated concept is *awareness*: "Sharpening my awareness by listening to my feet stepping on the flat road" shows an awareness used in the Gaga language sense, whereas "I became aware" (Noam) shows an awareness concept, which is not restricted to the context of Gaga. However, participants also use concrete characteristics of the anatomical Gaga body concept, for example, "Oiling the joints," and thus the movement possibility of "oiling the joints" has become a way in which participants experience, talk about, and perceive their joint movement: "the oiling of my joints" (Uri).

What remains to be mentioned is that particular components of a Gaga body topography and body concept, such as awareness, are not unique to Gaga classes: The vocabulary has been used in the context of other body practices, popular body discourses, and spiritual body discourses as well. The incorporation of the Gaga language into experience talk and the embodiment of the body knowledge concept seems to be facilitated by explicit and implicit body knowledge gained in other contexts. Sometimes this multisituationally discussed vocabulary coincides with Gaga vocabulary—awareness is a prime example. Other times, only the ideas coincide, not the vocabulary:

> When I meditate, I prefer to be with my eyes open because I feel like you can like there is more of like a continuous stream between your environment and your inside and you don't need to ... like when I close my eyes, I feel like it's harder for me to meditate. Like I'm not, it doesn't relax me, the opposite it closes me of, like there is no flow. (Dana)

Dana personally shared with Gaga's body topography the idea that with open eyes, there was a "continuous stream between your environment and your inside," or a "constant flow of information and energy," as the Gaga language would name it. Shutting her eyes "closes [her] of" and "shuts her senses down." It seems as if she thought that way before partaking in Gaga practice.

Furthermore, the longer people participate in Gaga, the more they seem to incorporate the Gaga language into their own verbalization and experience vocabulary: "And you always take the information on your new body, because your body is new every morning you wake up, you get older, you get stronger from practice, you're weak because of thickness, so all these informations are different" (Eli). The concept of "information" is used by Eli quite naturally; it is part of his embodied worldview, it seems. The use of thickness, however, might be a use only by chance: Eli might miss the English vocabulary for sore muscles, such as muscle ache. It could also be that he tried to remain with Gaga language metaphors in the context of a Gaga-bound interview.

Gaga Language as Most Accessible Vocabulary

The only way for participants to express is through the Gaga language itself, by developing a closed circle of meaning and experience reproduction. Somehow, participants were unable to express what they experienced in class or in the context of class without using Gaga's own vocabulary:

> Oh ya. It's oiling, it's strengthening, I think I'm better listening to it now. And I get more enjoyment from it ...
>
> And, ya, I believe with the practice and with the listening and if you're really in the experience, that happens. I think it's it happens. I don't need—it's like the echo. If it's there, it's just the echo of something you did, you don't think about it necessarily. (Uri)

The Gaga language becomes a metaphor to describe sensations and emotions— here, the "oiling." In addition, it is used in a metaphorical way to put experience into words, which is difficult to verbalize—here, "it's like the echo." This is a phenomenon that occurred with all interviewed participants. A possible

Narrating Body Knowledge   171

explanation is that when verbalizing their experience, the interviewee draws on a pool of shared knowledge and shared language between themselves and the interviewer, whom they know to be a Gaga participant herself. It is also possible that, because the experience in class is nonordinary, recounting it needs words outside of the narrators' ordinary spectrum, words they find in Gaga language itself.

The differentiation between the earlier described (1) embodied Gaga language, in the sense of an embodied worldview, and the aforementioned (2) Gaga language used as a metaphorical shared sign system is only theoretically possible—both aspects get mixed up in experience talk: "Ahm but ya I always, I think ya it's it's finding a balance between: studying, feeling of your skin or or how your feet are and also just letting go and just, you know, floa floating with it" (Dana).

Gaga Language as a System to Analyze Experience in General

Participants apply the Gaga language to life outside of class, and the metaphorical use of this language is not restricted to talking about Gaga classes. The transfer of the Gaga vocabulary, when talking about other body practices, is common, even though it often remains unclear whether the original source of the vocabulary is a Gaga-centered discourse, a common social or cultural popular discourse, or a discourse arising in the context of other body practices. This becomes clear when yoga practitioner Tamar describes yoga as a process of listening: "You know, yoga is let yourself be, listen to yourself, you know what's good for you."

In other cases, the Gaga language becomes an embodied way to view the world, even if only on the language level: "If we're really able to become available and really sense ourselves and sense around us, there is a potential I believe, you know, without anything else being said and knowledge about other people, there is the potential for a very strong connection to the others." (Uri)

In summary, what can be observed is a lack of possibilities to narrate and describe Gaga experience in research situations without using the Gaga language. Participants take on this language as a kind of "canonical language" (Stromberg 1993, 11–12), and it becomes a "set of symbols" (3) used when talking about experience. Language use seems to play a key part in terms of the effectiveness of a Gaga class and to hold the potential to transform participants' self-perception. The "ritual language" of Gaga classes influences their verbal output, oral and written. By verbalizing experience in canonical language, participants also interpret and store their experience using a type of "Gaga value system." It is important to remember that there are two different ways in which participants make use of the Gaga language: (1) They experience the Gaga language, and (2) they interpret their experience by using the Gaga language. Peter G. Stromberg (1993) observed the following tendency in the context of conversion narratives: "The canonical is the referential becoming constitutive [—Gaga language as experience,] and the metaphoric is the constitutive becoming referential [—Gaga language as metaphors]. Through the interplay of these two sorts of communicative phenomena, shifts between the referential and the constitutive may occur" (14). He adds, "As the canonical becomes constitutive, aspects of religious symbolism come to be real for believers. And as the metaphoric becomes referential, heretofore mysterious behaviors come to be replaced by religious convictions" (15).

The process of verbalizing experience in the Gaga language is thus an important part of the act of adopting Gaga as an embodied worldview:

> In part here the point is that a gradual transformation of identity may take place as a believer learns over time to construe herself and her life in terms of the canonical language. But it is also true and this is the process I want to investigate in this book that a particular identity may be acted out in the very performance of the conversion narrative. (15)

Nevertheless, using the Gaga language seems to be the logical consequence of the situation and nature of communication: English talk is requested by Hebrew participants practicing Gaga in classes, where teachers mainly teach in English. This situation appears to cause English words, which are "close at hand" to be used, to come up in English verbalization. Moreover, participants might use the Gaga language to make sure they are understood in the way they want to be understood. They know that the researcher and participants share the common experience of taking Gaga classes and that the researcher conducts a study on Gaga.

6.3 Experience Filters

Every participant enters class with individual body knowledge in the form of embodied filters, which shape embodied experience accordingly. Many of the filters are implicit and form part of a social and cultural network from which the participants come and in which they practice Gaga. Some of the implicit filters become explicit when participants talk about experience: in the way they formulate their experience semantically, grammatically, and narratively; in the way they interact with the interlocutor; and in the way they seem to interact with themselves, revealing the thinking and valuating principles of experience and emotions. The following draws attention to some specific linguistic characteristics of the experience "talk" of Gaga participants, which play an important part in how participants perceive Gaga or in how they experience and embody it, forming part of the embodied experience filters for future experience.

Reflecting and Deconstructing

This may be a typical filter of a postmodern participant and the "new middle class," as Dawson (2013, 135) characterizes, and it is most important in the context of a Gaga class, as it mainly influences how people experience and how they valuate and interpret their experience. Reflecting and deconstructing becomes obvious in how participants choose to present their experience to others and position themselves in relation to the experience. First, not unusual to a research interview situation, participants were found to be careful in stating definite opinions; they would always underline that they could only argue from their own restricted point of view. This could be shown by the frequent use of "I think." An average participant interviewed would use it between twenty and sixty times, once a minute. Tamar and Ester used it far less, only 0.4 time per minute, and Dana used it far more, around 2.6 times per minute. The function of "I think" was also fulfilled by other different verbs and phrases: "I mean, I guess, maybe it's" (Shira); "Maybe I'm wrong, but that's what I feel. That's what I feel" (Ester); "That's the way I understand it" (Ester); "That's my theory" (Eli). Second, participants also positioned themselves as nonexperts, assuring that what they said would not be taken as undiscussable truth, but rather as a personal opinion with the option to be mistaken: "But again, I'm a yo[gi/yoga practitioner], I don't know how it's ... but you, you know better" (Tamar). Third, participants clarified that they were aware of the fact that experience was just a construction happening in the context of class and that Gaga classes included cues to provoke this certain experience that they had. As Shira formulated, for example: "No, I cannot sperate my muscles exactly separate from my bones either, but it's just, part of it is just imagination, it's okay, it's not a problem." Fourth, participants wanted to converse with me, rather than just telling me their narration—"How do you feel, even if it's my interview?" (Shira). They showed interest in reflecting and deconstructing Gaga classes outside of the specific research situation. They also talked to one another or the teacher about what had happened during class.

Fifth, though they took the experienced as real, they retained the possibility of taking an outside view on it. This could appear in the form of mentioning self-reflection of one's own experiences—in the sense of taking a step back and viewing experience from the outside: "I think I started experiencing it like few months ago, half a year ago, like: it's so nice, you can do it again, and again, and twice a day, and it's like ... and I didn't like it" (Shira). The outside view could also consist of an individual's ability to be ironic about their own Gaga experience: Participants could accompany sentences such as "my wife said Gaga is my new religion" with a smile.

Embodied Discourses

First, data revealed that participants enter class with specific explicit and implicit knowledge on the body, gained in different discursive contexts, and that this specific knowledge influences their experience. It originates in contemporary spirituality practices such as yoga or other body and movement practices, or in popular discourses on well-being and the role of the body in terms of well-being. In these contexts, contemporary spirituality's knowledge is discussed alongside popularized scientific knowledge on the body, which exceeds scientific discourses and entered popular knowledge. Participants enter class with a body image and even a body scheme shaped by this discursive knowledge. The following represents some examples:

- *Body and mind are inseparable:* "I know that body and mind are tied together" (Uri).
- *Emotions are embodied:* Eli said the separation of emotions and sensations was not possible. His idea was that embodied emotions were stored in the body because of embodied conditions caused by specific situations. This embodied state could remain activated and "unsolved." Here, Eli seemed to portray popular knowledge originating in scientific ideas and findings. On the other hand, he still mentioned a "soul" and the releasing of "stuff" "from the past," which may be rather associated with contemporary spiritual language. Eli appeared to have gained most of his knowledge from other body and movement practices. His knowledge on embodied emotions thus mirrored the different knowledge sources, clashing and mingling in the popular discourses that individuals embody. Other participants, such as Shira or Sara, seemed to "know" about the embodiment of emotions or carry the body image of an inseparable body-mind.

- *The body is a project under constant construction:* According to Eli, the body needed constant training; as the body was constantly changing, there was no stationary body.

Second, due to the popularization of alternative spiritual and religious ideas, certain discursive concepts helped participants to interpret or describe what they have experienced: Tamar talked about Naharin "channeling" his teacher. Though self-reflected, she clarified elsewhere that her language revealed a worldview influenced by contemporary spirituality. She acknowledged that this worldview influenced her talking, experiencing, and interpreting. Noam mentioned the "pillars of practice." Many participants talked about "energy" (Tamar, Shira, Ester, Sara, Ariel, and Uri), and interestingly Gaga also participated in the discourse on energy, as energy was depicted as part of the Gaga body concept. When participants talked of "energy," the vast discourse on the term "energy" itself became apparent: There was the "good energy" in class and the "positive energy" of other participants (Uri). People could also have the wrong energy: A teacher was mentioned as having the wrong "energy" (Shira). The energy of a person was somehow part of them and their body (Shira, Tamar, and Uri), and people could add their energy to another, with the energy of the other adding up—as in the case of Naharin gathering and centering the energy of participants during class (Shira). Energy could also address a general energy in class, which could get "stuck" (Maya) or be "heavy" (Ariel). Energy comprised individual positive emotion and sensation: "Just take a Gaga class, (laughs) to have this feeling of a of a psychedelic joy and energy and fun" (Tamar). Energy was the sensation of a certain movement (Ester). Apart from this, energy was simply the physical force needed to fulfill a physical task (Noam). Another often used term was "guru"; this was how Naharin was commonly addressed (Shira, Uri, and Eli; it came up in many in-field conversations, too). However, there were people, for example Idan, who showed skepticism toward the use of what they thought to be alternative spiritual language, such as energy. Nevertheless, even Idan had incorporated ideas such as an "intuition" of the body, originating in similar popular discourse situations.

In summary, because of the individual participant being involved in a society, where all of this discursive knowledge is constantly discussed further in different media, the individual sources of knowledge are multiple and open, and difficult to trace back, and the experience filter is discursive and ever changing itself.

Remaining Individual

The self-responsible individual "I" defines itself as independent, and their own experience as a product of their own free choice. This is also a characteristic of the "new middle class": "The individualised character of the new middle class engenders a mobile, expressive and self-oriented demeanour" (Dawson 2013, 135). As observed in the data, participants always remained individual and in charge, not only explicitly by stating so but also by how they talk about their experience. For example, Ester and Shira mentioned that they would reflect on whether a movement was healthy and pleasant to them and adjust the enactment of instructions according to their needs. Idan said he would sometimes willingly zone out, become unaware—quite contrary to what Gaga's instructions demand. The wording in Mira's experience diary, on the other hand, reveals that she views experience, experience interpretation, and experience description itself as a conversational and discursive process carried out within her own body—an individual's perception of experience depends on that individual's interpretation mechanisms:

> Today in class I felt pressure in the beginning. I felt tired and I feel the teacher is quite intense and demanding, which in the beginning made me feel stressful. During the class I found some moments where I can let go and actually feel I'm getting much closer to the instructions then when I try hard and concentrate. (Mira)

It is only about the "I," how the "I" feels, perceives, interprets, and acts. This is not only a filter with which people enter class but also something Gaga trains by training self-awareness. Gaga is said to be about self-betterment, and this is where the Gaga discourse seems to meet what people seek—individual experience: "It's a sort of open that allows you to interact at a minimal level, but to still be within yourself and to be connected to the movement inside yourself and outside yourself" (Ester). When participants positioned themselves in experience narratives and an experienced setting, "I" also often gets a counterpart "they" to clarify their independence from other participants: "They do it like this, they are like this, but I do it, I am different"—as mentioned above.

The Individual Filter

An individual filter could consist of physical and psychological preconditions that participants carry along: the physical pain of Ester, or the challenging life situation of Dana or Tamar. It could be knowledge, such as Sara's psychological know-how, or Eli's somatic practice expertise. It could be Maya's view on beautiful movement, or Uri's love for Gaga. It could be one's profession, such as an artist, here Idan, who created and expressed and to whom Gaga became a new way to express. However, it could also be beliefs about one's own disconnection of the body, which Dana, Ariel, and others ascribed to themselves. The individual filter influences what participants narrate and how; what they want to emphasize and stress; and what is of minor importance. Moreover, the individual filter influences an individual's embodied experience.

I repeat, the way in which participants verbalize their experienced body knowledge is not random. On the previous pages, I demonstrated that:

(1) Language and content of narratives vary depending on the circumstances of verbalization. Especially interesting here is the formulation and translation of body knowledge immediacy. Here, for example, oral differs from written body knowledge reproduction.
(2) Language reflects the level of individual involvement with practice. Participants take on Gaga vocabulary and argumentative structure influenced by discourses originating with Gaga practice and the Gaga Movement Ltd.'s publications, when talking about their own experiences in the context of Gaga.
(3) It is possible to single out both collective and individual tendencies of language use: Collectively characteristic in particular is the way participants reflect and deconstruct on the said, while talking, or how they incorporate particular discourses in their argumentation. Language and content also reflect participants' urge to remain and be understood as autonomous and self-responsible individuals. Besides, the very individual preconditions reveal themselves, be they the professions or constituting biographical events.

Verbalization of experience, as verbalization of body knowledge, is an important research tool and data collection method, only if one understands its production and connection to the original experience and the original body knowledge. Only then can individual as well as collective experience tendencies as described by participants be deducted and systematized.

7

The Wow of Gaga

The detailed language analysis and systematization of narrated information shows that the context of Gaga influences participants' experience and body knowledge, as well as their experience and thus body knowledge narration. Experience narrations indicate and mirror the experienced body knowledge in three different ways: First, participants let the "audience" be part of an embodied effect, discussing the positively interpreted sensational experiences in class. Second, they argue for another level of the effect, namely, the long-lasting healing effect, which they connect to their participation in class. Narrations are then no longer only simple narrations of sensations, but stories constructed around healing. Third, the nature of narration reveals how Gaga practice enters participants' lives more broadly—as an indirect effect, incorporated into life sequences, events told, and into individual sense or reason constructions revealing themselves in narrative structures. These observances lead to the establishment of the categories "wow-moments" (Chapter 7), "healing narrations" (Chapter 8), and "worldview" (Chapter 9).

As wow-moments, I label highly positive emotional states that participants told me about having experienced in the context of a Gaga class. Wow-moments are experiences of body knowledge also commonly discussed and exchanged by participants in the context of Gaga class. When exchanging experiences of Gaga class, participants addressed momentary emotional-habitual actualizations of body knowledge perceived as extraordinary and as extraordinarily positive. The term "wow" emerged in interviews and conversations as an exclamation, filler, and adjective or attribute for these particular experiences. People seemed to lack other wording available to describe the experiences, or, rather, they seemed to find wow the most fitting. In consequence, the term wow-moments is endemic, stemming from the experiences of participants themselves—"Wow, you know, it's amazing" (Tamar). Gaga teacher Talia observed: "So and this is what what is like the most fun thing to see, someone go like WOW that's a WOW-moment that's amazing." Hence, not only could participants speak of their extraordinary experience as an explicit perceived transformation, but the embodied change could become explicit and visible to an outside observer. Wow-moments also related not to one specific and clearly definable perceived emotional-habitual actualization of body knowledge, but rather to a whole group of body knowledge, which could be singled out from other actualizations due to their "specialness." The perfect Gaga class was full of wow-moments, and the class was only as good as its wow-moments: "In the past, I felt like wow-moments, but now I don't feel it anymore," I was told by the clearly disappointed Maya during an in-field conversation.

The idea of extraordinary experience as such has long fascinated researchers, especially scholars dedicated to the study of religion. They have observed extraordinary experience phenomena, analyzed them, and conceptualized them under various names: Perhaps, as one of the first, Rudolf Otto (1920) and his "numinous" as a devotional, passionate, emotional state provoked by religious transcendence comes to mind. However, the state Otto intends to name remains indescribable with common words, as well as incomparable to an experience not explicitly religious in nature. Following Birgit Meyer (2015), a far more fruitful concept, which she herself terms the "'wow' effects" of religious practice, could be the concept of "awe" by Marett, who lived around the same time as Otto: "a powerful emotion produced and reproduced through specific and authorized methods," an "emotional thrill" (Marett in Meyer 2015, 17). Different from Otto, Marett's framework does not need an existence of a transcendent agent, but awe is "being effected through an authorized procedure that involves particular objects, spaces, and sensing as well as sense-making bodies in the context of specific power structures. Awe here is understood as a powerful emotion produced and reproduced through specific and authorized methods" (17).

Later, Abraham Maslow coined the term "peak experience": "a great range of mystical and ecstatic states, which he described in such terms as awe, humility, surrender, worship, ecstasy, and transcendence" and as "self-validating" (Meckel 2016). Maslow's peak experience as a concept, however, seems to denote only a specific embodied state. Daniel Meckel writes, "The very 'highest' of such perceptions comprehend Being as integrated, whole, unified, and so transcendent of all conflicts and dichotomies. Those who experience this know the world as fundamentally good and beautiful, and accept evil as an integral part of reality."

Moreover, from the twentieth century on, a whole branch of psychologists went after the research of extraordinary experiences united under the umbrella term "mystical experience." "The quest for the core" independently from a cultural or social setting was, as Taves (2020a) puts it, initiated by the "key theorists" William James, Aldous Huxley, R. C. Zaehner, and W. T. Stace. The focus of this quest had been laid not so much on mystical extraordinary experience, in general, but on "highly positive experience in which the sense of self disappears or is absorbed into something larger" (670). In the second half of the twentieth century, Stace's definition of mystical experience led to the establishment of the Mysticism Scale (M-Scale) and the Mystical Experiences Questionnaire (MEQ). The research focus remained on a narrow definition of mystical experience: In his M-Scale, Ralph Hood structured mystical experience according to "Introvertive mysticism (Ego loss): Unity, Timeless & spaceless, Ineffability)"; "Extrovertive mysticism: Unity, Unity in diversity, Inner subjectivity"; and "Interpretation: Positive affect, Sacredness, Noetic quality" (Hood in Taves 2020a, 674). Based on experience findings gained in the context of using psilocybin-containing mushrooms, Frederick S. Barrett, Matthew W. Johnson, and Roland R. Griffiths established four factors to their questionnaire (MEQ30): "mystical (including items from the internal unity, external unity, noetic quality, and sacredness scales ...), positive mood, transcendence of time and space, and ineffability" (Barrett, Johnson, and Griffiths 2015). As Taves (2020a) underlines, the categories of scale as well as the questionnaire evolved from Stace's narrow understanding of mystical experience. Howbeit, regarding the research on wow-moments, it seems important to highlight that both analytical frameworks, the original MEQ and the MEQ30, allow for the integration of data not only on a perceived self-loss or state of sensory unity but also already for an integration of data concerning "Experience of amazement. Feelings of tenderness and gentleness. Feelings of peace and tranquility. Experience of ecstasy. Sense of awe or awesomeness. Feelings of joy" (Barrett, Johnson, and Griffiths in Taves 2020a, 675). Additionally and based on this prior research, Taves, Michael Kinsella, and Michael Barlev provided their own (cross-culturally) valuable "inventory of nonordinary experiences" singling out their characteristics: "Absorbed, Out of body, Another self in body, Diminished self, Connectedness (others)," along "Items adapted from mysticism scales: Connectedness (all), Unity, Animated life, Not Existing" (684). Notwithstanding the applicability, compared to others, Taves, Kinsella, and Barlev seem to return to an even narrower definition of what can be seen as salient to a definition of "nonordinary experience," ruling out the possibility to include anything beyond what will be characterized as "moments of transcending" below.

A wow-effect of rituals and practices is still and all not only a research object of interest to a study of religion or psychology. Scholars of different fields are continually researching this particular effect of rituals and practices. All kinds of body practices have become transdisciplinary research objects. Karen E. Bond and Susan W. Stinson's (2000) work, "'I Feel Like I'm Going to Take Off!' Young People's Experiences of the Superordinary in Dance," and Lynda Flower's (2016) "'My Day-to-Day Person Wasn't There; It Was Like Another Me': A Qualitative Study of Spiritual Experiences during Peak Performance in Ballet Dance" are part of an interdisciplinary research field on extraordinary experience in dance practice. Simon Robinson (2007) analyzes experiences he had in the context of running a marathon, and he filters out some unique aspects of it. Bond and Stinson, and Flower, and Robinson's findings are interesting insofar as they match the extraordinary experience characteristics that Gaga participants describe. In the context of movement practices, a certain set of "wow-experiences" seems to be experienceable:

(1) According to Flower, professional dancers experienced "four major sub-themes ...: heightened positive emotions; altered states of consciousness; less self-awareness; and mastering technique" (2016, 70).

(2) Bond and Stinson use the following endemic categories to subsume their findings on what children and young people experienced in dance: "Bodily Resonance," "I Just Have to Dance," "Freedom," "Being Who I Really Am (or Might Become)," "I Forget about Everything Else but Dancing," "Another Place," "Magical or Spiritual Dimensions," "It's Hard to Classify," and "It's Hard to Say" (2000, 56–71).

(3) Robinson filters out the following kinds of experiences:

A sense of holism, with mind, feelings and body stretched together. A sense of being part of a greater community or entity. A sense of transcendence, being taken beyond the self ... A sense of ritual in the great public event, even of sacrament. Sacrament is an action which represents or embodies an underlying reality and meaning. A sense of transformation and development. (2007, 8)

In the context of this book, I use wow-moments to collect a broad range of narrated and verbalized momentary extraordinary experiences and momentary extraordinary body knowledge. As described above, its use is endemic insofar as wow as a title to the concept emerged in the data itself. I chose not to be restricted by prior definitions of religious or mystical experience, but rather focus on experience as part of an aesthetic process, part of aesthetics, and directly linked to body knowledge actualization narrated and verbalized. So, this chapter is, as in fact really the whole book, designed in a bottom-up approach: letting data speak. What enters under the category of wow-moments is what participants single out as extraordinary using particular wording (List 9).

List 9 Characteristics of Wow-Moments' Narrations

(1) Exclamations underlining amazement and wonder
(2) Changing the volume and tone of their voice
(3) Vocabulary linked to the transcendental experience of the religious or spiritual realm or popular vocabulary for extraordinariness
(4) Experience, body knowledge, and the cause of experience fuse while talking
(5) Very detailed description
(6) Description of either the embodied effect or the whole process

---

(1) Participants use various exclamations underlining amazement and wonder, which they appear to reexperience while talking. (2) They emphasize the importance of a specific experience moment by changing the volume and tone of their voice. (3) Participants single out an experience as extraordinary by using vocabulary linked to the transcendental experience of the religious or spiritual realm, such as "spiritual" (Maya) and "godly" (Sara), or by using popular vocabulary such as "love" (Uri), underlining how special the experience is to them. (4) Participants struggle to find the right words to describe what they experienced, and they then explain the experience with metaphors, images, or metaphorical adjectives, for example, introduced with "like." (5) The grammatical subject of the sentences dedicated to experience description is either "it," Gaga class in general, or Gaga class experience; experience, body knowledge, and the cause of experience thus fuse while talking. (6) The moment participants happen to mention a moment experienced as extraordinary, they discuss it in great detail, making sure the listener understands its importance. (7) Participants are found to either address only the embodied effect, the final emotional-habitual transformed state, or the whole process, the embodied process toward the transformed state. In a next step, the analysis of the data regarding wow-moments reveals different central families or fields of body knowledge experienced as extraordinary. Participants would not necessarily use the same vocabulary to describe what is subsumed under one and the same family of experience moments. Notwithstanding, experiences narrated

by different participants are still found to be connected via the content of the narrated.

Taves and Asprem (2016) provide the methodical and theoretical inspiration for closely examining the individual nature of wow-moments' different categories and experience families. They propose separating experience descriptions into smaller subcategories and then analyzing them according to the questions of "what happened," "what it means," and "why it happens" (53). In addition, they mention that assuming similar experience descriptions given by participants can function as a base for finding the collective perceivable aesthetical input provoking those experiences (54). Drawing on these ideas, I will address Gaga's wow-moments with three different questions in the following: What extraordinary (body knowledge) did people experience? How do they connect it to the happenings in class (not real happenings but perceived happenings, e.g., valued environmental conditions)? What could be the aesthetics causing the experience or the transformation of body knowledge?

7.1 Transcendence and Flow

Participants' discussion of experience reveals an experience field, which can be associated with "mystical experience" approaches as significant and distinctive alterations of self-sense (Taves 2020a). Participants described their experience as something that was significantly different from their everyday experience, in the sense that both their self-perception and the perception of the environment change. For some, it was a sensation of being carried away, "swept away" (Maya, Noam), dissolving the "self" (Noam), getting "completely lost" (Idan), whereas others experienced it as being totally present, concentrating all attention on the present embodied experience. The experience of "flying with it" seemed to bring the two together: letting go without letting go of self-sense. Participants described their transcendence as a place where only movement happened (Idan), and they dissolved in the "heightened sensation of being in class and really being completely into the movement research experience of it," where "time just stretches infinitely and there is only a horizontal pipe with free flow of sensations streaming from head to toe. That moment is the only pure love. That moment is God. That moment is everything. That moment is nothing" (Noam). As Tamar put it, "When I'm in a Gaga class, I'm totally in a Gaga class." As Ester put it, "You don't think about anything else, you're completely during that hour ... you're completely in it." Others interpreted their experience as being "possessed" by something. The way the transcendence experience was interpreted—implicitly via one's own body and explicitly via verbalization—caused different narrative varieties of experience output.[1] Moreover, the same individual used different descriptions to describe similar transcendence experiences.

Participants attributed the experienced moments of transcendence to (1) the Gaga teacher as well as to a particular stimulus in class, (2) the ritual environment, and (3) the movement instructions.

(1) The identification of or attachment to the movement of the teacher enabled transcendence. First, the perceived authority of a teacher played a significant role. Second, the enactment of their role as a teacher mattered: How did the teacher move, and could the participant connect to the movement? In the sense of: Did the teacher's movement have a positively perceived sensory-motoric effect on the participant? Were the movements perceived as beautiful? And, could participants translate the movement to their own bodies? In the sense of: Did covert imitation and embodied simulation explicitly work? Furthermore, the more participants admired the teachers, the more power and authority they accredited them and thus the greater the "wow": "He [Naharin] is taking us the one stage further of sort of flying with it" (Ester).

(2) Participants assured that "clean pure strong" transcendental Gaga experience only occurred on the setting of Gaga class as an ideal environment stimulating and effecting moments of transcendence (Uri). While music was explicitly neglected as the main stimulus in provoking movement in the context of Gaga's ritual culture, to participants it played a specific role. Transcendence seemed foremost bound to the movement possibility to "go crazy," stimulated by "energetic" music and the high volume of the music with a fast or better danceable beat, and initiated by the teacher's instruction to "not think and just move." Here the environmental stimuli seemed to leave no option but to experience transcendence. Howbeit, participants like Noam remarked that "soft" music and slow movements could potentially create similar body knowledge: "The quite soft music that was playing in the background and the slow-motion movement of the teacher immediately swept everybody down to a parallel universe."

(3) Participants reported that instructions "practiced intuition" in the sense of intuitive movement (Idan) and evoked an inner thinking process (Ester). As participants were constantly mentally involved, thinking, evaluating, and interpreting instructions, they experienced their mind being kept occupied and focused. Instructions in Gaga seem to be designed to lead to an extraordinary experience by constantly demanding focused attention or open monitoring. In addition, they contained imagery that guided the participant toward a state

of movement and self-ownership, which was not controlled voluntarily. The metaphor-based instructions seemed to have the power to make participants directly embody the imagery as body knowledge, which meant transcending the current embodied state (Tamar).

It makes sense to connect these findings to a broader interdisciplinary scientific context. The "moments of transcending" experience family is not unique to Gaga but known to occur in other settings as well. Mihaly Csikszentmihalyi (2014) acknowledges this phenomenon and names it "flow." The psychologist develops a theoretical approach to it: "We experience it [flow] as a unified flowing from one moment to the next, in which we feel in control of our actions, and in which there is little distinction between self and environment; between stimulus and response; or between past, present, and future" (137).

This matches the experience field of the interviewed Gaga participants: a kind of streaming along, being lost in this streaming along, being carried along, not caring about space and time, merging with "external forces" and instruction input, while nevertheless remaining present, attentive. Flow is said to be experienced as "enjoyable and intrinsically rewarding" (Csikszentmihalyi 2014, 233). During flow, self-sense alters: "What is usually lost in flow is not the awareness of one's body or of one's functions, but only the self-construct, the intermediary which one learns to interpose between stimulus and response" (141). As soon as one steps out to question one's actions from an observing unembodied perspective, the flow is lost. However, flow is usually only maintained for a short time; it happens, is lost, and happens again. Participants often described moments of flow in timely boundaries, using the past tense to describe their "getting into flow": for example, "swept away." According to Csikszentmihalyi, flow occurs in a setting where individuals encounter challenges they have to deal with and goals they can possibly accomplish (240). In the context of Gaga, this would have been the act of trying to embody and thus fulfill the purpose of the given instructions. Csikszentmihalyi also highlights that the initial "subjective state" the flow-perceiving individual has to be in must include "intense and focused concentration on what one is doing in the present moment" (240). This is what Gaga's working instructions and ritual culture demand and the instructions create: awareness in the sense of open monitoring as well as focused attention. If attention can be kept on a stimulus, such as instructions and their enactment, the movement of the teacher, or the music played, and the individual totally dissolves in accomplishing the sensory-motoric tasks posed by the stimulus, then the individual can reach a state of flow (242).

Other scientific discourses also exist that hold specifically "meditative and contemplative" practices, which involve techniques of "mindfulness," accountable for "spiritual" experience. The action of perceiving momentary sensory input without valuating the perceived seems to enable the experience (Kohls, Walach, and Lewith 2009). The training of awareness and availability during class would thus play an important role in reaching such an experience state. In addition, this specific training could enable participants with ongoing practice to reach the state of flow faster by focusing on the enactment of instructions and their sensations, stopping their minds from wandering (Russell and Arcuri 2015).

All of this is probably particularly effective in the context of a Gaga class because participants self-control their focused attention: "If you find that your mind wandering away from the class is something you want to deal with, you will deal with it, you will notice it first, and when you notice it creates discomfort for you because you're missing out on something here, and then you'll turn your attention back and it will happen less" (Uri).

7.2 Freedom

The experience of freedom is another positively valued experience: freedom from the physical and psychological hinderances posed by one's own body, as well as from restrictions by the perceived environment. For many participants, the freedom to "express oneself" (Tamar) was a wow-moment as well as a very "addictive" aspect of Gaga class. Like Sara, they "hungered" for it. Sometimes freedom meant freedom to be creative: "Like I really feel like I can have fun and be, you know, imagine and be creative when I'm when I'm dancing" (Dana). Furthermore, freedom was doing what seemed to be right for the body, what brought pleasure to the body. As there was no set form, but only movement qualities given in the instructions, participants could adapt their movement to their own bodies' needs, and this was perceived as a wow-moment of class: "You can just find the movement that is already there and just let it happen and it's your own things it's it's only, the teacher doesn't tell you to do this or that usually" (Ariel). The opposite to that freedom would be a given set of forms that one has to accomplish during class: "I went to a ballet class maybe twice, and that was terrifying. I don't have that lightness" (Idan). Freedom also meant taking advantage of class and the freedom of form to move in a way one would not usually move, because of what was perceived as boundaries to one's own body and movement, for example. The instruction design, as well as the environment in Gaga, offered an opportunity to break those boundaries: "I am already in a state, that I'm free with myself to go places, that I won't usually go" (Idan). Furthermore, Gaga's "absolute freedom" was related to "a release" from what bothered outside class (Tamar). Gaga class created an experience of freedom because it generated a place free of "judgment" and "competition," free of certain movement conventions, "allowing weaknesses" (Tamar): "I thought about why Gaga was so good for me, because it removes the causes of frustration and judgement from the dance class … and this gives you a lot of space to be what you are, in movement" (Eli).

Following the data from participants, the experience of freedom seems to depend on the ritual characteristics of Gaga: the implicit and explicit rules leaving space for free-form movement, only adjusting the movement quality; the setting without mirrors and audience; the structure involving not only ongoing movement, ongoing task and self-occupation, and flow creation, which inhibits reflection on one's own movement, but also the constant variation of aesthetical input, having no fixed class concept; and the knowledge that different people from different backgrounds with different stories are coming together with the goal of just moving, binding together, and creating a safe social space by sharing movement, emotions, experiences both implicitly and explicitly before and after class. All these components of the ritual space, including environment and interactions, somehow led to perceiving a Gaga class explicitly as a space of freedom.

7.3 Ongoing Discovery

Alongside the experience of a special connection to the body during moments of flow and the experience of a freedom of movement, a Gaga class offers an experience that could be referred to as "ongoing discovery," in the sense of a "never-ending body knowledge acquisition" or "endless practicing and enhancing attention." This already implies that the experience remains exciting, as there is always some new sensory information and body knowledge to discover. Participants see this discovery as rewarding. It becomes the aim and goal of a Gaga class, a pleasurable experience, and an argument for why practicing Gaga never gets boring. Eli, for example, described the experienced body knowledge during the enactment of the instructions as an "ongoing investigation" because once something was experienced, there was nothing one could be sure of keeping; it was a momentary, fleeting sensation. At another point, Eli tried to explain the fleeting character. First, he said that sensations were fleeting because the body was in a different physical state every day, and the physical state was momentary. Second, he compared the enactment of the instructions, the practicing of movement, and the finding of sensation to strength training, where muscular strength could not be kept without ongoing training. Likewise, to Sara, "It's all the time a discovery and the feeling of discovery." Like Eli, she attributed this experience to different characteristics of a Gaga class: Gaga classes always looked different because of their structure and changing teachers, and every Gaga class was always experienced differently; body knowledge constantly changed. To Sara, this "is like just godly, in a way. Because like every day I can explain to my husband what is Gaga, and I can explain it in a different way." Tamar offered a similar argument: "The beauty in Gaga is that every time it's another teacher, and every teacher brings other things, and every class is totally different."

What participants recounted matched my own observations: (1) Class is always different: From a variety of movement qualities, teachers were free to choose the ones they want to apply during a Gaga class. Teachers instructed the qualities enriched with their own personal images and vocabulary. Instructions were combined in multiple ways, and actions were combined with multiple body parts and multilayered with other actions. Moreover, as Naharin was still developing Gaga further, and thus introducing new instructions and movement vocabulary, Gaga had been constantly transforming. The script of a Gaga class was only roughly structured. The teachers in Suzanne Dellal rotated; a teacher usually only taught several times per month, and teachers came from different body knowledge backgrounds. (2) The body as the base to sensations during class is different every day due to physical activity or absent activity, optimal or poor health state, hormonal changes, amount of sleep, and other factors: As doing Gaga included bodily awareness, the experience varied according to the body state. (3) The body knowledge transformation acquired has a fleeting character: Only in the context of participatory observation, in the context of frequenting Gaga classes nearly every day, I started floating while walking and applying Gaga to other body and dance practices. The longer the time without practicing Gaga, the more my body seemed to "forget." (4) Finally, because there is no form to reach, no limit, and no defined goal of the actions that instructions initiate, an action can never be "fulfilled": In the way instructions were verbalized and given, something always remained to be discovered.

7.4 Release

Some participants describe extraordinary moments of Gaga class as moments where they feel a release of physical and emotional tension—the latter connected to the former. The physical release was described by a participant as follows: "One day, my body felt really wah (stiff) because of so much Gaga, but the Gaga helps; at the beginning it was hard, but then it felt good (it loosens) after a short while" (in-field conversation, October 4, 2017). Tamar talked about a broader sense of release than only the physical. She talked about how Gaga experience helped her to cope with her difficult life situation, a problematic marriage.

Participants' observation helped to trace the relationship between the physical and emotional release experienced:

- Enactment of movement in Gaga class can provoke body-bound emotions: "Yeah, there'll be moments where I just feel like, you know I touched something inside of me that, that felt special" (Idan).
- Gaga class seems to offer the possibility to release anger throughout movement: "You know when there was a war some years ago, many people were coming to Gaga angry. It was an existential [life-threatening] situation. And Gaga helped them to release their angry feeling. Their way to deal with the situation" (Iris).
- A Gaga class can bring participants to shed tears: "Yeah, I did cry, I did cry. Yeah, I did cry. Yeah, I think last week maybe two times" (Shira). Or: "I ended up the class with tears. So, and I've had that happen many times, and in a situation where I was in difficult spiritual places, the classes were even more meaningful" (Uri). Uri described crying especially in connection to certain movements, such as shaking. As shaking is a physical tension-loosening action, the release of physical tension seemed to be directly connected to setting emotions free or "very strong mental sensation," as Uri called it, and thus to the action of crying.
- Another hint at the relation between physical and emotional body state and physical emotional release is the observed absence of wow-moments in certain classes: "Class today was heavily crowded, which means a smaller territory to work on, which ultimately influenced the way I carried myself in space. I don't think I reached my maximum stretch—not physically nor emotionally" (Noam). Noam saw the emotional effectiveness of class connected to the physical effectiveness of class, and he related both to the action of "stretch"—reaching the physical maximum of movement

while reaching the maximum range of emotions. Stretching is a muscular tension–releasing action. For Noam, a class without the possibility to release lacked a central positive experience.

I take crying as a prime example to demonstrate how Gaga's body knowledge is connected to the experiences people have throughout class: Crying is tear-shedding accompanied by alterations of the sensorimotor and interoceptive states in the rest of the body, the tensing of muscles in the face and/or muscles attached to the respiratory system (Patel 1993, 206). "Crying is necessarily a complex interaction of emotions and the neurological substrate of the secretomotor phenomena" (206–7). Crying is provoked by sensory input, possibly imaginary, and it is also experienced as body knowledge in the form of sensory information and emotional state. There are different theoretical approaches toward crying that link crying to a perceived relief: Either (1) crying is experienced as relieving, or (2) crying is accompanied by the embodied emotional and sensed relief (209). Both theories correspond to what participants mentioned as experiences: (1) For Uri, the act of crying became meaningful in difficult times—he probably experienced a "release" of emotions similar to Tamar's case. These could have been sadness, anger, and "not being free." (2) On the other hand, Uri's crying accompanied an emotional release following a physical release, the "very strong mental sensation." Crying can be understood as an integration of physical and psychological processes coming together in body knowledge.

The findings suggest that the release of tension forms part of this integrated physical-psychological process. One can consequently look for muscular tension-releasing actions, as well as mentally releasing actions in Gaga techniques, to understand where the wow-experience of release originates: (1) Throughout class, instructions offer different tools to "break patterns" and to let go of physical and mental boundaries, both physically real and perceived as real. (2) Furthermore, Gaga works with stretching and broadening the movement range. (3) Muscular tension release is reached by alternately "tensing" and "relaxing" the muscles—known from Jacobson's method, for example, to be psychologically efficient (see Koch 2017, 397).

7.5 Happy Aftermath

Participants do not only feel a release of emotions such as sadness or anger and "break free" of emotional tension, but also report a heightened positive emotional state of mind after class. Participants such as Ester talked of happiness to the degree of laughing: "I usually end the class and I'm laughing. With every teacher the end of the class, I laugh. Yeah ... I finish an hour; I always find myself laughing; in other words, it makes me happy." Shira experienced this happiness not only as a state of mind but also as a state of the whole body: "Sometimes it's just being happy after the class, and feeling the body being happy." This "happy aftermath" is experienced as being so great that "everybody" should be able to experience it: "I really wish everybody to be able to dance Gaga ... The people would be happy! It just brings you happiness and joy" (Tamar). Tamar also compared the happiness a Gaga class evoked in her—the "psychedelic joy and energy and fun," as she named it—with the experience she observed other people having doing drugs or drinking alcohol. From Tamar's point of view, the state of happiness a Gaga class put her in was "transcendent" compared to taking drugs or drinking, which she herself did not do and did not need; yet she valued it as something incomparably positive and unreachable via other means.

Furthermore, Tamar talked about happiness being the result of an emotional-habitual transformation undertaken throughout class. This transformation again was "mind-blowing" and extraordinary. From being "really tired, or a bit ill, or a bit sad or depressed," she reported reaching a state of lightness, "flying," and happiness, leaving behind the previous state: "You know, now I'm coming out, I'm light, I'm flying, I'm happy, and I manage to forget or to leave the shit I'm dealing with somewhere else and ah it's just amazing." This therapeutic effect Tamar indicated seems to be closely related to the happy aftermath Sara perceived as "so empowering."

The happy aftermath was also observed by Idan, who felt "completely" better after class. Idan, though, highlighted the role of "going wild" to "energetic" music as the trigger for his heightened emotional state. If the teacher ended the class with "really slow" movement, then Idan did not reach the same state and, in consequence, was "disappointed." Interestingly, however, Idan used his own wow-experience and experience filter to deepen the explanation of the observed: In his eyes, the transformation could not take place if the moment of high movement energy was missing, because people were not given room to express themselves. The aftereffect was connected to the experience of freedom. During participatory observation, similar observances were made: The more exhausting the class, the more physical energy people wasted throughout class—which happened especially in moments of "going wild" to an "energetic song"—and the more energized and happier, while exhausted, they seemed to be after class. They would, for example, clap longer and louder for a teacher who brought them to a level of total exhaustion and thus show their satisfaction with class. This also resembles Ester's observation that her wow-experience directly depended on the amount she sweated, thus on her physical exhaustion.

The fact that exhaustive physical training can potentially lead to such an effect is popularly known as the so-called runner's high: "a euphoric state resulting from long-distance running" (Boecker et al. 2008, 2523). Long-distance running implies ongoing movement, which is extraordinarily exhaustive, for a long period of time. The runner's high effect is attributed to the "release of endogenous opioids [occurring] in frontolimbic brain regions after sustained physical exercise" and "its close correlation to perceived euphoria of runners" (2530). In the runner's high context, the therapeutic effect of endurance training leading to such experiences and the addictive effect of the experiences themselves were also recorded (2530)—something Gaga participants' statements would affirm. The same physiological effect as during the runner's high was observed in other contexts of high-intensity aerobic training: This kind of training (1) potentially controls the "release of catecholamines, which control attention, mood, movements, and the responses of the endocrine and cardiovascular systems [, and] stress response," or (2) leads to "the production of endogenous morphines or endorphins that promote a good mood" (Krivoschekov and Lushnikov 2011, 510). So, what does Gaga have in common with practices such as long-distance running or high-intensity aerobic training? Gaga requires ongoing movement, since participants are never allowed to stop. In addition, Gaga requires switching between movements needing high energy and low energy—fast and slow, large and small—described as the "stamina" component of a Gaga class. As data from participant observation revealed, the raising of the heartbeat, leading to a rise in body heat and perspiration, plays an important role in creating the happy aftermath. Gaga offers such an example to prove the effectiveness of "the thermogenic hypothesis [, which] supposes that exercises enhance body temperature, which results in decreases in muscle tone and somatic anxiety" (510). The happy aftermath would thus be bound to the experience of the release described above.

7.6 Power of Instructions

Two different types of wow-effects can be related to the "power of instructions": First, the instructions create an aesthetical space for participants to connect to optimal sensations or the optimal emotions of former experiences, memorized body knowledge. Uri, for example, expressed his love for the "letting a good taste spread." He experienced this as especially pleasant because it gave him enough freedom to connect to the memories he wanted to connect to—if the "good taste" was clearly defined and bound by the image of "Nutella" or "honey," it did not have the same impact.

Second, instructions offer participants a philosophical framework to deal with former or ongoing experiences outside of class. For Sara and Tamar, Gaga class instructions were not solely about physical experiences. Instead, they were experienced as "true paradoxes," "the way you would think about life," as "wisdom" beyond sensations. Sara mentioned Gaga's imagery of floating as enlightening, in the sense that one never falls down but is always carried by one's own engine. The experience of having "so many engines" and being able to start over and over again was also special to her, and it seems as if this, especially, originated in enacting instructions and not just listening to them. Sara even related the image of the engines with the "circle of life and dead." To Sara, the most important instructions dealt with two contradictory things, such as inhibiting destructive power or restarting from destruction. In Sara's eyes, the language used in a Gaga class, Naharin's language, became "meaningful," "true," and "empowering"; it conveyed "worldly wisdom," which made it "genius." Tamar seemed to find importance in similar input. To her as to Sara, instructions contained "a lot of wisdom." Though Tamar did not address the sensation of floating, she named the action of just restarting with ease after a fall as a central important idea she had adopted for life. Tamar also hinted that other ideas from class were useful to her in life. Moreover, she took what she experienced throughout class "on a very spiritual level."

The findings indicate that the individual embodied experience filters of participants receiving the instructions were highly important to experience an instruction as a wow-moment. However, some instructions initiated a positive experience equally in different participants: floating, "not being shaped by gravity," and continuing to move, "finding different engines." These instructions seemed most likely to be experienced as meaningful. A possible explanation for this could be that some instructions in Gaga use what Lakoff and Johnson (2003, 14–21) call "orientational metaphors" attached to collective cultural experiences:

> Most of them have to do with spatial orientation ... These spatial orientations arise from the fact that we have bodies of the sort we have and that they function as they do in our physical environment. Orientational metaphors give a concept a spatial orientation; for example, HAPPY IS UP. The fact that the

concept HAPPY is oriented UP leads to English expressions like "I'm feeling up today." Such metaphorical orientations are not arbitrary. They have a basis in our physical and cultural experience. (14)

Regarding floating, for example, participants spoke about crushing, lying on the floor, and being dragged down by something or somebody, among other things, when a difficult life situation arouse that someone had problems coping with. In Gaga, participants were told "not to collapse into gravity," but instead were offered an embodied solution, namely, the action of floating, to overcome gravity. Participants connected the "collapse into gravity" with their outside Gaga experience, saved in orientational metaphors, and thus were able to take the experience of floating not only as connected to the orientational metaphor of an "uplifting" experience but also as an embodied solution to their very own "down." In addition, in class, participants encountered much imagery describable as "playful" and light, in the sense that the imagery asked for the enactment of commonly believed joyful experiences: eating sweets, indulging, yawning, being childish, and being "silly."

7.7 Relational Wow

The way in which the relationship with other humans is perceived and experienced is an important aesthetic in deciding on positive or negative experiences during class. Different kinds of relationships are found to exist: (1) interactions between participant and participant or (2) interactions between participant and teacher. Both interactions can, on the one hand, be passive in the sense that participants react to aesthetical input offered by others without necessarily having to interact with them directly, offering an input to them in exchange. On the other hand, interactions can be active, which means that participants are part of a situation of communication between two people. Interactions in the context of Gaga class for nonprofessional dancers never included touch in the sense of skin or even cloth's contact of one body with another. The medium, transmitter and receiver, of interaction were movements in space, including emotional expressions, the voice of the teacher, and the bodily senses, which received the information and enabled its perception.

(1) Participants feel connected to other people in a Gaga class, and experience in the class is wow because of the class being a shared body practice. Uri believed it to be essential to Gaga classes that the experience was not an

individual but rather a shared, "interpersonal" one. The experience was shared and "interpersonal" because of the "meaningful" "connections ... made between people," as Uri said: "And that's okay, because ... some of the connections that I made in the classes in this family are very meaningful, I don't even know how to explain in what way." Uri saw the connections happening in moments of focused attention on the surroundings. He described how other people's moods could be sensed and understood. However, Uri did not describe only the sensing and reacting to others as a passive reaction; for him, connecting was already a situation of active communicating, which eventually led to verbal or corporal communication after class: "It's the people who come to you at the end of the class and and they hug you, because of the positive energy that they received." Part of "the wow" of a class, then, was the experience of being connected to others, as well as possibly taking this mere feeling of being connected and elevating it to a situation of communication by finding someone to communicate with. The way Uri formulated it, the experience radius increased by the experienced connections to others.

If certain coparticipants, to whom one is emotionally attached, are not in class, then the class is experienced as less positive. Sara, for example, mentioned her disappointment upon entering the space of class and realizing the "right" people were missing. On the other hand, seeing the people to whom one is emotionally attached and partaking in class with them enhances the experience significantly. Noam described the positive effect of seeing his friend as a significant wow and mood-changing; the connection became emotional-habitual transformative. From a state in which he "felt really weak," he turned to being energized by "all those small, medium and big engines" until experiencing a situation of practically "flying," letting go into experiencing the moment—a wow-moment only caused by seeing his friend. Noam stated that what he experienced in this moment before class, he took as an emotional-habitual state to class: "That was Gaga class for today." The interaction, remaining passive and not yet in a situation of active communication, was "the wow" of this class.

Positive verbal feedback in the form of "nice words" from other participants ignites positive experience. Tamar described heightened emotions when other participants paid her compliments on her movement and her appearance in class. The compliments were especially important to her when the participants communicating the feedback had perceived power and authority. Why the positive feedback was so special to Tamar remained unsaid; however, it seemed that by the feedback, she had the possibility to identify herself as a dancer, or that she did not receive many "nice words" outside of class these days.

Another interesting aspect of the relationships formed in Gaga class is that they were described as existing and remaining mainly in the context of class, as if relationships were part of the setting.[2] This seems to be the reason that, as the aforementioned arguments show, the relationships have such a high impact on experience; they are part of the aesthetical environment of class. The relationships belong to the Gaga "world," as Sara described, and usually do not extend beyond it. This defines and secures the safe and therapeutic space that Gaga offers.

(2) A participant's relation to the Gaga teachers plays a central role in creating the wow-effect of class in various forms. Teachers are the central agent of class. The production of body knowledge depends on the teachers' descriptive body and movement, their instructions, their choice of music, their character, and their perception through participants' experience filters. Participants measured class experience in terms of being able to "connect" to the teacher or not: no experienced connection meant a negative experience. The term "connection" was used for interpersonal connection, as mentioned above, but the idea of connection extended to connecting to instructions, music, the atmosphere, and the whole class. Similar vocabulary used would reflect the same aspect of relation between participants and different "parts" of class. An established relation was always a success in the sense of a positive experience.

The connection does not seem to be mainly about the instructions teachers give, but rather about the explicit mood teachers are in, the images they use, and the "energy" they share with the participants. The individual experience filters of the participants also play a main part in how participants experience teachers. The teacher as input can only reach participants through their filters, such as admiration of the movement or the background knowledge about a teacher, affection or empathy toward a teacher, and the possibility to match one's individual experience with the teacher's instructions. Maya's experience filters, for example, seemed to include certain conventions on "aesthetically-ideal" movement and possibly some affection for the teacher because of his "artistic background." She said she could identify with the movement of the teacher and with his "effort." Moreover, "his energies" had a strong impact on her experience. Her described result of the situation was that she had "meaningful interesting, invigorating movement experiences," and she experienced the class as "spiritual!" Maya's relationship to the teacher, alike teacher–participant relations in general, depicts an exemplary passive relationship: Maya is reacting to the given input of a class setting. Though their quality and character of movement and instructions vary, the teachers are always there to potentially guide all participants. What Ariel observed was also interesting: He said it was easier for him to take the movement input and Gaga body knowledge—what he called "connecting"—from a teacher whom he knew than from an unknown one. Supposing that "connecting" to class also meant taking part in the positive effect, being able to bring oneself in line with the teacher was as important for Ariel as it is for Maya. For him, however, it was not about instant affection toward the teacher, but a process of learning; connecting with new teachers "might take longer." The ability to empathize could take time.

Via the teacher–participant relation, teachers also hold the agency to inhibit wow-experience. Experience diaries captured it as follows: First, the teacher did not create an atmosphere and environment that allowed for opening oneself up (Maya). Second, the teacher was too "demanding" (Mira), "manly," "passive aggressive," too "serious" (Maya), and not fitting the emotional-habitual state of the participant. Third, the teacher interrupted the natural flow of the movement and let "the energy get stuck" (Maya). Fourth, the teacher created instructions and movements that seemed to be "not honest" and "superficial" to participants, in the sense that, instead of listening to the sensory information offered by the group and by their own body, the teacher just "showed off" (Maya, Dafna). Fifth, the participant—very simply yet importantly—could not establish a visual connection to the teacher, because the teacher was standing at the side of the group and dance space, for example.

Shira described how she left class because of her teacher. She singled out two characteristics of that especially negatively experienced Gaga class: First, the teacher had the "wrong," too "harsh" energy. Second, the teacher chose the wrong music—music that Shira could not stand to the extent that she asked for it to be changed. However, Shira mentioned that the music chosen by her teacher seemed to directly reflect the teacher's energy, in the sense that perceptions of music and energy were difficult to separate. She also took the music as a metaphor for the energy of the teacher: "Changing the music is changing the energy." Shira felt what happened was that the class and the participants "echoed" the teacher. Shira also mentioned another time she left a class, when it was not the fault of her teacher but her "own" in the sense that she did not enter class with the right emotional state; she was too sad. As a consequence of her negative experience, Shira started to reflect on the role of the teacher. For Shira, what teachers did was "activating" participants with their energy and instructions. This activating, in her opinion, was supported by the place the teacher took in the room, namely, the middle. She compared the role of a Gaga teacher to that of an Israeli folk dance teacher. However, according to Shira, the amount of feeling being activated depended on the teacher's "energy," which also reflected in the teacher's movement: The more "powerful" the energy, the greater the activation, the greater the wow, and the greater the effect. Teachers possess the agency to provoke and inhibit the wow by how they behave and are being perceived; they hold the agency for the ritual effect of wow.

A teacher's wow-agency not only depends on their actions, the movement, the mood, or the given instructions, but certain teachers are also addressed with additional characteristics enhancing their potential agency. Naharin, known as the founder of Gaga, as already discussed, has been granted special agency by all participants. To Ester, Naharin owned special agency because he established the "philosophy and method," and, unlike other teachers, he was not teaching the method, but he represented the method. Taking his class, Ester had an enhanced, positive wow-effect, which she did not experience with others. She explicitly mentioned that she had more trust in him than in the other teachers and therefore could dive deeper into the experience.

As with many of the other wow-moments, the wow of interpersonal relationships in class relates to observations, research, and findings from a scientific background. Embodied cognition conceptualizes the perception of actions and the interpretation of emotions of others as embodied: The actions and emotions of others are simulated in the body of the perceiving individual. The sensorimotor system and the affective emotion areas of the brain are activated while watching others, and they establish a bond of similar experience between the one who is moving and an experiencing person or observer. What is taking place is an embodied simulation of the observed motor activities in the form of a somatosensory and emotional experience (see Oosterwijk and Barret 2014). The embodied simulation is not bound to positive emotions; therefore, negative emotions of others can have an embodied negative effect (Preston and Waal 2002, 14). This is said to be caused, when visual perception triggers mirror mechanisms including mirror neurons (Craighero 2014, 54–5). Different people influence and enhance each other's experience. However, there is difference in how one individual can connect to another via embodied perception. It depends on the amount of perceived possible identification with the other individual through the interdependence of "feeling alike" and affection toward that individual. Simulation ability and mirroring activity are greater with emotions or movements the observer is familiar or can identify with (56). This explains why certain Gaga teachers could provoke wow-experiences in participants, while others could not.

All of these interactions between people as embodied reactions to each other's bodily states could be termed passive interactions. There is the possibility that Gaga instructions in general enhance the effect of these types of interactions: Gaga instructions direct participants' attention toward the others with whom they share the class. Instructions tell participants to actively observe the others and be attentive to them, thereby paving the way to empathetic processes (see Preston and Waal 2002). The teacher is to be listened to, activating the sensorimotor system and evoking embodied simulation by language perception; watched, enhancing the activation of the somatosensory and emotional areas of the motor system through vision; and copied, further enhancing the experience and identification through action requirement and thus action-oriented perception. Furthermore, instructed movements play a role in how the individuals are related to one another in space: When told to enhance their bodies in the space, such as in "evaporating," "connecting to external forces" or parts of the environment, "becoming very fat" or "have a too large skin," and "sensing others with the back," participants practice prosthetic perception and could probably momentarily alter their peripersonal space. They expand the space that they can influence with their actions. Other participants are made meaningful components of an individual participant's peripersonal space, as they constitute and flank it (see Vignemont 2014). Situating them in the peripersonal space alters their importance to the perceiving individual.

As intrapersonal relationships establish and grow with time, they have the potential to become crucial parts of a Gaga class experience. A class experience will naturally be enhanced by positively experienced relationships. Other participants become part of the aesthetics of the Gaga class; relationships become aesthetically effective. In addition, the possibility of talking with other people who have had a similar experience or who share the same code and language seems to be an important way to interpret and store one's own experience. All this might also be the reason that certain relationships, though highly important in the context of class—as well as before, during, and after class, are not taken into another non-Gaga context. Aesthetics remain in their corresponding context.

7.8 Being a Dancer

Partaking in class, participants perceive heightened positive emotional-habitual embodied states when experiencing themselves as being a dancer. First, many participants enter class with admiration for Batsheva dancers. They take class in Suzanne Dellal, home to the Batsheva company, and they perform Gaga, which is the "movement language" of Naharin and which they know as the

Batsheva dancers' central training method. They experience a becoming part of Batsheva. Second, Gaga offers a space with music playing and the possibility to move to given movement qualities, but without a specific form—a space without "judgment," as many participants experienced it, and a space with "freedom to express."

7.9 Addiction

While discussing wow-moments, many participants mentioned the possibility of becoming addicted to them. They observed an experience of not being able to "get full of it" (Sara), and they needed the experience to be happy—to the extent that they started structuring their life around Gaga classes. Why is that? Sara, for example, informed that she could deal with negative emotional states through her body. The emotional-habitual transformation she underwent became central and extraordinarily important. She described this transformation as an "endless" process. For Sara, the Gaga experience was "satisfying," it fulfilled her need for "therapy," yet she was never satisfied, the class left her with the feeling that she wanted to repeat the experience as often as possible:

> At the beginning I used to like maybe once a week for a few months and then two times a week and then I saw that I just needed more and more, and know I'm like signed on for, so I can go to as many lessons as I want, and I would go to every single lesson, if I could.

For Uri, on the other hand, instead of emotional-habitual transformation, the experience of transcendence became the reason why he needed to repeat Gaga practice daily so as to be happy. He described it as an experience he could only gain during a Gaga class. He observed a strongly negative emotional experience: He "hate[d] missing class." In consequence, Uri structured his life around Gaga classes. He self-reflected: "I'm hooked on that, it's important for me to start my day that way. I hate missing the class ... I work my schedule around my classes." Uri added, "If I made more time, I would do more Gaga, even than what I do now ... I haven't yet filled the cup so much that I feel like: okay ah enough," and "it's it's become more important than other things, I've I've become SO ah involved with this practice that I reduced my yoga practice." Shira, too, reported experiencing an addictive effect. Shira noted that she felt like she wanted, or needed, to increase the number of Gaga classes; although she remained critical and self-reflective and underlined that the addiction was not a merely positive experience.

Matching Shira's self-report, it became obvious to me in the field that certain people were frequenting Gaga classes daily, sometimes even twice a day, or taking double lessons in the evening, and if not daily, then at least planning to take them regularly. Eli was one of those usually found in class. He self-reported that from three times a week, he increased the amount to taking classes every day. He also mentioned waiting the whole day after class for the next Gaga class to happen. However, as it became clear when he further talked, Gaga lost part of its attraction due to disappointing Gaga experiences, which led to partial substitution with other practices.

The phenomenon of increasing the number of classes was observed with other participants as well: Dana said she wanted to start taking double lessons in the evening. Other participants, such as Tamar, revealed the dilemma of wanting to do more Gaga, but not being able to do so due to lack of time. Tamar even seemed to feel the need to justify this lack of time during the interview:

> I got so much into this movement in two years, or two and a half years, of going—at the beginning once a week, and now I go twice, but never more than three times a week, I don't have time because I've got a daily yoga practice, I also started now Ido Portal, it's another movement ah language, so I really don't have time—and I'm a mother of two kids, I'm forty-five years old, you know, and so I just manage to do it once or twice a week.

As Shira, Eli, and others disclosed when telling their Gaga stories, the Gaga addiction seemed to come in waves: from taking classes every day to taking less or not wanting to take any.

In search for an explanation for this peculiar addictive effect, I came across what Marks Griffiths (1997) identifies as the characteristic steps of exercise addiction: (1) "salience," (2) "euphoria," (3) "tolerance," (4) "withdrawal syndrome," (5) "conflict," (6) "relapse."

> Salience. This is when the particular activity becomes the most important activity in the person's life and dominates their thinking, feelings, and behaviour. For instance, even if the person is not actually engaged in the behaviour they will be thinking about the next time they will be.

Eli's behavior of waiting for the class to start could be categorized here.

> Euphoria. This is the subjective experience that people report as a consequence of engaging in the particular activity (i.e. they experience a "buzz" or a "high").

This is clearly something all Gaga participants mentioned when talking about the happy aftermath of class.

> Tolerance. This is a process whereby increasing amounts of the particular activity are required to achieve the former effects

The data showed that it was common that Gaga participants felt the need to increase the number of classes.

> Withdrawal Symptoms. These are unpleasant feeling states and/or physical effects which occur when the particular activity is discontinued or suddenly reduced e.g. shakes, moodiness, irritability etc.

Participants like Uri reported they "hated to miss class."

> Conflict. This refers to conflicts between the addict and those around them (interpersonal conflict) or from within the individual themselves (intrapsychic conflict) which are concerned with the particular activity.

Talking to Uri, for example, I had the impression that his wife seemed at least a bit skeptical toward his increased involvement in Gaga class and in Gaga class context; for him, it was clear that his passion for Gaga was something she did not and could not share. He did not mention openly, however, whether his Gaga practice turned into a point of argument. Intrapsychic conflict seemed to arise when participants like Shira felt the need to increase Gaga training but did not like that feeling; or when Shira and Eli felt the need to stop classes; but also when Tamar seemed to have to choose on which practice to spend her spare time.

> Relapse. This is the tendency for repeated reversion to earlier patterns of the particular activity to recur and for even the most extreme patterns typical of the height of the addiction to be quickly restored after many years of abstinence or control. (Griffiths 1997, 163–4)

Gaga participants like Shira or Eli always came back to Gaga practice or even for an increased amount of Gaga practice.

Even though, a "Gaga addiction" seems only a light version and far from the strong body knowledge transformation connected to Giffith's exercise addiction, Griffith's different stages of addiction can serve as a guideline to understand, what is happening to body knowledge in the context of Gaga. Notwithstanding, it is important to notice that rather than Gaga classes as such becoming addictive, the transformation of body knowledge is addictive. As they stand, wow-experiences people had during class could also have occurred in other practices and rituals—though, Gaga seems to culminate in many of these moments of "euphoria." Hence, the possibility cannot be ruled out, that people could possibly substitute Gaga with practicing something else or practicing something else with Gaga without breaking a chain of "addiction."

7.10 Individual Wow

All interviewed participants and those who wrote experience diaries revealed individual wow-moments. Even though there was congruence in certain aspects of experience—participants did experience similar wow-moments—variations in individual experience filters and individual interpretations existed. It seemed as if every participant had a certain disposition—individual pre-experiences leading to individual preferences and individual experience mindsets—through which they were able to judge and describe their experiences as well as filter them as needed.

What I propose by my listing of the wow-moments in this chapter is expanding the search for "nonordinary experience" (Taves 2020a) by what I learned from my own research on extraordinary experiences. I am convinced that limiting the research on nonordinary experience to predetermined categories of experience, will cause to overlook significant parts of aesthetics. Experiences of effective momentary body knowledge actualizations, which are socially and culturally important, will be missed. Embodied effects playing a major and significant part in understanding the social and cultural impact of practice will be overseen. For example, the "happy aftermath," described above, seems to be at least as powerful an experience as "flow" or "loss of self-sense." Moreover, predetermined experience categories can never be clearcut, but are interrelated in their body knowledge origins. This makes it unwise to prioritize any kind of narrated experience and assign it into a category. One needs to find new endemic categorizations without repeating what Taves calls "the quest for the core" (671), which I tried by elaborating "wow-moments." Ultimately, an aesthetic approach can advance religious experience research. It not only allows for an identification and labeling of a momentary extraordinary experience under wow-moments, it also allows for making a connection of these momentary extraordinary experiences to other longer-lasting effects of practices described in the following chapters.

8

Gaga's Therapeutic Impact

You know, they say at the end of the class: take it with you for the rest of your day ... with the practice and with the listening and if you're really in the experience, that happens. ... It's just the echo of something you did, you don't think about it necessarily. (Uri)

Here Uri observed that, when he tries to enact the given sensory input, the actualization of body knowledge, which happens to his body in Gaga class, somehow stays with him after class, like an "echo." He is not the only one: Participants mentioned the experience of lasting physical and psychological "healing" provoked by the Gaga practice. Participants addressed the perceived bodily transformations as overtly positive; they experienced their embodied state as better with the enactment of Gaga practice than before and the bodily transformations as transitions from a negatively interpreted emotional-habitual state to a "better," positively perceived state of body and mind. Gaga's healing effect consisted of physical and psychological pain relief and an increase in physical and psychological well-being. Yet, participants did document not only the embodied state that was "healed" but also the whole "healing narratives" created around the embodied state. They explained the causation of the healing effect in connection to Gaga practice, as well as the life-changing impact of the healing experienced. The experienced embodied state of being healed and the healing narratives were apparently filtered by implicit and explicit, and individual and collective filters. Apart from individual body knowledge, body schemes, and embodied worldviews, not only explicit personal biographical details but also discourses such as those initiated by Naharin or Gaga Movement Ltd. on the health benefits of Gaga seemed to serve as interpretative and narrative filters for body knowledge interpretation and verbalization.

The following explores how long-lasting transformations as healing effects of Gaga practice are narrated. The analysis assumes that even though understanding the possible embodied therapeutic effect of physical transformations is interesting and it is addressed below, comprehending the perceived therapeutic effect is not a necessary requirement. It is participants themselves who create the therapeutic effect by which they are affected.

8.1 Gaga Body Product

In terms of body knowledge transformations, participants mention themselves enacting and perceiving on the basis of Gaga's body topography. It is mostly described as an experience of suddenly realizing that the body is moving in a Gaga way. This is also what I experienced during my field research: sitting somewhere, or walking somewhere, realizing that my body was enacting Gaga movements, without me having explicitly initiated them. The vocabulary used by participants to describe this experience was, for example, "you just find yourself" (Uri) or "I (suddenly) realized" (Ester), reflecting the sudden revelation of unconsciously performed movement and implicit body knowledge as explicit sensation. During my initial field research in Tel Aviv, my first time doing approximately three Gaga classes, I experienced a specific form of this "revelation": I woke up during the night and found myself enacting floating. It was a strange experience; it somehow seemed as if my body was dreaming Gaga. Gaga teacher Talia described a similar experience: "And once actually during the teacher program, I woke myself up, because I was like moving floating in bed. So, it was like, I was doing like all these like wiggly things, and I woke myself up and I was like: freaking egg, this is going too far!"

Gaga participant Uri talked about how Gaga body knowledge would pop up during everyday situations—"sometimes you just find yourself on the chair ... floating." He observed for himself that the embodied transformation was something like an "echo," carried along afterwards, outside of class. Uri also mentioned the power of key words like "floating," which allowed explicit and implicit embodied knowledge to come up, showing the extent to which the movements were embodied.

So, there is an implicit body knowledge transformation taking place toward a Gaga body. The body starts enacting body knowledge acquired in class outside of class. It eventually becomes explicitly noticeable as a movement style. One movement in particular has heightened potential to fulfill this role: the action of floating—Uri, Talia, and others mentioned it; I experienced it myself. Participants also reported experiencing other sudden movement sensations out of context, such as the "shoulder blades are exploring something" (Uri). Moreover, they reported a heightened awareness within their bodies. While not paying mind to this heightened awareness in the form of focused attention on their bodies, they experienced heightened sensitivity as body knowledge and an embodied state of awareness of, for example, "even the cloths on my body and the sensation of how my body moves inside my cloths" (Uri).

In the same way that they experience sensory transformation, participants experience motoric transformation. Ester reported, for example, that she experienced accidentally scrubbing herself with a sponge using the left hand, or differences in how her feet touched the floor while walking. She said, "I realized that different parts of my body, different members, and I'm sure that the inner members and the outer members are no different, are learning new things that they can do, something that was always passive can suddenly take an active part in something."

There is yet another part to the embodiment of Gaga's body knowledge. Not only does it happen that implicit body knowledge becomes explicit, but it can also happen that the action of embodiment is explicit. This happens when the individual deliberately takes body knowledge or body topography into different practices. Gaga teacher Hannah, for example, talked about how she would think of Gaga's body concept and body knowledge in yoga practice:

> So, even if the teacher isn't saying something in yoga, I can do it for myself, I can recognize that: ah this will help me, if I lift my pika here, I will have more support, if I engage yoyo, if I'm playing with that, that's what my body needs to do now. Or I might just find it interesting, you know, I don't know, maybe being in downward dog and feeling like I'm pulling my sit bones out.

Doing yoga, she thought about Gaga and deliberately used the knowledge gained therefrom to adjust her practice. For Hannah, Gaga's body concept and body knowledge were, on the one hand, a guarantee of a physical healthy practice, which is why she applied it. On the other hand, to her, the ability to apply it represented an action of experimenting, "playing," and testing the Gaga body in different contexts. She went on: "So, I do bring it into other contexts and into my regular life occasion ... this has become a way that I conceptualize and experience my physical existence."

Finally, the embodiment of Gaga body topography is by no means only observable from the internal individual point of view. As already mentioned, participants started enacting the movement they were talking about during the interviews, and I perceived enacting the movement I was writing about. The level of embodiment thus becomes explicit to the outside observer. Gaga teacher Ayala affirmed that she could even observe the degree to which participants were enacting the body knowledge provided by the techniques:

> I can see more when it's after two classes or three classes ... in the first one it's too much information ... they don't know what to do, there is a kind of uncertainty, there is not—but then after, definitely I would know; if I was working many days with one group and then ... two new people come, you can see that the other people are listening more to their body in difference of the other two.

Ayala reported an increased observable embodiment with an increase in the amount of Gaga practice, which leads to another question: How are perceived physical transformations connected to Gaga practice? Gaga practice not only leads to the embodiment of Gaga body knowledge but also incorporates techniques to support that embodiment beyond the frame of class and provides participants with the necessary sensory awareness to realize embodied transformation. Gaga practice produces the body knowledge needed to produce further body knowledge and to produce it in a lasting way.

Furthermore, the long-lasting transformation of body knowledge is not an instant transformation; as with the experience of positive momentary transformation, it needs time to happen. Participants were aware of the not-yet-embodied body knowledge, and they were explicitly working on being able to perform it: "There is one thing I haven't yet been able to do or to grasp, when they say something like: caress your rips with your shoulder blade ... That's something what I'm thinking about ... I'm not yet sure of that" (Ester).

The participant is thus an active part of the embodiment of body knowledge and transformation. As soon as the transformation occurs and is experienced as something positive, it could form part of the addictive effect of Gaga classes, leading to an increased number of Gaga lessons taken. Ariel felt an emotional-habitual change with Gaga practice. He attributed it to the "discovery" of and becoming connected to the body, especially in the first year of practice. From what he said, the transformation became long-lasting and natural with ongoing practice until it did not feel like a transformation anymore. Gaga teacher Hannah mentioned something similar about the teaching practice: With ongoing teaching and Gaga practice, she had more fun while teaching. "Tools" were incorporated to an extent that she no longer had to reflect on them, but they were at her disposal to be discussed on another level; she had become fluent in the Gaga language.

The transformation is long-lasting yet not ever-lasting. Only ongoing practice guarantees that the transformation would last. When Ester, for example, talked about experiencing the embodiment of Gaga's body knowledge, she added:

> There've been several days when I've been very busy and happy with the visit of my family and with work and with other things and ah, I feel that I need a little more Gaga in order to get that back because my mind is just so busy with other good things right now that it's a little, so I hadn't had that feeling in two days or so now ... I feel like I'm fat, and you know, I feel, the whole thing ah and I'm glad that I'm going ... tomorrow morning.

The body transformation had vanished or was at least perceived to have vanished. Ester reflected that this was likely due to being "busy" with other things, and the body and mind consequently having forgotten Gaga. To get it back, she had to do Gaga again. Eli attributed this long-lasting yet not ever-lasting transformative effect of Gaga classes to the constant change in a body enacting Gaga's body knowledge. From Eli's point of view, Gaga's body knowledge consisted of a constant process of "finding." However, he also grounded this nonpersisting character of the physical transformation acquired in the fact that body transformation was never lasting if the conditions to provoke the transformation disappeared: "You have to train. Ya. If you don't train, it deteriorates and goes away."

With ongoing Gaga practice, enactment of instructions, and movement, participants reported an embodied effect of practicing outside of class context, or, rather, they associated experienced body knowledge with Gaga class because that is where they experienced it. The aesthetics of Gaga class expanded. Frequent Gaga participants enacted Gaga's body topography, body concept, and movement style not only in Gaga class but beyond, not only as unconscious movement or body schemes but also as conscious (re)experiencing of certain proprioceptive sensations, for example. The key to this production of a Gaga body seems to be an ongoing and frequent immersion and participation of participants at Gaga classes, which causes a certain aesthetical "training." It seems of interest to bridge this training and its effect to Tanya M. Luhrmanns' observation on the possibility to train and increase by training what psychologists address as the "human capacity for *absorption*—a capacity to be immersed in the world of the senses, inner and outer" (2020, 85). Luhrmann herself introduces the psychological concept of absorption to the study of religion in a quite different context: to enable the understanding of believers experiencing the presence of "invisible beings." She describes how this specific kind of experience seems to be facilitated by an "inner sense cultivation," "the deliberate, repeated use of inner visual representation and other inner sensory experience" (93). While Gaga participants never reported any experience of such kind, of course, they did indeed report the experience of a heightened proprioceptive sensation or the (re)experiencing of prior experienced proprioceptive sensations like the action of floating with ongoing and especially frequent class participation. Also, while it does not make sense to talk of cultivation of inner senses in the context of Gaga, sense cultivation in general is a substantial Gaga training method, and absorption into sensory information is a central element of Gaga class. Consequently, it seems highly possibly that this kind of Gaga sense cultivation partially accounts for the success of the Gaga body product and a heightened capacity of absorption that accompanies it. The other way round, Gaga observances might enable to broaden Luhrmann's concept by not only explaining the why but the bodily how of the occurrence of such phenomena as seeing invisible beings or experiencing the extraordinary in everyday life.

8.2 On the Therapeutic Effect of Gaga

Looking at data, the answer to the question of whether Gaga practice has a therapeutic effect can only be "yes." Not only called participants Gaga their "therapy" (Tamar, Uri, Sara, Rahel, Ada), but Gaga was also generally connected to an emotional-habitual transformation, from a negative emotional-habitual state to a positive one. Answering why this is so, however, requires a multidimensional answer: On the one hand, it was shown above that the Gaga body is part of a social and cultural context, where the individual is culturally required to care for the health and fitness of their own body. This is not only because it will lead to enhanced social acceptance in all areas of life but also because popular scientific knowledge suggests that a healthy body means emotional health, a higher quality of life, and a longer life. Gaga practice and its participants form part of a larger "healthism" movement (Koch 2014, 10, also 13–19). Thus, a body transformation is never only the experience of a physical transformation, but rather a physical transformation experienced through cultural, social, and individual experience filters, which attach additional meaning to the body transformation apart from the physical.

On the other hand, natural sciences' findings underline the fact that it is legitimate to search for the therapeutic effects of Gaga in body transformation occurring in a Gaga class itself, primary and implicitly before experience interpretation, even though this might only be hypothetically possible: Different research suggests that emotions are embodied. What is commonly termed poor posture—collapsed or contracted—can lead to depressive thoughts and a rise in cortisol levels, commonly experienced as negative emotions or a negative state of the body-mind unit. In contrast, not only do positive thoughts stem from a "good," erect posture, for example, but positive thoughts themselves also seem to have the potential to provoke this posture from which they stem, as Peter Payne and Mardi A. Crane-Godreau (2015, 4) mention in their article on the preparatory set. Apart from posture change affecting emotions, a more subtle habitual change such as conscious awareness can also affect emotions: The autonomic nervous system is a network linking sensory input from the environment, afferent nervous reaction, to an emotional state. When focused attention, or conscious awareness, is paid to sensory input, emotional self-regulation becomes possible (4–5). The embodied negative emotional-habitual states can be helpful to solve, for example, situations when the individual perceives ongoing stress. Stress arises in the preparatory set, which "involves integrated action of the subcortical systems controlling muscle tone and posture, autonomic/visceral state, affect, attentional arousal, and expectation" (2). When stress ends the embodied situation, the preparatory set usually returns to its normal state. A maladaptive preparatory set, traumatic/ongoing stress, and other factors, however, might inhibit the preparatory set from turning back to its initial state. By working on posture and interoceptive awareness, thus the embodied solution, the stress situation can be solved (11–12). The combination of movement and awareness also influences mind and experience by directly engaging and affecting different brain regions, as other researchers have found out (see Schmalzl, Powers, and Henje Blom 2015). In addition, movement practice bears the potential to alter a body scheme: Some of the brain's characteristics are neuroplasticity, its ability to change neuroplastically, and its structural specialization, resulting in microstructural differences within the white matter of the brain (see Roberts et al. 2013). A change in the body scheme potentially directly influences experience. Cognitive scientists suggest that thinking and perception are organized like the body and depend on implicit and explicit body knowledge. Learning new skills could influence embodied cognition (see Casasanto 2014). The different forms of awareness enacted during practice appear as highly effective transformation techniques: alerting attention, orienting attention, executive attention, which are variations of focused attention, and open monitoring (Schmalzl, Powers, and Henje Blom 2015, 8). A specific case of attention required is metacognitive awareness, meaning that one consciously monitors one's own emotions, thoughts, and experiences. Metacognitive awareness plays a special role in creating self-regulative nonjudgmental awareness of the individual (9).

As demonstrated from analyzing Gaga techniques, Gaga practice incorporates the following actions that are transformative in nature: "Proprioceptive or interoceptive imagery; Affective imagery; Adopting a specific posture; Performing specific movements"; and "Paying attention in certain ways" (Payne and Crane-Godreau 2015, 12). First, Gaga works a great deal with "breaking" movement "habits" to create an upright posture and a strong, fit, healthy body: The tools used are stretching, expanding the movement range outwards into the space, engaging the "correct" muscles and the "right" amount of muscular effort, and exploring the movement of posture-crucial body parts, such as the shoulder blades, head, or spine, and bringing them into the optimal position. Second, Gaga instructions and movement create awareness in all its variations: awareness of sensory input from the environment, such as people, place, and things, by seeing, listening, and sensing with the skin; kinesthetic awareness of one's own movement; interoceptive awareness of the sensations inside the body; and the play with sensory perception of peripersonal space. Alerting, orienting, executing attention is enacted in all variations as "listening" is made the base and goal of all actions. What a Gaga class requires from participants is controlled movement and controlled movement adjustment, referring to the controlled correction of movement, awareness and control of the whole body, or movement attention. On the one hand, there is focused attention on body and movement, which Gaga practice creates and which inhibits mind-wandering. On the other hand, open monitoring of the environment, space, and people and constant availability to react are required. The intake of sensory information in class is heightened in a twofold way. First, due to the constant movement, alteration of posture, speed, and movement quality, the sensory input from the own body is substantial, and the body is forced to react, for example, by adapting balance. Second, Gaga instructions draw attention to the perception of sensory input, enforce concentration, and inhibit distraction. As in other practices, participants are asked to monitor sensory input while simultaneously executing movement. In addition, participants are asked to monitor their attention and evaluate their movement execution. The working memory is fully engaged in different ways. Instructions are constantly given and repeated, while the teacher embodies instructions through their own movement. Participants are guided in maintaining their attention (see Russell and Arcuri 2015).

Potential therapeutic effects of Gaga could thus be that, first, physical change due to Gaga practice—especially efficient because of attention training methods—leads to enhanced perceived emotional well-being. Second, participants gain the tools to self-regulate, self-evaluate, and self-monitor without self-judgment. This also leads to enhanced emotional well-being.

Since the accomplishment of well-being is experienced as a transition from a negative to a positive state, it seemed useful to address the transformation as a "healing" process: This implies that the process "make[s] free from injury or disease" as it "make[s] sound or whole," "make[s] well again" as it "restores to health," and "cause[s] (an undesirable condition) to be overcome" as it "mends" (*Merriam-Webster* 2019a). Participants believe Gaga has therapeutic effects, which can be subsumed under this definition of a "healing" process. The main therapeutic effects addressed are (1) overcoming physical restrictions that affect one's life, (2) feeling an emotional-habitual release, (3) experiencing Gaga as support during difficult life situations, and (4) finding a different positive mindset.

Overcoming Physical Restrictions

Participants mention that Gaga helped them overcome physical restrictions causing pain. Ester, for example, described how she started Gaga practice with her body still hurting and being mainly restricted due to a struggle with a robbery attempt on her three years ago. She explained that Gaga was a special challenge to her, as she could hardly do many of the movements required. Yet, with each lesson, and even though she did not even reach her movement limits at all, she felt her movement range growing. Gaga helped her acquire what other methods such as physiotherapy could not. What amazed Ester the most is that she could still undergo such a body change, as the "mugging" happened years ago and the restrictions were lasting.

Iris, with whom I conversed in the context of Gaga class, told me the following:

> I was suffering so much in my whole body and Gaga slowly relieved in more and more places. For example, at first I couldn't stand on my feet, I had pain. Then slowly it got better. I couldn't stand on my toes and now I can walk on my toes. And when I'm not suffering, I'm also happy in other areas of my life, I'm happy with my family, with people at work, in my errors.

Iris described how with Gaga practice, the pain she was suffering while standing slowly relieved. She said she was now able to do things she could not do before.

Most importantly, she connected this relief with an increase of happiness in the rest of her life.

Emotional-Habitual Release

Participants observe that Gaga practice has a direct effect on emotions, which they experience and imagine as being held in their bodies: "Gaga ... raises a lot of things, good and bad, okay, because a lot of people are holding in their body good and bad things. So, some people are coming good out of it" (Eli). Eli mentioned that Gaga's possibility to have such a therapeutic effect originated in the assumption that emotions, "good and bad," were stored in the body and the "muscles," and that muscular tension was connected to "soul" tension "from the day, from the past"—a belief Gaga shared with Feldenkrais and Greenberg, among others. He observed how by working the whole body in the same way as other practices from the context of body and movement therapy, these stored emotions could surface in the context of Gaga class: "When you release something in your body, you're also releasing some tension you have in your soul." When Eli talked about the therapeutic releasing effect of Gaga, he argued using the knowledge from his background. As someone interested in body and movement practices and somatic therapies, he was an expert in theories circulating discourses on embodied emotions within the knowledge groups he was part of.

Sara, as someone skilled in psychology and therapy, approached the therapeutic effect of movement from a psychological point of view. She said the constant movement in Gaga had the same therapeutic effect as psychoanalysis: "More things can come up." She believed the "subconscious" and the "unconscious" can surface because movement makes "room" for them "to enter." Gaga was as "life changing" as doing psychotherapy. Sara also experienced this effect of Gaga on herself. That Gaga had the potential to be a substitute for visiting a psychologist was also mentioned during in-field conversations with Rahel and Ada—the latter of whom formulated the following:

> You know, I had a lot of problems, and I was supposed to go to psychotherapy. And I went and I felt like talking was not my way to, I couldn't talk about my problems. And then I started to do Gaga and Gaga became my therapy. I could deal with my problems physically in Gaga, I'm the person to deal with my problems physically.

The actual form an emotional release can take is shown above: It could happen in the form of crying in the context of class. The emotional release made up one part of the therapeutic effect of Gaga.

Support in Difficult Life Situations

Participants report an especially significant positive impact of Gaga during difficult life situations, and even though these situations could not be solved, they were experienced as more bearable. Tamar, for example, emphasized several times throughout the interview that she was in a "difficult" life situation at the moment and confronted with "negativity": "My life right now is difficult, really, I'm dealing with shit in my life right now," "my life is a bit shit"—this negativity seemed to be due to a difficult marriage situation. Betterment came with taking Gaga class. She said, "I manage to forget or to leave the shit I'm dealing with somewhere else and ah it's just amazing." Gaga offered Tamar a safe space to forget the difficult situation. Moreover, she noted some long-lasting effects, making difficult situations more bearable:

> As I told you, my life is a bit shit, and I feel sadness, and it's okay to feel sad, you know, I observe, but I know it's not gonna be forever, I know it's not even me, you know, but while there it's there, and I have to embrace it, I cannot run anyway of it or pretend it's not there, and it's okay, you know. But today I managed to feel that in the past I would have been maybe numb, you know ... and it's interesting.

Accepting sadness was a long-lasting effect of Gaga practice to Tamar: "I really learned to feel ... and I—(changes voice) today in my outside world, I start feeling, I feel people, I feel myself."

Dana, too, found herself in a difficult situation due to a transition from one stage of life to another. Whereas Tamar talked about the situation as something that was going to change again and that would not go on forever, Dana already saw a change in her situation and life. Dana broke up with her boyfriend of more than five years, the separation was recent, and she still seemed to miss him. However, Dana said what she missed most was that person. She now had to find her "own comfort" and her "own safety" in a situation and at a time when other areas of her life also held difficulties: "I started work, I finished school, I had like a crazy semester where I didn't sleep for almost half a year and then started working immediately, so—I think it's, all my friends are like depressed right now (laughs), like it's a crazy crazy crazy time." Dana seemed to generally be in a situation where she had to define her identity anew. It was only Gaga that helped her to cope up with the situation well: "It's the only that helps my mind set like I think." In addition, Dana described Gaga as offering her a solution to identify herself in a new way. She mentioned trying to spend time dancing, as it was "creative and intellectual," different, and still related to her former life.

She observed Gaga as a possibility to transform her life and body toward a new identity.

In general, Gaga's support in difficult life situations seems to be most relatable to momentary wow-moments—feeling "really tired," "sad," or "depressed" can be overcome in a Gaga class; one comes out "light," "flying," and "happy" (Tamar). Gaga becomes an extraordinary experience space. Over time, however, Gaga practice can also lead to long-lasting, increased happiness, a happier life, and a more positive mindset—maybe in overcoming the difficult situations.

Different Mindset

Participants see their mindset, their approach toward life, changing with Gaga practice. Tamar said Gaga taught her to raise her voice. With the "unleashing" she experienced in Gaga classes, with being forced to reset her physical and mental limits, Tamar became more confident. She was now able to yell and scream. In Eli's eyes, Gaga had the potential to change mindsets because it forced confrontation. In a Gaga class, one had to confront one's shyness of moving in front of others, and Gaga offered the perfect conditions to confront shyness, as the cause of shyness was "left outside because: okay, we can watch you, okay; and everybody that is in the class is in the class, he is not watching you, he's doing it." To Ester, changing one's body image had the potential to create a different mindset in terms of body perception and body scheme.

Dana and Idan both mentioned, independently from each other, that practicing Gaga made them become less "cynical": Idan criticized Gaga teachers for using exactly Naharin's vocabulary, especially "those phrases of encouragement" because "it feels false," but then he instantly reflected on his critique, saying, "but I'm cynical." Having said this, he stated, "You know, that's another thing I'm learning, it helps me to be less cynical." In Idan's eyes, being less cynical was an outcome of dealing with the embarrassment he felt for himself and observing others in Gaga classes. Being less cynical, to Idan, meant learning to accept without judgment—or talking about something without judgment:

> But sometimes I'm embarrassed in that room, too. I'm embarrassed for myself, and I'm embarrassed for others. yeah. I was like, this guy is like, it's like embarrassing, but then I'm like, you know at the end of it the what's more important is, he's allowed he's here, he's getting something out of it. He's allowed to embarrass himself. I'm allowed to embarrass myself.

Dana said she used to be more cynical in the sense of being "sarcastic" for the "past five years." She listed the following as things possibly causing her to be sarcastic: "My school is very hard and my friends from school are the best and they are very smart, but they are also kind of sarcastic." Dana clearly did not want to be sarcastic, she emphasized. She said she was overcoming this mindset: "And like I'm not like that, but I think I have been for the past five years." She mentioned that Gaga was helping her to change her mindset: "I mean just, have no you don't need a reason to be happy kind of thing? So, I've really enjoyed that." During the interview, she also talked about how she was affected by other people's moods; for example, over "the last five years," she would feel responsible for other people having fun. However, Dana recently experienced, when going out on a "Thursday after class," that she could allow herself to have fun even though nobody else was having fun. For Dana, the therapeutic effect of Gaga practice was a change from a negative mindset that she saw herself as having been stuck in. Dana was in the process of "learning" a more self-confident mindset and being "comfortable" with herself.

I want to conclude with Uri, who stated that the perceived therapeutic effect of Gaga is nothing he discovered in Gaga only but in body and movement practices in general. Gaga's therapeutic impact is indeed and again nothing singular and unique but comparable to the aesthetics and body knowledge of a range of other contemporary practices.

9

Gaga Goes Worldview

"My wife said, Gaga is my new religion" was one of the first things interview participant Uri told me about himself. And, while he was clearly aware of the impact of Gaga practice on his life, he also seemed to quote his wife to position himself as a "believer."

Body practices such as Gaga provoke momentary body knowledge transformation narrated as an extraordinary experience and, at the same time, bear the potential to provoke long-lasting transformations that, in a next step after being recognized by a transformed individual, could be interpreted and adopted as a worldview. Gaga goes worldview when what participants experience during class influences their narrations of class. In narrations, Gaga class becomes "central" as a background motif and as a structuring element (see Schröder 2013, 110–16). The way participants spoke about Gaga showed that it took a fundamental position in their lives. First, participants told narratives about "converting" to Gaga and the life-changing impact of Gaga. Second, participants reported the urge to do as much Gaga as possible—they described their well-being as depending on the Gaga practice. Third, participants characterized themselves in opposition to the others by highlighting their particular level of awareness as having fully embodied the Gaga body concept. They depicted themselves as the ideal Gaga practitioner and the ideal descriptive body for Gaga's body topography. In this context as well, participants seemed to be influenced by the Gaga practice in multiple ways: consciously, as they were able to reflect on the role of Gaga within their life and use it as an explicit narrative resource, and unconsciously, as continuously enacted body knowledge implicitly defined and shaped their narrative output. On the one hand, participants saw the impact of Gaga on their lives and were able to analyze or deliberately use this fact. On the other hand, they were influenced on an implicit level, which was not—at least not easily—accessible by themselves in an explicit way of knowing.

These patterns observed in narrated data can be exemplarily connected to two different phenomena occurring in religious and spiritual practices: (1) conversion, especially in the sense of a practice gaining centrality in the life of an individual, and (2) the worldview potential of religion: (1) As with experience, there is a long-standing interest in what provokes humans to "believe," to become "religious," or to radically change their beliefs, to convert. Especially scholars looking at religion from a psychology perspective have been interested in understanding what seemed to be a psychological transformation process: "In classical psychology research on conversion, religious conversion (i.e., the practice of changing religion in the broadest sense) was perceived as a fairly radical personal change related to the adoption of a new interpretative framework" (Popp-Baier 2001, 1). However, for nearly half a century already, the focus of conversion studies has shifted to conversion stories as narrative constructs and effective speech acts, and to what could be learned, from how people spoke of their adoption of certain religious beliefs and practices, about the places of those beliefs and practices within their individual life and meaning-making (2). Still, as Anne-Konstanze Schröder (2013) points out in her work on conversion, there has never been a clear definition and agreement on what the definition of conversion is. She adds that conversion in any case remains a "multifaceted" process to be researched (98).

To fill this theoretical gap, Schröder builds her own approach to religious conversion on the definition of conversion as a process of centralization, "Zentralisierungsprozess." During this process, religious "things" start to dominate individual concepts of self, and they turn into "Personal Religion," "Persönliche Religion" (Schröder 2013, 109–10). The then "Personal" religion starts to provide an interpretative source to the interpretation of a nonreligious environment. The religious environment is more often frequented and consulted, and the originally nonreligious environment is understood as part of the religious environment or context (110). In consequence, emotions are interpreted religiously, and behavior is shaped by religious norms (111). Schröder points out that conversion is triggered by a change in the social and cultural "setting" of an individual and a change in the individual meaning system connected to a change in perception and behavior; body-extern and body-intern conditions influence each other (113). Also, conversion is not a radical shift in terms of an abrupt change or transformation; rather, it is radical because it influences the whole person—a holistic transformation. It is only perceived, experienced, or described as abrupt because the characteristic of abruptness is what is socially, culturally, and individually searched for (115–16). Even though the Gaga practice lacks the crucial characteristic of being a "religious" setting in the sense of Schröder (30), it seems possible to understand part of the observed effect in terms of this process of centralization that Schröder unfolds. Gaga participants introspectively verbalize it when they describe how Gaga practice increases in importance and life centrality. Not only does the narrative content and wording indicate a centralization of Gaga practice, but centralization also happens while structuring and designing the narration.

(2) "Worldview," as presented by Taves, intends to be a practical concept on how to understand and analyze the meaning-making effect of "religious" as well as "nonreligious" practices (2018, 13): "It will allow us to ... conduct our analytic, comparative, and explanatory work without worrying about (a) defining religion or (b) whether those we study consider themselves religious" (Taves and Asprem 2018, 297), which makes an exploration of Gaga as worldview particularly interesting. It is a "naturalizing" framework, as it is about "connecting [religion as a worldview] to a cognitive and ultimately biological explanatory scheme" (299), which is especially interesting for an aesthetic approach focusing on body knowledge transformation.

Primary worldviews are ways of life that, as trained or inherited and constantly updated "self-models," structure the interaction between the individual and the environment, and thus also individual perception (Taves and Asprem 2018, 300–1). However, "'Way of life' is the larger, more encompassing concept. All humans [and other animals] have a way of life with many taken-for-granted beliefs and ways of doing things, but not all have an explicit worldview" (Taves 2018, 19). Ways of life are "implicit, intuitive, nonlinguistic and nonconscious processes of meaning-making" (Taves and Asprem 2018, 302). They remain as implicit perceptual guidance, even when individuals adopt worldviews as explicit meaning systems, while, nevertheless, worldviews possibly function on an embodied and implicit level as well. According to Taves and Asprem, worldviews as explicit meaning systems are able to answer to "(1) ontology (what exists, what is real), (2) epistemology (how do we know what is true), (3) axiology (what is the good that we should strive for), (4) praxeology (what actions should we take), and (5) cosmology (where do we come from and where are we going)" (300). A concept such as worldview could function to explain another part of the effect of neo-spiritual practices. Explicit and implicit body knowledge transformation itself seems to have the potential to become a "worldview"—not so much in terms of the extraordinary becoming an ontology, or epistemology, but indeed an axiology or praxeology to the ordinary. Participants appear to take on Gaga as a possible perceptual cultural order. Body knowledge updated in class influences narrations on a language level, concerning the mode of verbalization such as the vocabulary chosen, and a content level, concerning the topics participants told me about. Gaga participants self-identify with Gaga's collective body knowledge, body topography, and movement style not only via their behavior, talking, and movement but also by telling biographical "Gaga stories." They implicitly incorporate a Gaga body scheme, while they explicitly self-affiliate with Gaga's implicitly and explicitly discussed collective values.

9.1 Gaga Stories—Binding Oneself to Embodied Experience

In order not to bring any subjective evaluation of Gaga practice in terms of fulfilling any religious or spiritual needs, the baseline to analyze Gaga stories is a close look at the text: What do participants tell as their Gaga story? Participants' Gaga stories are different and yet similar in the following story "components."

Time Consumption of Gaga Practice

Participants talk about how their initial Gaga practice increased after some time, reached a peak, and eventually decreased. Gaga practice thus becomes central in terms of time investment. Most of the people interviewed told me that they started off with less classes and then increased the number to as many as possible; the majority then owned a monthly pass with as many entries as possible. Tamar told me that in the beginning, she went once, then twice, and now three times per week, which was the maximum she could do. She added, almost as an excuse, that she was also frequenting daily yoga classes and other movement practices and was a mother. Sara told me that she went once a week for a few months, then twice per week, and, as she saw that she "needed more and more," she bought the monthly pass and tried to go as often as possible, "every single lesson," if she could. Dana, who was relatively new to Gaga practice, practicing for two months at the time of the interview, said she went to one to four classes per week. She noticed her tendency toward three times per week over the last weeks and mentioned that she would like to do "double classes"—in her case, two evening classes in a row— likely because she could not come on more days. Eli, participant with the longest time practicing, described his time investment as follows:

> It began like, you know, I thought that okay I like it so I'm do it like ah three times a week like as a, for shape. And I found myself like waiting every day to the end of work to go and do Gaga. And then [how often are you doing?] I started

doing—actually this year I'm doing the least that I'm doing in the last ah nine years. Usually I do every day, ya, if not more than once a day. Depends a lot on the time I have, of course.

Whereas Eli only described a slight decrease in time spent on Gaga classes, Shira's Gaga story revealed an on-and-off time investment. Shira started Gaga, stopped but kept it in mind, restarted, and stopped when she experienced a loss in her close family; although she described the second stop as taking a break rather than as stopping. Since she did not know what her class participation would be like in the future, she did not own a monthly pass at the time of the interview. However, Shira discovered that she went to class nearly every day anyway:

> Now I just took like ten classes I bought so —I came occasionally, I didn't come so much, but then I came on Sunday and now it's always like—so, because those two classes were free on Sunday on Monday and then today, and then yesterday I wanted to see Ohad Naharin. This always to have sometimes, from time to time to have a class with the master (laughs).

The amount of time participants dedicated to Gaga is important insofar as it reflects the centrality of the practice in participants' lives—either by the amount of time they dedicate to Gaga practice or, indirectly, by their wish to dedicate even more time to it. While, as we have seen, many participants mention an addictive effect of momentary positive experience, wow-moments, in the context of a Gaga class, the effect of this "addiction," reflected in time spent, itself has a life-transforming potential: People begin to structure their lives around Gaga classes, and Gaga class participation becomes time-consuming, not only experience-wise but also timewise. Gaga seems to bear the potential to be a substitute for other activities and other experiences. This transformation is a moment where the self-reflection of participants reaches its limits: The participants would talk about their intent to frequent classes more often and perhaps their daily class participation—most without questioning their behavior.

Moments of "Revelation" of Bodily Transformation

Another important component of Gaga stories is the moment of "revelation" of the bodily transformation. Participants narrate a transformation from an emotional and physical "numb" state to a newly found connection to their bodies that they do not want to miss anymore. They narratively construct an embodied identity, which consists of being aware of their own bodies, and they talk about a transformation from a prior preaware state to a later aware state. Narratively, this awareness transformation is related to an experienced emotional-habitual transformation and the transformation of relationships with the environment. Though this physical revelation is a clear turning point in participants' lives, it is not necessarily a turning point of the narrative. It rather underlies the narrative as a motif, which participants address while talking about many different transformative aspects. Some people, such as Tamar or Ester, told me, without being questioned, about experienced emotional-habitual transformations; they were eager to share the perceived change, such as from sadness to happiness, from pain to release, and to increasing the movement range and altering the body scheme. In the case of others such as Ariel, Dana, or Uri, I needed to ask whether they experienced a transformation or "change" in their lives due to Gaga practice, hinting at them to talk about an embodied life-changing transformation experience as part of the interview's guiding thread. Then they answered by talking about life-changing aspects similar to those mentioned by Tamar and Ester (for detailed descriptions of the different bodily transformations, see Chapter 8). Content-wise, the moments of revelation that participants narrated corresponded to the body transformations analyzed above: For some, the revelation was the unification of body and mind, overcoming a quasi-dualistic perspective, and the newfound bodily awareness; for others, it was the healing effect of Gaga in overcoming difficult emotional-habitual stages. In any case, the revelation respresented a moment of change toward something better.

Participants and Their Gaga Practice: A Vivid Relationship

Gaga stories also tell of setbacks, obstacles experienced, and obstacles overcome. Participants are in a vivid relationship with "Gaga" and Gaga practice, including emotional ups and downs. Participants go through different stages of relationship (List 10).

List 10 Different Stages of the Practice–Participant Relation

(1) The euphoric/in-growth—these participants are highly enthusiastic about Gaga, telling me about having "new" and exciting experiences
(2) The ongoing fan—these participants have generally been practicing Gaga for more years, and they still enjoy it; to them, it is a routine that they need to "survive" everyday life

(3) The skeptical—these participants mention some criticism concerning Gaga
(4) The temporarily deconverted—these participants stopped doing Gaga because they no longer enjoy it.

In their Gaga stories, participants revealed that they underwent different stages in an ongoing process. Participants could also take on the stages as standpoints from where they argued about and narrated their Gaga experience. The stage they took as a standpoint while talking seemed to affect the centrality of Gaga to their biography and the narrative outcome to their Gaga story.

Gaga Practice as a Narrative and Biographical Turning Point

Narrating about the time before Gaga practice takes up a special place within the narratives that are told. The life narratives of some participants clearly accelerate toward Gaga practice, and the time without or before the start of Gaga practice becomes addressed as a kind of lost time. For example, participants wished, mentioning various reasons, they had started Gaga earlier: "I'm very sad, I must say, you know, it's still, it's stupid what I'm going to say, I wanted to say, I'm sorry I didn't start this fifteen years ago, but I didn't ... so I started it now ... I'm sure I would have benefited" (Ester).

Moreover, the bodily state before starting Gaga practice was mostly described in a negative way. Dana described herself as having been "cynical, like sarcastic" before starting Gaga practice. Now she could be "happy" without a reason. Idan became less "cynical," yet in the sense of being less judgmental.

The different narrative characteristics culminate in Uri's personal Gaga story: First, there is the story of a dance admirer fulfilling his dream of dancing by doing Gaga; Gaga offers him the potential to become part of something he admires. Second, there is the story of an aware yoga practitioner to whom doing Gaga yet adds another level of awareness. Third, there is the story of someone who—though he does not tell why—needs therapy and finds this therapy in Gaga's movement and Gaga's social community. The centrality of Gaga to Uri's life was observed by himself quite clearly: He said he structured his life around his "religion," Gaga, and he still could not get enough Gaga class experience. It was not only the great experience of class, "the wow," that Uri did not want to miss but also the long-lasting embodied effect. Uri was at a stage in his "relationship" with Gaga practice where he did not criticize the practice at all; during the interview, he switched between being an "ongoing fan" and describing some "euphoric" experiences. The interview revealed a level of embodiment of Gaga body knowledge, where Uri's everyday life seemed to be shaped partly by this embodiment. Uri did not say directly that he wished to have started Gaga earlier; however, by the way he talked about the time until he started—it "took" him time—and how he described the explanatory narrative episode of yoga being preparation for Gaga practice, one could tell that he saw the time without Gaga, if not lost in a way, at least as having been less enjoyable.

9.2 Taking on Experienced identity: Tendencies of Positioning and Othering Processes

Identity is a central concept in current debates that refers to a host of meanings. I understand "identity" to mean belonging to a particular social formation that is inclusive as well as exclusive. Identity ... creates boundaries and promises clarity and security in a world characterized by distraction and fragmentation (Meyer and Geschiere 1998). In this sense, identity needs to be placed in a dialectic of flow and closure. I suggest that it is important to take into account the importance of the senses and sensations in invoking and sustaining identities that people feel to be natural and thus beyond questioning. I do not, of course, want to claim the existence of primordial, essentialized identities. The point is, rather, to understand why and how personal and collective identities, though constructed, are perceived as "natural" and "real." (Meyer 2012, 170)

I cite this identity definition Meyer (2012) offers, even though she only lets it to enter her book chapter as footnote, because I feel it can be ideally applied to what participants do and what happens to them when they take on Gaga as a worldview and consequently take on a "Gaga identity." Gaga as a worldview seems to have reached another level of embodiment and influence when participants make use of Gaga-related ideas, concepts, and ontologies in creating a narrative identity for themselves. This happens in different ways of "closure" (170): Either participants position themselves as insiders to the perceived Gaga identity, or they position themselves by setting themselves apart from others whom they see as not being part of the perceived Gaga identity—a process of othering. Two things seem to be suitable for identity creation and thus highly effective worldview components: First, participants take on a *dancer identity*, positioning themselves as insiders to the dance world; second, participants position themselves as *bodily "aware"*: mainly in the sense of enhanced proprioception, but also nociception and thermoception, for example. They present themselves as demonstrators of Gaga's and society's striving for this bodily awareness. The identity of belonging to the dance world with all additional consequences and an identity bound to awareness share the characteristics of being an identity continuum between implicit, only embodied, and explicit, verbalized knowledge shaping cognition. Awareness, however, seems to have a particular potential to become an implicit embodied identity: Gaga participants state that they experience their bodies differently and more intensely; they discover new things about their bodies; their bodies behave differently; and they experience a body change. Due to their manifold implicit and explicit expressions, as well as the implicit and explicit input of a varying nature, "dance" and "awareness" identities could be seen as discourses rather than defined and closed groups with static identity features. Yet, the discourses still define and bind together a group of people who implicitly and explicitly identify with the embodied characteristics of a dancer or an aware person. Different from establishing oneself as a dancer and becoming a legitimate part of the dance world, establishing an identity as an aware person seems to work mainly by setting oneself apart from people who do not belong to the group of the aware. The dance identity seems to have been introduced into the Gaga worldview from the outside by participants admiring Naharin's work and the dancers of the Batsheva Company. Awareness, on the other hand, is something that Gaga explicitly claims as its goal and center of practice and that it implicitly creates through its body knowledge. Awareness is the central worldview component that Gaga participants take on during Gaga practice to influence their meaning-making. As soon as participants experience through their embodied identities or rely on their identities to position themselves, Gaga as a worldview becomes unquestioned and an unquestionable baseline for constructing their identity.

The "Dancer"

Implicit and explicit dancer identities merge in talking—it is impossible to tell why someone is positioning oneself as a dancer, though the narrative aim of being identified as a dancer is clear. Moreover, the discursive nature of "dancer" manifests itself: For some, it is the identity of a dancer in general, whereas for others, it is the identity of a Batsheva dancer, which seems to be used for individual identity construction.

Uri, as discussed in detail above, presented himself as a dance lover and dance admirer. Some of his teachers were his "idols," and Naharin was his "guru." Then, Uri's dream finally came true, and he was able to learn a piece of choreography and perform it to an audience, the other half of the class. Whereas this specific situation of performance was new to him, he clarified how, during class, he would no longer even bother about being watched in general; Uri positioned himself as a self-confident performer inside Gaga class. Dancing in front of others had become normal to him.

Another "strategy" to identify oneself as a dancer, or at least one's dance potential, is speaking about being identified as a dancer by other participants. In this regard, Tamar talked about getting positive feedback from people whose opinion on her dancing in Gaga class she valued. Due to this experience, and by how she experienced herself moving, she even considered, "I even think I was a dancer in a previous life." Not only was Tamar a dancer today, as others with knowledge and the right to judge (insiders to the dance world) told her, but she might as well have been a dancer for all her life. Especially in Tamar's case, but in other cases too, the reason for her to recount narrative episodes such as this did not solely appear to be because she wanted to be viewed as a dancer. Rather, Tamar seemed to tell me this because she experienced being addressed as a dancer as a wow-moment. Eli, too, seemed to have received positive feedback on his dancing after his first years dancing Gaga: "And then a girl came to me, and … she asked me if I don't want to do anything with." Yet, different from Tamar, probably because the event lay further back in time, Eli already worked this event into his narrative: This experience was the initiator, the reason he got into the dance world. He remembered a dance project with other Gaga participants:

> It kind of failed the project, but it got me closer to dance and it got me start thinking about creating stuff and ah and ah and I was … there was another project I initiated, with two dancers, that I was actually managing it—I don't like the word choreographer, I don't know, I don't know. I feel it's too big it's too big. I created, I don't know and also it was quite clear that I was missing a lot of stuff. (Eli)

Throughout his interview, Eli appeared to be in an in-between situation of identifying himself with the dance world, "Since the beginning it seems that … me and a moving had good connection. Like people noticed me and I noticed them," on the one hand, and talking about himself as not being "good" enough to be part of this dance world, "missing a lot of stuff," on the other. The not being "good" remained from his old, embodied worldview, which changed due to

Gaga practice: "If you would ask me ten years ago, if I would dance, I would say no that's not my talent (laughing) and today I dance." This takes us to something else that Eli and Tamar had in common: Rather than just presenting their dancer identity, they were presenting it as a process, as a developing narrative. In this narrative, Gaga practice made them become dancers:

> So, this improvisation has brought, is waking a lot of creativity in me, because I had a lot of blockages and a lot of believes of: I cannot dance. I'm not worthy to dance. I was looking at dancer wow, you know, that this is not for me. And suddenly I became a dancer, I really became a dancer. (Tamar)

Other participants had childhood dance stories to tell to identify themselves as dancers: Ester clarified her expertise in dancing by talking about her strict ballet education. She mentioned her extraordinary talent for dance, which made her dance teacher offer her free additional dance classes:

> That gave me a lot, and here I think it connected to something that I have from the ten years old nine years when I did ballet dancing—and I loved it, it was the center of my life, I was dancing— ... and I went four times a week. It was really the center of my life. I went twice a week because I paid for it, and twice more because the Russian teachers called my mother and said: bring her for four times. Without paying. Just because she's got dancing material. (Ester)

Apart from this "outside" identification as a dancer, comparable to Eli's and Tamar's experiences, Ester also talked about her self-identification with dance in childhood: "I danced from the age of three to the age of twelve, that was the main part of my life, I wanted to be a ballerina, that was the idea, yeah, on my toes; and then I didn't dance for decades. I didn't continue, I stopped, when I was young, and I, I didn't continue."

Whereas Ester seemed "fast forward" in presenting her childhood dance history—the power of judgment of the Russian ballet teacher was unquestionable—other participants presented their childhood dance stories differently. For Sara, for example, mentioning her childhood dance experience became a possibility to create a history and narrative for her self-chosen belonging to the dance identity: her love for dance. She said, "Well I always kind of a little, you know, I was young I did ballet, I even had jazz and modern dance and dance on the toe, when I was younger, ya, I've always." Sara added that she really missed dancing and that she compensated her need for "expression" through dance by going to Gaga class.

Idan, too, experienced the need for "expression" and found it to be answered through Gaga. When he talked about himself in the context of dance, Idan made use of different narrative topics that others mentioned as well: He described his intense experience as a child watching a dance piece by Naharin on television. Thus, Idan had a long history as a dance admirer and was someone who knew Batsheva. Idan mentioned that becoming a dancer had been something he always wanted to be: "I think that I always appreciated moving, movement, and I think there is a part of me that always wanted to be a dancer, and somehow, I ended with—ended! Somehow, it went to visual art and that just gives me this place to explore myself through movement."

However, different from Uri who talked about his adult dance identity, Idan described it as if the dance identity was already part of his childhood story. Idan not only mentioned that he could possibly have become a dancer but also said he just loved to dance: "I love dancing—like dancing for me is super important, I used to go out and dance a lot, and now a structure like Gaga kind of replaced that need to go out and dancing." Idan talked about his experiences in the context of so-called conscious dance practices, here 5rythms. He described 5rythms as his first found alternative, being able to live his love for dance and acquiring the transcendental feeling dancing brings with it without going out, drinking, or taking drugs. Idan replaced his 5rythms practice with Gaga, which he enjoyed even more because of the possibility to dance alone; in 5rythms, people would try to make physical contact. Idan clarified that he could best connect to a dance practice such as Gaga, which, to him, is about "style" and not about "technique."

What the data from interviews could not tell was that there are various nonverbal strategies to create a dance identity for oneself. Identity could be established via clothing, for example: At the Suzanne Dellal Center, tourists could buy Gaga t-shirts from the Gaga staff; teachers and Gaga staff themselves would sometimes wear the t-shirts, which, as I overheard, were usually handed out to professional dancers who participated in intensive Gaga workshops in summer or winter. Identity could also be established by how people moved. As an Israeli who did not practice Gaga told me during an in-field conversation on September 17, 2019: "You can tell by looking at people—even when they are sitting—by the way they move [that they are doing Gaga]." Finally, social media offers manifold methods to identify oneself as part of the dance world: I witnessed participants posting videos of themselves doing Gaga-style dance improvisation at home, for example.

The "Aware" (in Bodily Control)

First, the implicit self-identification as someone who is aware manifests itself mainly in the way participants talk about their bodies: the way in which they describe their bodies and the use of Gaga language, the position they choose for their bodies within the narrative, perhaps as the narrative focus, and the evaluation of their own embodied change as positive, as something to strive for.

Second, the explicit and reflected self-identification as someone who is aware manifests itself in the following ways: In Uri's eyes, people "who are not necessarily at the same level of intimacy [like him] with their own body" were not able to enjoy Gaga class that much: "With someone who is not familiar with their body, Gaga can cause concern, can limit the participation and the experience." He also mentioned it to be potentially dangerous; one could get hurt if not knowing enough about one's own body. This was interesting for different reasons: Uri clearly valued his bodily awareness as an achievement to be made. Having achieved it, the body was better prepared for Gaga practice, and the experience is superior. The awareness of one's own body thus became a necessary step to be taken. Uri legitimized his long way to Gaga through yoga as something that guaranteed him a "better" Gaga experience than others. He was an insider; he could fully profit from Gaga. Uri's point of view might not have originated in Gaga discourse but in discourses related to other practices in which he was involved, such as yoga.

For Idan, being connected to or disconnected from one's own body made a difference in terms of art. "Good" art needed uniqueness, and this required connection to oneself:

> The way that I judge art in general, is that yes, as I said before, the most important thing is having your uniqueness. But I think that what's different about people, is how much they're connected to themselves. And you can see it through art. You can see art of people that are influenced by other things, and are not connected to themselves, and you can see it with—in movement too. If someone is a hundred percent in fantasy, and they don't have a sense of how they are in the space it's present. You know, that's what makes a better dancer, a dancer better, right? (Idan)

Without talking about himself, Idan, a freelance artist, revealed that he thought of himself as being connected, or at least trying to be connected, otherwise his art would not have any raison d'être. From Idan's point of view, lacking bodily awareness was visually observable and undesirable. Connectedness observable from the outside was the state to be reached.

In Dana's case, first, her whole narrative was about becoming aware of her own body, becoming connected. She described it as a process that she deliberately underwent. The not being aware and not being in control of the body was a state to be overcome and one that she was working toward overcoming. Second, as with Idan, there was an aesthetical question involved. However, Dana did not address it as being "connected," but being "illustrative": "That I saw people being very literal and very like illustrative, being illustrations of something instead of trying to be the idea, and in my school, because I'm a design student, the worst you can do is be illustrative."

Dana expressed her fears that she might look like those people, when moving. What Dana called an "illustrative" movement could be connected to Gaga's explicit and implicit claim that the Gaga practice is about not portraying the instructions and metaphors but enacting them, thus enacting quality rather than executing forms. This is probably an occasion where Dana's individual worldview, feeding on embodied social and cultural knowledge, met Gaga's worldview, feeding on similar social and cultural sources. Dana's meaning system was not shaped by Gaga here, but rather by Gaga-underlying discourses.

Tamar approached bodily awareness from another angle. She talked about people at trance parties who needed to take drugs to be "happy." Tamar said she did not need to take drugs at parties, as she could have the same experience without them. Her own body could be a source to the transcendental experience that people not doing Gaga would need drugs to attain.

Rather than othering, Ester was identifying herself with "proven" facts:

> I mean, you know, ah it's a known fact that the people who live to be a very old age very often, if they don't to physically activity, at last then what they do, they think a lot. They have creative ideas, they write or and as long as you have this inner activity, mental or physical. It's a good thing against gravity (smiling), you know, dragging you down, it uplifts you, that's the word right, it uplifts you.

Ester addressed people who were physically active as "they," yet she talked about being active at writing, being creative, and living to be very old—all things directly connectable to her own life. In another context, she claimed more clearly: "You know, I'm a physical person." According to her, being physically active and in bodily self-control was a better way of life—in terms of creativity and becoming old—and she formed part of this "physically active as bodily aware" community.

Eli presented himself as a demonstrative individual for the bodily aware: He took dance classes apart from Gaga, studied other somatic movement and body practices. He spoke about himself as someone who really investigated alternative knowledge on the body discussed in body and movement practices, and he had clear opinions and advice on what to do with Gaga: Gaga was not enough as a training method; it needed other training as well. Eli further explained how Gaga's body knowledge was just seen to be part of the same knowledge as other body and movement practices, not only because Naharin incorporated their knowledge—reflected and nonreflected—but also because people entered class with a body that was the same body with which they engaged in other practices. As with other participants, however, in Eli's bodily awareness and his awareness about specific awareness discourses, he thought himself to be different from most people: "I guess most of the people that you will talk to won't have a clue about the things and about other forms…"

Observing all these examples, a general line of argument seems to be as follows: I am bodily aware and thus superior to the others who are not. Furthermore, people seem to think the following: I am doing it right, and the others are doing it wrong. Not being bodily aware and in bodily control is clearly devalued. Whether this stems from Gaga, or whether it rather originates in general social and cultural values, is not possible to say, but it is also not important. The Gaga worldview and participants' worldview merge in these main ideas. What is interesting as a remark is that there seems to be a form of "competition" taking place when describing how aware one is, possibly in comparison to others.

9.3 Gaga Language Goes Worldview

As shown above, Gaga's embodied effect depends on the given instructions and their design. Moreover, for some participants, talking about Gaga seems to be impossible without relying on the vocabulary presented by Gaga-centered discourses, be it instructions, conversations with other participants, or material from media such as the website. Still, Gaga's instructions bear another transformative potential. Its instructions are taken by participants to provide a system of values and guidelines, which can be applied to life in general: Gaga language turns into a worldview, as the language successfully provides participants with answers to five "big questions" of "ontology," "espistemology," "axiology," "praxeology," and "cosmology" (Taves and Asprem 2018, 300).

This process looks as follows: Participants would listen to something the teacher said, which they thought to be a "true" observation of life in general or which they deemed to be advice they could take for their everyday lives and which they would keep in mind as such, as useful advice to remember and to allow oneself to be guided by. Perception and enactment of this advice, or rather their performance outside of class, happen to different extents.

As mentioned before, especially Sara and Tamar took part of their interview to frame Gaga language as particularly efficient in effecting wow-moments. In this context, they also took time to describe how, to them, Gaga language provided an attractive worldview applicable beyond Gaga class:

> I really think it's genius, cause I think that … there is an essence, which is like just godly, in a way. Because like every day I can explain to my husband what is Gaga, and I can explain it in a different way, and there is so, just so many true paradoxes that are so meaningful like: floating and falling, and, you know, to like fall down, which is like free-falling, the way you would think about life, you know, kind of. Free-falling but that you have such a strong engine that makes the free-falling like a float. You know, fire going up, but you're going down, like a hot-air-balloon, or … it's genius, it's really—and like one time I told him [her husband], it's, you know, to be able to find so many engines in you to start, because all the time, you know, all the time in a way you're dying and starting again, stopping and starting again, and, you know, dying and living again. So, to find that you have so much in you that you can start, and that you can start, and that you can start, it's mind blowing … It's so empowering. It's like empowering and humble at the same time. Everything is a paradox, I think, that's what's so genius, that's what Ohad, about the language. It really manages to hold all the time things that are, have tension between them. (Sara)

Sara expressed her impression that Gaga "language" was "empowering and humble" at the same time; it successfully incorporated many contradictions, which she knew from life. The amount and variety of "true paradoxes" she found in Gaga was endless: Every day she could explain Gaga differently to her husband. This meant she always experienced Gaga differently; she found an always changing connection between Gaga and her life. When talking about what she explicitly took from class to life, she named falling-floating, stopping-starting, associated with the "life cycle" of living-dying, and empowering-humble. Gaga's "mind-blowing" effect was due to this variation of instructions and contradictions, which she found her life reflected in.

Though Sara named this as characteristic to Gaga, the ever-changing experience probably depended on the ever-changing individual emotional-habitual state in which she entered class. Rather than the power of the language of the instructions themselves, potentially applying Gaga language as ethics to situations outside class seems to be connected to the experience filter with which participants enter the class. Nevertheless, the individual experience filter echoes in Gaga language in a way that shows collective tendencies. How Gaga language is understood, also in a "life ethics" context, is collective, not only individual. This is because individual experience filters arise in the context of culturally and socially shaped meaning-making, where a specific experience is addressed using specific language metaphors (see Lakoff and Johnson 2003). For example, not only does the Gaga language contain instructions to move, but instructions could also be understood as metaphors. Since Gaga is a movement practice, many instructions convey movement advice. These instructions could be understood as "orientational metaphors," to use Lakoff and Johnson's (14–21) terminology, and their understanding is shared by the social and cultural community that Sara was part of.

An orientational metaphor that Sara mentioned was "falling." "Free-falling" was how she experienced life, her specific metaphor for life, yet falling as a downward movement is likely to be understood by more participants in a similar way. Gaga offers metaphors such as the image of a "hot-air balloon," an image of something moving and staying upwards, to overcome the sensation of free-falling, which held the potential of a pleasant image not only to Sara alone. Sara did not stop here; she then connected the floating instead of free-falling, probably through the image of hot-air balloons, to the metaphor of finding engines to start over again from stopping, which she then connected with dying and living again. Still, it remains the same idea. In the context of Sara's interpretation, overcoming a fall or stop by not falling or starting again is understandable as overcoming difficulties, but also as acknowledging the circular and repetitive character of the whole process of overcoming difficulties. When Sara switched from inhibiting falling to being able to restart the engine again and again and again, she connected an orientational metaphor to an "ontological metaphor," "our experience of physical objects and substances" (Lakoff and Johnson 2003, 16), such as "engines" and their "starting," "stopping," and "restarting." Ontological metaphors, too, are shared by a social and cultural community.

The ethical guidance Tamar took from Gaga was similar to that of Sara:

All those learnings, I'm take them in my outside world, of course, it doesn't stay in the thing ... There is so much wisdom, so much wisdom. One of my first teachers ... she said something so simple and so stupid, and she said: and when you fall you fall, and if you fall you fall, and it's true, if you fall you fall, you stand up and you carry on. And so many things that you can take from the directions about your dance in your life, you know, it's lot of wisdom, a lot of wisdom. and consciousness basically, I take it on a very spiritual level this Gaga—but again I'm a yogi, so, (laughs) I don't know.

Tamar stated clearly that she took the Gaga language "on a spiritual level" and into her "outside worlds"; Gaga was "learning" and "wisdom" for life. She, like Sara, was especially impressed by the metaphors around falling. Yet, she did not describe it as falling and inhibiting the fall by the float, but as falling and standing up again. However, this carried similar signification to Sara's starting, stopping, and starting again. Gaga's instructions seem to hold one key movement theme with great metaphorical potential: the instructions trying to make people overcome gravity. The orientation downwards appears to be connected to life situations in which one is experiencing a negative emotional state due to having problems originating in physical pain or eventually leading to the experience thereof, physically feeling heavy. An instruction giving uplifting advice, just from the metaphorical content, thus has the potential to be taken as a metaphor to overcome all kinds of experienced down situations. The ontological metaphor of the engine and the restarting covers the same intension; the ontological metaphor seems to become a metaphor to an orientational metaphor.

Other parts of the Gaga language are also used as advice to overcome unpleasant moments in life. There is more to Gaga than overcoming being "down" or "stagnating." Idan, for example, chose the "effort" addressed in Gaga instructions as a useful idea in his life:

> Or it's funny how they sometimes, they disconnect you, how they connect you to effort. And how to experience effort, and those moments of that really requires you to work hard. when you associate something positive with effort, it's already not that bad. You know, when they're like, when you are doing something and it's really difficult and then like: connect to the sense of effort and just like, kind of like: make peace with the sense of effort; it's already, it's already becoming effortless, cause it's like, you feel like you're in control of the effort. You choose to do. You know it's like, it's not just because I was told to do this task, that is difficult, it's like I take charge over the effort. Or just associating joy with effort ... And it's [a] super important lesson to life. Because we all, we all have to constantly do things we don't like, or there is hard—you know life's hard (laughs). Life's hard for everyone, and if you just learn to associate everything that's hard with joy, just becomes much better. That is... the clichés ... you know Ohad's piece of cake.

Interestingly, for Idan, the metaphor he could take from class was not only about the verbalization in instruction but also about the instruction carried out, the enacted instruction. It was about the actual effort experience that was made positive. Idan incorporated this embodied experience of doing something that required much effort, where the effort was then addressed with positive evaluation, into everyday effort situations. First, Idan described how, in running, he could convert his effort experience as an experience of fun. Second, Idan mentioned that "life's hard for everyone," and being able to still see it as "joy[ful]" would make it "much better." At the end, he made a connection to an actual verbal metaphor used in Gaga to make effort more supportable: Idan experienced "piece of cake" as a metaphorical equivalent to "enjoy the effort."

Uri, on the other hand, took "silliness" as advice for his life:

> One of the first new sensations I had going to Gaga classes was the opportunity to be a child. To be happy and carefree and to move around like a child without inhibition to be silly—I love the silly word. I think it's a fantastic metaphor. He's a genius it's really so much about being silly, and let yourself be silly, and enjoy the silliness. And it's in the spirit, it's not the silly movement, it's the silly sensation, it's the silly mindset, not to be serious. So, ya, I experienced a lot of things that are completely in the spirit in the mentality in in the area of feelings and ... that's completely not physical, and it happens in the class. And you asked about taking away and a view, ya, it goes with me ... it's not that you need—but there is an opportunity to be silly in other ways, in life, and not to take things too seriously in life and to take pleasure in simple things like movement and so, ya, I take, I think I take more balance with me.

According to Uri, what he gained from class was the possibility to move around like a child, "happy and carefree." He connected this experience to the "fantastic metaphor" of silly. In his eyes, the invention and introduction of "silly" characterized Naharin as a "genius." Silly did not refer to "silly movement," but the "silly sensation," which represented "not to be serious"—here Uri used the Gaga language to explain Gaga language perception. Uri stated that, in class, he experienced specific emotions as embodied reactions to instructions, such as the "silly mindset," that were "completely not physical." Uri told me about this episode because I asked about "taking away," and he mentioned that from "silly," he took away being silly in life: "not to take things too seriously in life," "to take pleasure in simple things like movement," and to find "more balance."

In conclusion, the ethical potential of the Gaga language can be connected to the concept of a worldview. Gaga instructions are becoming a guiding principle to one's life on a different level than body transformation: on a more explicit psychological level, it seems. Yet, the whole body is involved in perception, thereby experiencing, enacting, and attributing the Gaga language worldview status. This is due to both language's metaphorical character and the embodied character of experience in general. Participants see "life topics" reflected in Gaga, and a self-reflected participant can explain the whole thing:

> Gaga is a good tool for many things, I think. but also I think it encapsulate inside of it a lot of philosophy as well, which helps you to cope. and I think it helps you to cope in ah since I think that inside body movement we actually—that's my theory—weak or—guess a lot of people have this theory—a lot of our behaviors are actually body behaviors that we translate into be a mental behavior. translated to body movement: ... we're talking this way, ya, he's a flexible person, we don't mean that he is flexible in his body or ya. So, I think that a lot of the methods that are used in Gaga ... you use in other fields of life ... when I'm doing the dishes, I can indulge the effort and then I can really enjoy life more ... or falling into movement, or how do you translate the body things that happen into your own life. And, of course, also in Gaga you deal with separations ... I separate between my hand and my shoulder, but I can also separate from my mentality, you know in mentality I can be flexible in the body and unflexible in my soul, but so, there are people like that. (Eli)

The explicit worldview potential of Gaga seems to be perceived as the "genius" component of Gaga, or, as Tamar put it, the Gaga language has "so much wisdom." The other way around, Gaga's metaphors, especially orientational metaphors concerning gravity, can also be used to describe life experiences: "It's [physical activity] a good thing against gravity (smiling), you know, dragging you down, it uplifts you, that's the word right, it uplifts you" (Ester).

9.4 The Mastering Gaga Component

The "mastering Gaga component" was one of the first things observed in contact with participants and recorded as an interesting phenomenon to address. It revealed much about the impact Gaga practice had on participants' lives, as well as the impact participants' lives had on their Gaga practice. With Gaga entering their lives—or, better, their life narratives—participants (1) mentioned conditioning their bodies for Gaga practice, (2) started to search for a change in lifestyle that would bring them closer to the Gaga world or the dance world with which Gaga is associated, and (3) felt the desire to become Gaga teachers.

Having discussed Gaga practice in connection with an Israeli society and culture shaped by so-called neoliberal topics, the idea of mastering Gaga practice seems a logical consequence of contemporary social and cultural discourses and tendencies. The main principle of Gaga practice, namely, the body as a yet-to-be finished product under constant construction, guarantees the participant who really "listens" self-betterment in many ways: The result is a more enjoyable life with a more enjoyable body. Moreover, as shown above, the participant also has the possibility to connect via body knowledge transformation to the identities of a dancer or a bodily aware person. The Gaga practice enables participants to present themselves as they want to be seen by others. While there is said to be no such thing as being "good" at Gaga, participants believe they could reach a different Gaga practice level by preparing their bodies for it. Furthermore, for some participants, the embodied output of Gaga class does not seem to be enough. Either they enjoy the experience of Gaga during practice (the embodied output) and are so "consumed" by it that they want to make it the center of their lives, or they seek another level of identification with Gaga—more from a self-perceptive perspective—by becoming a teacher and reaching a higher level of legitimation and unquestionable certification, which helps them, as members of the "new middle class," justify and clarify their identity to themselves and to others and to keep self-optimizing.

Getting Better at Gaga

The data also reveals that it is commonly believed that an embodied effect only comes with time and involvement in practice, and one must make an effort to get there. Some participants, such as Uri, mentioned that their yoga experience and ongoing yoga practice was the perfect way to prepare their bodies for Gaga practice. The preparation culminated in a peak experience during Gaga class. Tamar mentioned that she had just started a new movement practice that she found to be "terrible difficult" and more "gym oriented." She hoped and legitimized her doing it, which she needed to do because it was "so not yogi" and Gaga, that it could have a positive effect on her "dance": "My dance gonna improve, my yoga gonna improve." Tamar reported that she experienced a "journey" in the other movement practice, too. The practice, like yoga or Gaga, had the potential to fulfill the specific needs to become a setting for extraordinary experience: "A new journey. And it's difficult and I force myself to go and now it's already three four weeks that I'm going and I feel wow, it's getting easier and I'm already excited to go." Yet, Tamar chose not to give the non-Gaga practice the same significance; she emphasized, "It's like, just now it's a practice to enhance my other practices." Another perspective was added by Eli. He stated that Gaga is even not "enough" training to have a fit and healthy body: "Enough for what? Gaga alone is enough for fun, is enough for a good time recreation, for a bit … of physical activity." In Eli's eyes, Gaga did not offer proper cardiovascular training, nor did it make one's body particularly flexible compared to the effect of other practices. Gaga's techniques did not practice enough switching between calming and relaxing one's body and being dynamic. However, at another point of the interview, Eli appreciated the "flow of movement" as the main and great idea of Gaga, and he even said, "So, I think Gaga has it all inside." Eli's guiding argumentation throughout the interview, as mentioned above, was presenting his Gaga identity or his desired Gaga identity, alongside his identity as someone who knew and could talk much about the body in general, one who was already one step beyond and "wiser" than a common Gaga participant. Eli mentioned that he overcame Gaga's "limitations" individually not only by doing other practices but also by bringing his body knowledge from other practices into Gaga. He then practiced Gaga differently, more effectively, and thus "better" than others.

Gaga as Entry to a New Life

Eli mentioned that doing Gaga made him strive to become a dancer. Due to all of the experiences in the context of Gaga, his life changed: "Of course, it changed my life. The, ya, only the fact that it introduced me into a world of movement, that's one thing." Eli told me that due to his Gaga experience, he started studying dance: "It's a school for grown-ups who want to study dance and they don't have any background." He intensified his Gaga participation during a phase of unemployment. Inspired by the Gaga environment, Eli even became a professional somatic practitioner. He made movement the center of his life. Eli said he grew up in an environment where "definitely boys didn't dance," and he would never have thought to become a dancer. In this context, becoming a dancer meant a maximum transformation. Eli described it as a psychological transformation invoked by his Gaga practice. He changed his attitude toward dance and learning to dance: "Because if you would ask me ah ten years ago if I would dance, I would say no that's not my talent (laughing) and today I dance. … So, I don't believe in talent anymore, I belief that a you learn everything." Gaga practice impacted Eli's life not only by influencing the activities he chose to occupy himself with and dedicate his time to, his "outside" identity, but also by transforming his mindset, his "inside" identity. Throughout Eli's narration, Gaga practice remained central to the life change and to his changed lifestyle and mindset. Not only did he state that Gaga was still central to his movement practice and that his changed lifestyle was acted out in the context of Gaga classes, but he also connected all his changes to Gaga practice: By his newly gained knowledge on the body, he "demystified" what was going on in Gaga practice. By becoming a somatic therapist, he started doing something "quite close," or as close as he could get, to becoming part of Gaga Movement Ltd., Batsheva, or the professional dance world in general, whose dancers turned to somatic therapy for treatment.

Gaga practice is an entry into a new life for other participants as well. Several people described how doing Gaga brought them to deepen their relation to movement and body practices. Rahel, for example, became a somatic therapist, too; Dana started frequenting dance and choreography workshops in Europe up to creating performances and participatory movement formats herself; and Idan mentioned that he wanted to get more artistically involved in the dance world.

Becoming a Gaga Teacher

Another motif that I came across was Gaga participants being particularly interested in becoming a Gaga teacher. Especially after having had extraordinary experiences as wow-moments during an intense weekend or weekday workshop, participants would ask the Gaga teacher about the procedure to become a teacher. Others mentioned during in-field conversations that they had considered becoming Gaga teachers. It seemed as if participants required a certified identification with Gaga, which gave them such a heightened experience. Potentially because participants find that they are not able to become Gaga teachers, they start searching for other ways to "certify" their identity as body and movement therapists, experts, or choreographers:

> I'm not a Gaga teacher, I guess if I would fight for it, I would be—I find a dissonance between Gaga the organization and the Gaga language; the Gaga organization I find is as a very rough organization, ya, you have to go to this procedure to be a teacher, blabla blabla, you haven't been a dancer, have been a dancer. (Eli)

9.5 Gaga Passion

It was shown that Gaga practice has the potential to become central to participants' lives, and that participants would transform their lives to make Gaga practice central to their biographies, undergoing and narrating conversion toward it. Gaga was shown to play the role and function of Taves and Asprem's (2018) worldview in participants' lives. However, the greater the extent to which participants acknowledge the part that Gaga practice plays in their stories and thus in their lives, the more the phenomenon seems to fit another phenomenon that psychologists describe and try to understand: dedicating extraordinary amounts of time to leisure activities, especially sports. Conversion and worldview thus seem to be inseparable from what psychologists claim as characteristic of the phenomenon commonly termed addiction. This phenomenon, already partially discussed above in the context of wow-moments and their potentially addictive effect, could possibly explain why conversion to Gaga becomes traceable or why Gaga takes up the role of a worldview in narration. From the data described above, it is possible to deduce that conversion toward a worldview, and this new worldview's potential, is bound to a particular "investment" made by the participants. Not only is it an investment of time, but it depends on participants deliberately choosing a Gaga "mindset" or, without explicitly choosing it, still being influenced by it in thinking and acting.

In the above, I used the concept of addiction to grasp different sorts of (narrated) body knowledge related to addiction as a developing process and to show how extraordinary experience, addiction, and body knowledge were related. Here I introduce the concept of passion as an alternative and open framework to lay out the interrelation of practicing and a practice's worldview potential. "Passion toward an activity is a notion that refers to engaging in a beloved activity that one finds important, and invests time and energy into it" (de la Vega et al. 2016, 326). I propose "energy" as standing for the necessary holistic, physical-psychological involvement of participants in the form of deliberate self-identification and self-preparation. The passion concept includes the notion of "harmonious" passion, "when one likes the activity, freely selects to engage in it, and when internalizes the activity into the self" (326), and "obsessive" passion. In the latter, the individual is no longer able to choose their involvement freely; rather, the engagement is "rigidly controlled," and the function of the activity in creating "self-esteem" and helping to "escape problems" plays a main part in the individually felt need to go on practicing and the inability to stop it. Obsessive passion causes an individual to spend time on the activity that would otherwise be spent on "other important life activities." Different from harmonious passion, obsessive passion leads to an inability to control the time spent, as the individual might experience "withdrawal" effects, for example (326).

From this point of view, Gaga does not only occupy the place of an activity for which participants can develop a harmonious passion, but from what participants told and what was just discussed, the potential also exists for Gaga practice to lead to obsessive passion. However, there is no need to state that participants experience obsessive passion when they "convert" to Gaga and Gaga becomes their worldview: As the data shows, there is no such thing as either/or; the transformation of passion from harmonious to obsessive found to be reflected in the context of Gaga takes place on a continuum. If the passion concept is translated as such a process, instead of as a concept of two existing categories, then "conversion" could indeed be understood as a process of becoming "passionate" to different degrees, resulting in different stages of worldview incorporation.

Conversion, worldview, and now passion—what is the take-away? To an academic study of religion, it is, of course, of great interest to see how body practices like Gaga without explicit or spiritual reference, affiliation, or leitmotif, even without explicit secular framing, take such a fundamental place in narrated experiences, biographies, and identities. This observation supports approaches of scholars like Taves (2020b), who asks for a reframing of the study of religion as a study of worldviews. Moreover, it indicates that the narrative action of structuring "life" around a fixed, consciously or unconsciously chosen set of enacted and experienced body knowledge, a fixed set of aesthetics, is socially and culturally inscribed. Vice versa, it proofs that a quest for the fundamental "life" impact of certain aesthetics on people's experience is inevitably met with (1) the narration of conversion, (2) establishing an aesthetic-related worldview, and (c) the verbalization of passion from those who are interviewed. Still, the real strength of this chapter lies not in general observations but rather in an in-depth analysis of data; in showing how conversion, worldview, and passion manifest in narration; in demonstrating how and what kind of conclusions can be drawn from narrations regarding the unfolding of a practice's aesthetics.

10

Concluding Thoughts

As initially mentioned, the research and the book that stems from it aim to be, above all, an encompassing analysis of neo-spiritual aesthetics, exemplified on Gaga practice, with a cultural studies and study-of-religion perspective—no more and no less. This analysis was thoroughly carried out in the preceding chapters. The research was conducted and the book written based on the assumption that practices affect senses; and via senses—bodies; and via bodies—cognition; and via cognition—the social and cultural participation of individuals—an assumption confirmed by the results found and described. The analytical methods of choice, body knowledge, ritual studies, movement analysis, and qualitative narration analysis, helped to uncover the mechanisms at work that produced an embodied effect of neo-spiritual Gaga practice, which consequently influenced participants' lives and worldviews beyond class.

Aesthetics of Gaga

The book unveiled an embodied effect caused by practicing Gaga of different levels of "intensity"—from a temporary change in the emotional-habitual state of participants to a perceived healing effect and lasting increase in well-being, and the incorporation of Gaga-related values or embodied transformations as a central way of life and worldview. People had moments of extraordinary experiences. They felt very different, in a positive way, after having taken class; they discovered their identity as a dancer; and they considered Gaga to have a healing effect. They also observed their bodies changing; they connected more to their bodily sensations and attributed their significant improvement in well-being to this fact. They also saw this body state as something to be achieved, a goal in life. They found themselves applying their "Gaga body" to other areas of life, outside of class, and they became demonstrative bodies for Gaga's body concept and movement possibilities. Finally, they were even influenced in their meaning-making.

As already mentioned, participant observation led to the assumption that this effect was related to and created in an aesthetic interplay of incoming sensory information and bodily change induced by (1) the movements that participants enacted in class—Gaga's techniques, (2) how and by whom movement was introduced in instructions, (3) the ritual environment, and (4) the individual preconditions. (1) Gaga's techniques included the following: focused attention on particular sensory stimuli in or outside the own body alongside open monitoring, the play with and expansion of peripersonal space, the use of prosthetic perception, an emphasis on the skin's sensory system, willingly controlled versus uncontrolled movement, an increase in movement range, the creation of Gaga-specific strength and posture, movement-efficient strength, "balanced tone" in the sense of relaxed or only necessarily tensed muscles during action, a switch of movement qualities, ongoing movement, and endurance of effort with "pleasure" as an emotional reinterpretation of body knowledge. The techniques became effective as participants enacted the instructions. The enactment of instructed movements introduced body knowledge related to an experience of flow, losing the sense of time during class, or a runner's high, a heightened positive emotional state after class, for example. It also led to an embodied change, physically and psychologically, in implicit or explicit character, where physical pain and tension and, in relation to this, psychological pain and tension were released. Moreover, it helped to create implicit and explicit Gaga-typical body knowledge that participants could use to represent themselves outside of class and which affected their body scheme and perceptual order. (2) However, the enactment of instructions was found to be directly related to the teachers' particular "technical" role. Verbal instruction, visual body topography enacted by the teachers, and the teachers' emotional-habitual state were successfully simulated in participants' bodies. They directly became body knowledge effective and transforming. They enhanced the experience caused by kinesthetic sensations of the own movement. (3) Besides, the ritual environment contributed to a setting that made Gaga extraordinary to its participants. It provided many different aesthetically effective sensory stimuli and helped effective body knowledge transformation along. Ritual characteristics entailed, for example, the dance studio known to the participants as the training place for the admired Batsheva dancers, the perceived agency of teachers, or the rules and spacing that rendered teacher movements and instructions the main sensory stimuli. (4) Finally, incoming sensory information affected already affected bodies, bodies with individual and collective (due to socialization and cultural enculturation) body knowledge, bodies with physical and psychological preconditions. The longing for self-optimization, self-betterment, and well-being and the individual's responsibility to it; a demand for certain aesthetics and aesthetic experiences; the admiration for arts and the search for belonging, but also embodied stress, sorrow, happiness—all this and more formed body knowledge and embodied base to incoming sensory stimulation and the creation and transformation of body knowledge.

Furthermore, Gaga explicitly, verbally and nonverbally, revealed a specific body and movement concept that participants were led to enact. In Gaga practice, the body was understood and visualized in a way that highlighted the core muscles as central; the body was depicted as being in constant movement; traditional body parts became regrouped in new ways and under new names, allowing for a holistic perception of the body as a sensory system. Now, placing the findings in relation to social and cultural discourses or phenomena described by others demonstrated that these explicit aesthetics were not random, but Gaga shared its aesthetics with other practices.

Aesthetics of Neo-Spirituality

I will end the book with generalizing some of my research results toward the characteristics of neo-spiritual aesthetics beyond the context of Gaga practice:

Neo-spiritual aesthetics incorporate a group of relatively (!) fixed technical characteristics and are thus comparable to each other on the meta level of body knowledge:

- awareness training—focused attention and open monitoring of bodily (intern) and environmental stimuli
- alteration and relaxation of bodily tension (introduced, e.g., via the changes of muscular contraction and relaxation, or moments of deep muscular contraction) and creation of a bodily state of "balanced tone"
- creation of movement efficiency—regarding the muscular effort involved in relation to the movement result
- creation of proprioceptive control by training fast reaction, by alternating between self-willed and spontaneous movement, or by training the ability to enact all kinds of movement qualities
- increasing flexibility and movement range

- alteration of body scheme and peripersonal space
- creation of strength and stamina
- introduction of postural changes toward a commonly perceived optimum posture—grounded, erect, with a strong core
- and alteration of (embodied) emotional states.

Many neo-spiritual practices, though not Gaga, also use specific breath techniques or moments of stillness in combination with techniques of contemplation. Specific to Gaga is the focus on enhanced skin sensation and the incorporation of the skin as a main sensory system into the body scheme. Depending on the neo-spiritual practice, the techniques are designed to raise heartbeat and body temperature and to create a situation of flow, causing perceived emotional highs and moments of "transcendence." Neo-spiritual practices also often explicitly aim at enabling participants to free themselves from movement-restricting thoughts of judgment, or they invite the practice of nonverbal self-expression and moments of individual creativity. Additionally, though neo-spiritual practices can be seen as sharing these techniques of body knowledge creation and transformation, the realization of such techniques is practice-subjective, as each practice uses its own version of vocabulary and its own variation of practical anatomy of the body. Even the technical methods like touch/no touch vary from method to method. Nevertheless, typical to neo-spiritual practices seems to be the use of embodied imagination as the main technical method. Finally, while neo-spiritual practices can be characterized as sharing some techniques in common, however, not all the practices that share the same techniques can necessarily be characterized as neo-spiritual. This is the case with t'ai chi, qigong, postural yoga, the Alexander technique, and Feldenkrais, for example, which share techniques with Gaga, but only are to be understood as neo-spiritual under particular social circumstances.

In a next step, similar techniques of practices can be observed to establish a canon of neo-spiritual body topographies. Body parts of great importance and emphasis in Gaga practice, for example, are the core muscles in the lower stomach—addressed by the concept of lena—and the pelvic floor muscles—addressed by the concept of pika and activated by the concept of yoyo or by playing with the distance between the sitting bones. These body parts, core muscles and pelvic floor muscles, are equally central to body concepts in other practices such as Pilates or t'ai chi: Pilates aims at training the "powerhouse"; the powerhouse has been addressed in various ways by Pilates techniques (Brignell 2009, 33). In contemporary t'ai chi, the "tan t'ien" is emphasized as a place where movement initiates (Newth 2006, 27). T'ai chi further shares with Gaga other similarities, such as the grounded body position with slightly bent knees, the head imagined as floating up from the spine, or the idea that there is an immanent and hidden bodily energy, the "chi," activatable as needed (25–8). The ongoing and fluid movement required and practiced in Gaga is something Gaga shares with t'ai chi (26). The "animalistic" movement range and movement possibilities—introduced by moving like an "animal" or crawling on the floor—appear to be a commonly shared feature of new body practice approaches subsumed under the category of "animal movements," such as "Animal Flow."

Techniques hold a particular place in neo-spiritual practices, as they are a possibility to create collective body knowledge implicitly and tacitly via the enactment of movements that participants are encouraged to follow. This guarantees the creation of collective body knowledge and thus collective experience. The techniques form an important part of the practice's aesthetics. In neo-spiritual practices, the situation might be that there is no fixed script of techniques to follow in the sense of literary instructions to be repeated, yet there is a technical meta-canon guiding the instruction design and instructed movement. In Gaga, for example, teachers appear to be free to choose instructions from a variety of techniques, which are adaptable, according to their judgment based on observations of their own body and that of the group of participants. The collective effect of neo-spiritual aesthetics such as Gaga depends on teachers' own body knowledge, which they acquired by following the technical canon and which remains with them as an implicit or explicit memory source from which to lead the classes.

(Neo-spiritual) aesthetics evolve in a network of interrelating sensory inputs of which neo-spiritual practices' techniques and worldviews only play a minor part. Though neo-spiritual practices focus on body movement and bodily transformation achieved by a self-responsible participant, it is not only and mainly the enactment of movement that affects participants' bodies and creates neo-spiritual aesthetics and a neo-spiritual experience effect. Rather, neo-spiritual aesthetics evolve in a network of relations, where the enactment of movement interrelates with many other sensory inputs affecting the participants. This is, on the one hand, because aesthetically effective body knowledge is created not only in conscious movement but also before. The main sensory input for the creation of body knowledge is not the enactment of movement, though this would play a significant role in the perceived body change and explicit body knowledge. The main sensory input seems to be provided by the movement instructions given by the teacher and, more generally, the ritual environment.

On the other hand, neo-spiritual practices' aesthetics are foretold by the preconditions of participants entering the practice. Neo-spiritual aesthetics expand beyond the time and space frame of a practice, and even beyond any material or immaterial practice context. They are to be searched for and found in collectively and individually shaped preconditions of an individual participant. Popular discourse about body practices might tend to depict the conscious and explicit bodily participation of participants as causing the embodied effect of practice. However, it is the unconscious and implicit consumption of sensory input arising in the context of class that mainly impacts body knowledge and the resulting explicitly noticeable and narrated experience.

Neo-spiritual aesthetics carry and transform neo-spiritual worldviews. Even though neo-spiritual practices do not openly state explicit worldviews, they cannot but carry out a certain worldview via the bodily transformation they evoke. For first, they do not exist in empty space, and culturally and socially relevant discourses implicitly and explicitly shaped those who developed the practices' techniques, shaped the techniques that formed the source for the development of the practice, and continue to shape neo-spiritual practice participants' bodies, body knowledge, body schemes, perceptual orders, and social and cultural modes of interaction. For second, by transforming bodies according to relatively fixed ritualized techniques and an agenda—be it implicit or explicit—neo-spiritual practices nevertheless reveal themselves as practices with a worldview. The worldview is transformed to participants by affecting and changing bodies and therefore their cognitive mechanisms. The worldview therefore appears in the implicit and explicit body image and movement style, the body topography, promoted by a neo-spiritual practice.

Neo-spiritual aesthetics typically recreate social and cultural standards. Though neo-spiritual practices seem to offer (and want to offer) their participants extraordinary alternatives to ordinary cultural and social norms and experiences, via their own aesthetics, they reestablish the norms and answer to aesthetical demands: Neo-spiritual aesthetics typically guarantee and promote "self-optimization," "well-being," and "healing" by offering bodily transformation toward a physiological and/or psychological ideal. Moreover, congruent with an aesthetization discourse inseparable from an aesthetization demand and aesthetization used as commodity, neo-spiritual practices become spaces for "extraordinary experience."

Neo-spiritual aesthetics are intrinsically interwoven with embodiment discourses and popular scientific knowledge. Another characteristic of neo-spiritual practices is that they all depart from an embodiment framework and embodied understanding of the body-mind unit. They do not only build on the knowledge that body, environment, and cognition are inseparable entities; they seem to use this knowledge as a basis for the development of their own techniques. They guide participants' sensory focuses, they use embodied ways of learning, they dehierarchize established sensory orders and introduce new sensory systems, always oriented toward the goal of letting participants achieve a certain body topography and thus worldview. By doing so, neo-spiritual practices function as examples and diagrams of contemporary societies' state-of-the-art discussions and knowledge production and show how popular and accessible the embodied cognition paradigm has become.

Furthermore, open-access natural science journals hold numerous neuroscientific and (neuro)psychological research conducted on the effects of neo-spiritual practices' techniques under the headline of "somatic" or "meditative" movement practices. These scientific papers depict the possible effects of participation on the mental and physiological well-being and the therapeutic impact of practices using embodied techniques that potentially resolve as traumatic, stressful, and painful perceived embodied states. The articles in these papers tell another story: There seems to be a downright social need to prove the "worth" of neo-spiritual practices, the need to explain their supposedly positive effect, on the one hand; on the other hand, there is a particular group of scientists dedicated to and interested in understanding the creation of perceived "well-being" from an embodied cognition point of view. Natural science, too, has become dispositif for the tradition of social and cultural discourses without a cultural studies meta-reflection of the social and cultural trends. Neo-spiritual practices profit from their own "scientification," as they can use research results to promote participation by claiming a scientifically guaranteed effect of practicing on well-being.

Neo-spiritual aesthetics are not what they appear; neither are they secular nor are to be taken leisurely. Neo-spiritual practices present themselves as secular leisure-time activities—secular here used in the sense that they do not state or promote an explicit worldview, but also because they explicitly refrain from addressing anything beyond the "safe zone" of participants' bodily sensations. They seem to be designed to not promote or evoke any political and cultural discussions. Besides, they seem to try to set themselves apart from the "religious" and "spiritual" sphere, not only by remaining "neutral" and without declared viewpoints as in the case of the political or cultural, but rather by connecting their techniques to popular discourses marked as scientifically provable and objective knowledge. The latter is important insofar as neo-spiritual practices are, of course, practiced by individuals with undeniably individual viewpoints: Neo-spiritual practices can thus never remain neutral-ground but do always become dispositifs for nonsecular, non–leisure-time discourses. However, due to the secularizing function of scientifically provable, objective knowledge discourses that practices structurally connect to, they maintain a secular stance and participate in processes of secularization themselves.

In addition, framing neo-spiritual practices as leisure-time activities causes to oversee their great impact on practice participants. Neo-spiritual aesthetics cause participants to experience signs of "addiction," or at least "passion." Neo-spiritual practices' participants centralize practicing and aesthetics; they attribute them with extraordinariness and hold them in high esteem. Finally, neo-spiritual aesthetics unfold their worldview potential via participants' bodies, especially if participants repeatedly partake in practicing.

Final Words

In conclusion, is neo-spiritual aesthetics even a thing to an academic study of religion? I wholeheartedly argue "yes." First, talking of neo-spiritual aesthetics puts the focus on socially and culturally relevant phenomena that are often overlooked. Neo-spiritual aesthetics not only influence an individual's social and cultural participation, but they also reflect the state of the art of social and cultural norms. None of the humanities seem to be better equipped to understand these phenomena with experience focus and worldview impact than the study of religion. The study of religion in turn can profit from the framework of neo-spiritual aesthetics, as it paves the way for an alternative understanding of study-of-religion research objects by their aesthetics, which needs neither a functional, based on social demands, nor a phenomenological definition of religion or neo-spirituality and which, most importantly, by being a cultural studies approach, remains a critical stance on the tendencies of naturalizing religion on body level. However, the ultimate argument to taking neo-spiritual aesthetics into focus might be: Neo-spiritual aesthetics are everywhere. They are not limited to the aesthetics of neo-spiritual practices. The somatization and aesthetization of traditional "religion" and its practices, the "technical canon" of neo-spiritual aesthetics and embodied imagination used by ritual leaders, has become incorporated in traditional religious rituals or added to the religious sphere via the invention of new rituals. To understand any kind of contemporary religious phenomena now seems to involve the understanding of neo-spiritual aesthetics.

Notes

Introduction

1 I found that this was handled differently depending not only on the cultural and social sphere but also on the teacher, it seemed. In Israel, people would leave the room if they had to go to the toilet urgently and then return. Furthermore, in some Munich workshops, for example, the rules were followed more strictly: Leaving the classroom meant having to wait for the next class to start.
2 At workshops in Munich, I experienced that if there were mirrors, they had to be covered.
3 For a more vivid impression, have a look at the YouTube channel of Gaga Movement Language (2022): https://www.youtube.com/channel/UCJuG8LobRKuB D0134W6hoBA/featured.

Interlude: A Body-Focused Research Method

1 In the context of the research on Gaga, in terms of AoR, some interesting data collection methods had to be excluded: (1) No video-taping during class was allowed, meaning that there was no possibility to use audiovisual media to enhance memorizing of what had taken place or to transcribe the videos as source for a detailed description of class (see DeWalt and DeWalt 2011, 164), or even to use the audiovisual material as source for innovative interviewing methods, as Gore et al. (2012) propose. (2) There were no financial and knowledge resources to conduct a "medically informed research program," as Koch (2015) demands, which could have included the measurement of heart rate, hormones, and muscle tone, for example, though this could be a possibility for a further elaboration of the research project in future.
2 An interesting point, however, is that when remaining self-reflexive as the observing researcher, what I never reached was a moment of flow. I could only experience it in Gaga classes, in which I participated not as a participant observer and researcher but just as an ordinary participant.
3 Being an Israeli-Jew is understood as partaking in Israel's high culture and customs, which, due to Israel's history, are influenced by Judaism. It is not necessarily

connected to observing Jewish rites or sharing Jewish beliefs (see Shavit and Shavit 2016).

1 Influential Culturescape

1 Yossi Naharin even wrote his master's thesis on "the therapeutic benefits of Gaga" (Friedes Galili 2015, 386).
2 The "injury" theme, too, is a recurrent theme of different movement and dance practice founders, to whom their injury or illness is said to have become the impetus to develop a new practice approach, which is based on what they perceived as having helped them to heal from a condition, where common medicine told them they would never be able to dance again, such as Moshe Feldenkrais' or Gabrielle Roth's (founder of 5Rythms) knee injury.
3 In addition to several places in Tel Aviv, Gaga in Israel is practiced at two places in Jerusalem and Haifa, at Givat Olga, Kfar Blum, Kibbutz Ga'aton, Misgav, Moshav Herut, Ramat HaKovesh (Kfar Saba), Ra'anana, Rehovot, Tal Shahar, and Kiryat Tivon (Gaga 2022).
4 Based on these considerations, Gauthier (2017) asks for research on religion to shift focus toward the "sensory dimensions" of religion (447) along with a shift and establishment of a new definition of religion, which defines religion by its aesthetical dimension, design, and functioning (453). A definition based on this could potentially include practices such as Gaga for the commodities, experience, and values they provide, and Gaga could become researchable as part of the contemporary religious landscape.

2 Ritual Environment Shaping Enactment

1 At the time of writing, the Gaga Movement Ltd. has been offering classes via Zoom. What started off as donation-based classes to support Gaga teachers in Israel and New York at the beginning of 2020 in times of the SARS-CoV-2 pandemic was professionalized by the Gaga Movement Ltd. in autumn 2020 as the pandemic situation with its lockdown and travel restrictions remained. Participants could now access classes for a fixed fee from anywhere.
2 In-field conversation in May 2018 with a Gaga teacher.
3 Participant observation in Metodica/Methodics class, May 26, 2018, and participation at Gaga/dancers workshop at Tanzwerkstatt Europa Munich, hosted by Joint Adventures, from 2016 to 2019.

Notes 253

4 Excerpt of the "Statement and Declaration" received (July 16, 2019) and signed by participants of Gaga/dancers workshop at Tanzwerkstatt Europa Munich, hosted by Joint Adventures, with name, passport number, address, signature, and date prior to their workshop participation. It was addressed to Ohad Naharin, Gaga Movement Inc., and drafted by Gaga Movement Ltd., Tel Aviv.

3 Body Topography in Discussion

1 The usage of "flesh" instead of muscles occurred in the context of nineteenth-century guides for the bodily "education" of girls, for example (Hortense de Goupy [1893, 2], "Unserer Töchter Erziehung zur Schönheit," in von Steinaecker 2000, 64). While today apparently still known and used to describe "the soft parts of the body of an animal and especially of a vertebrate; especially: the parts composed chiefly of skeletal muscle as distinguished from internal organs, bone, and integument" (*Merriam-Webster* 2022), it seems to have been a more commonly used term in the context of earlier body practices—though possibly with pejorative connotation.
2 It invites to think about yoga's *mula bandha* (see Maehle 2011, 11–12) or the initiation of contraction as a signature movement in the Graham technique, developed by dancer and choreographer Martha Graham.
3 Whereas some terms such as *pika*, as "the place between pipi and kaka," are named after the original idea or image, some specific terms are named after persons: "Lena was the daughter of then rehearsal director Aya Israeli" (Friedes Galili 2015, 371). "When Aya was pregnant with her daughter Lena, Ohad developed Lena, the center of life" (Gaga class 2018). Other terms such as *yoyo* were inspired by the Japanese, though not necessarily of any sense. Galili (2015) offers a list of Gaga vocabulary attached to her essay; nevertheless, I experienced only a small amount of it being used in class. As Friedes Galili (2015) writes, "Some of Naharin's invented terminology has faded from use in recent years, with more common language being ascendant; the words 'available' and 'ready to snap,' for instance, are often used alongside or sometimes substituted for the term 'dolfi.'" In still other cases, Naharin "bypassed invented words and strung English words together to describe a concept or to denote an action, for example, the 'snake of the spine' or 'move your hands from your heart'" (371).
4 Thinking of the *powerhouse* in Pilates, for example, "the center of the body" is "the location from which all movement is generated" (Brignell 2009, 33), or, according to *tan tien* in t'ai chi, it is "two inches below the navel"—the home of the energy, *chi* (Newth 2006, 10).
5 This is similar to the starting position, the neutral position, in t'ai chi, for example, where the weight is said to fall in the *tan tien*, keeping everything above light,

"floating" away from the tan tien, bringing the head up and away (see Newth 2006, 68).
6 The importance of movement quality instead of movement form and body shape is not unique to the Gaga and Batsheva styles, but is part of an overall development in body practices and dance techniques from the late twentieth century on, where the dance world developed a "critical stance toward dance technique itself" (Bales 2008, 2).

5 Transformation in Movement

1 In the movie *Mr. Gaga* (Heymann 2015) Naharin explains that he used this saying when his father had problems getting out of a chair, to show him that it's nothing difficult, nothing he cannot accomplish, nothing to take too seriously, nothing to worry about. Since it worked, he incorporated the concept into class.

6 Narrating Body Knowledge

1 Because the following is about closely examining the characteristics of verbal experience narration, I stick to a literal and detailed transcription of my interview data, including slips of tongue, moments of consideration, and filler words. Emphases are capitalized; punctuation marks are used intentionally to depict the flow of words.
2 Because the following is about closely examining the characteristics of written experience narrations, I stick to the exact text from experience diaries as it was sent to me by the participants—including incorrect grammar, spelling, and vocabulary and other formalistic uncertainties.
3 However, in Hebrew, the present tense verb is identical to the present participle.

7 The Wow of Gaga

1 Tamar, for example, is familiar with contemporary spirituality's vocabulary and worldview; she not only uses it and takes part in it but also reflects on it and experiences a "possession." She seems to be familiar with the metaphor of possession; contemporary spirituality is her experience filter, and she displays a certain level of embodiment of the metaphor of "external forces," becoming the powers that possessed her.

2 Yet, as Noam's diary extract or the data from participatory observation shows, the context and setting of a Gaga class expand beyond the actual hour of class. The context of class, or rather the experience of class, begins when people meet other participants outside Suzanne Dellal or enter the building, and the context of class ends when participants go on to conduct their everyday business, which could even be just having a coffee with other participants at Café Dallal.

References

Abe, Naoko, Jean-Paul Laumond, Paolo Salaris, and Florent Levillain (2017), "On the Use of Dance Notation Systems to Generate Movements in Humanoid Robots: The Utility of Laban Notation in Robotics," *Social Science Information* 56 (2): 328–44. https://doi.org/10.1177/0539018417694773.

Aldor, Gaby (2009), "Margalit Ornstein," in Jewish Women: A Comprehensive Historical Encyclopedia, Jewish Women's Archive. https://jwa.org/encyclopedia/article/ornstein-margalit (accessed October 1, 2021).

Alibali, Martha W., Rebecca Boncoddo, and Autumn B. Hostetter (2014), "Gesture in Reasoning," in Lawrence Shapiro (ed.), *The Routledge Handbook of Embodied Cognition*, 150–9, New York: Routledge.

Aristidou, Andreas, Efstathios Stavrakis, Panayiotis Charalambous, Yiorgos Chrysanthou, and Stephania Loizidou Himona (2015), "Folk Dance Evaluation Using Laban Movement Analysis," *Journal on Computing and Cultural Heritage* 8 (4): 1–19. https://doi.org/10.1145/2755566.

Aschenbrenner, Lina (2019), "Three Become One: Three Israeli Stories, One Arena," in *Shahar Binyamini: Ohad Naharin. Today I Will Do What I Want/Ballroom/Decadance*, translated by Paul Richards, 14–17, St. Pölten, Austria: Festspielhaus.

Aschenbrenner, Lina, and Anne Koch (2022), "Do Gaga, Be Well? Well-Being as Intersectional Dispositif in the Neo-spiritual Israeli Movement Practice Gaga," in Géraldine Mossière (ed.), *New Spiritualties and the Culture of Well-Being*, New York: Springer.

Aschenbrenner, Lina, and Laura von Ostrowksi (2022), "Embodied Neo-spirituality as an Experience-Filter: From Dance and Movement Practice to Contemporary Yoga," *Body and Religion*.

Bales, Melanie (2008), "Introduction," in Rebecca Nettl-Fiol and Melanie Bales (eds.), *The Body Eclectic: Evolving Practices in Dance Training*, 1–3, Urbana: University of Illinois Press.

Barrett, Frederick S., Matthew W. Johnson, and Roland R. Griffiths (2015), "Validation of the Revised Mystical Experience Questionnaire in Experimental Sessions with Psilocybin," *Journal of Psychopharmacology* 29 (11): 1182–90. https://doi.org/10.1177/0269881115609019.

Bartenieff, Irmgard, and Dori Lewis (2002), *Body Movement: Coping with the Environment*, 2nd ed., New York: Routledge.

Batsheva Dance Company (2015), "About: Ohad Naharin." https://batsheva.co.il/en/about?open=ohas_naharin (accessed October 1, 2021).

Batson, Glenna (2009), "Resource Paper: Somatic Studies and Dance," International Association for Dance Medicine and Science. https://iadms.org/media/3599/iadms-resource-paper-somatic-studies-and-dance.pdf (accessed October 1, 2021).

Blacking, John (1984), "'Dance' as Cultural System and Human Capability: An Anthropological Perspective," in *Report of the Third Study of Dance Conference, University of Surrey*, 2–21, Guildford: National Resource Center for Dance.

Boecker, Henning, Till Sprenger, Mary E. Spilker, Gjermund Henriksen, Marcus Koppenhoefer, Klaus J. Wagner, Michael Valet, Achim Berthele, and Thomas R. Tolle (2008), "The Runner's High: Opioidergic Mechanisms in the Human Brain," *Cerebral Cortex* 18 (11): 2523–31. https://doi.org/10.1093/cercor/bhn013.

Bond, Karen E., and Susan W. Stinson (2000), "'I Feel Like I'm Going to Take Off!' Young People's Experiences of the Superordinary in Dance," *Dance Research Journal* 32 (2): 52–87. https://doi.org/10.2307/1477981.

Bourdieu, Pierre ([1977] 2005), *Outline of a Theory of Practice*, translated by Richard Nice, Cambridge: Cambridge University Press. https://doi.org/10.1017/CBO978051 1812507.

Brignell, Roger (2009), *The Pilates Handbook*, New York: Rosen.

Butler, Judith (1997), *Excitable Speech: A Politics of the Performative*, New York: Routledge.

Butler, Judith (1999), *Gender Trouble: Feminism and the Subversion of Identity*, 2nd ed., New York: Routledge.

Casasanto, Daniel (2014), "Body Relativity," in Lawrence Shapiro (ed.), *The Routledge Handbook of Embodied Cognition*, 108–17, New York: Routledge.

Coello, Yann, and Martin H. Fischer (2016), "Introduction," in Yann Coello, Martin H. Fischer, and Hong Yu Wong (eds.), *Perceptual and Emotional Embodiment: Foundations of Embodied Cognition*, 135–48, New York: Routledge.

Conradson, David (2005), "Landscape, Care and the Relational Self: Therapeutic Encounters in Rural England," *Health & Place*, Special Section: Therapeutic Landscapes: An Evolving Theme, 11 (4): 337–48. https://doi.org/10.1016/j.healthpl ace.2005.02.004.

Corrywright, Dominic (2009), "A New Visibility? Wellbeing Culture, Religion and Spirituality." https://www.academia.edu/572387/A_New_Visibility_Wellbeing_ Culture_Religion_and_Spirituality (accessed October 1, 2021).

Craighero, Laila (2014), "The Role of the Motor System in Cognitive Functions," in Lawrence Shapiro (ed.), *The Routledge Handbook of Embodied Cognition*, 51–8, New York: Routledge.

Csikszentmihalyi, Mihaly (2014), *Flow and the Foundations of Positive Psychology: The Collected Works of Mihaly Csikszentmihalyi*, Dordrecht: Springer.

Csordas, Thomas J. (1993), "Somatic Modes of Attention," *Cultural Anthropology* 8 (May): 135–56. https://doi.org/10.1525/can.1993.8.2.02a00010.

Cusack, Carole M., and Alex Norman, eds. (2012), *Handbook of New Religions and Cultural Production*, Leiden: Brill.

References

Davidson, Joyce, and Hester Parr (2007), "Anxious Subjectivities and Spaces of Care: Therapeutic Geographies of the UK National Phobics Society," in Allison Williams (ed.), *Therapeutic Landscapes*, 95–110, Farnham: Ashgate.

Dawson, Andrew (2013), "Entangled Modernity and Commodified Religion: Alternative Spirituality and the 'New Middle Class,'" in François Gauthier and Tuomas Martikainen (eds.), *Religion in Consumer Society*, 127–42, Farnham: Ashgate.

DeWalt, Kathleen M., and Billie R. DeWalt (2011), *Participant Observation: A Guide for Fieldworkers*, Plymouth: AltaMira.

Eddy, Martha (2009), "A Brief History of Somatic Practices and Dance: Historical Development of the Field of Somatic Education and Its Relationship to Dance," *Journal of Dance and Somatic Practices* 1 (1): 5–27. https://doi.org/10.1386/jdsp.1.1.5_1.

Eshel, Ruth (2003), "Concert Dance in Israel," *Dance Research Journal* 35 (1): 61–80. https://doi.org/10.1017/S0149767700008779.

Flower, Lynda (2016), "'My Day-to-Day Person Wasn't There; It Was Like Another Me': A Qualitative Study of Spiritual Experiences during Peak Performance in Ballet Dance," *Performance Enhancement & Health* 4 (1): 67–75. https://doi.org/10.1016/j.peh.2015.10.003.

Foucault, Michel (1972), *The Archaeology of Knowledge and the Discourse of Language*, translated by A. M. Sheridan Smith, New York: Pantheon Books.

Foucault, Michel ([1979] 1995), *Discipline and Punish: The Birth of the Prison*, translated by Alan Sheridan, 2nd ed., New York: Vintage Books.

Friedes Galili, Deborah (n.d.), "Dance in Israel," https://web.archive.org/web/20190801111521/https:/www.danceinisrael.com/. Archived August 1, 2019 (accessed October 23, 2019).

Friedes Galili, Deborah (2013), "Reframing the Recent Past: Issues of Reconstruction in Israeli Contemporary Dance," in Melanie Bales and Karen Eliot (eds.), *Dance on Its Own Terms: Histories and Methodologies*, 65–90, Oxford Scholarship Online. https://www.oxfordscholarship.com/view/10.1093/acprof:oso/9780199939985.001.0001/acprof-9780199939985-chapter-4.

Friedes Galili, Deborah (2015), "Gaga: Moving beyond Technique with Ohad Naharin in the Twenty-First Century," *Dance Chronicle* 38 (3): 360–92. https://doi.org/10.1080/01472526.2015.1085759.

Gaga (2019a), "Home." https://web.archive.org/web/20190520143409/http://gagapeople.com/en/. Archived May 20, 2019 (accessed October 1, 2021).

Gaga (2019b), "About Gaga." https://web.archive.org/web/20190821162127/https://www.gagapeople.com/en/about-gaga/. Archived August 21, 2019 (accessed October 1, 2021).

Gaga (2019c), "Gaga around the World—Ongoing Classes—Gaga," https://web.archive.org/web/20190821184202/https://www.gagapeople.com/en/gaga-around-the-world-ongoing-classes/. Archived August 21, 2019 (accessed October 1, 2021).

Gaga (2021), "Gaga/Seated Classes." https://web.archive.org/web/20210510100250/https://www.gagapeople.com/en/gaga-seated-classes/. Archived May 10, 2021 (accessed October 1, 2021).

Gaga (2022), "Gaga in Israel." https://web.archive.org/web/20220426081439/https://www.gagapeople.com/en/gaga-in-israel/. Archived April 26, 2022 (accessed April 29, 2022).

Gaga Movement Language (2022), YouTube, https://www.youtube.com/channel/UCJuG8LobRKuBD0134W6hoBA/featured (accessed April 29, 2022).

Gaga Movement Ltd. (2017a), "Work Instructions." https://web.archive.org/web/20170608195808/http://gagapeople.com/english/about-gaga/work-instructions. Archived June 8, 2017 (accessed October 1, 2021).

Gaga Movement Ltd. (2017b), "About Gaga." https://web.archive.org/web/20170703181701/http://gagapeople.com/english/about-gaga. Archived July 3, 2017 (accessed October 1, 2021).

Gaga Movement Ltd. (2017c), "Gaga | People.Dancers." https://web.archive.org/web/20170802002754/http://gagapeople.com/english/. Archived August 2, 2017 (accessed October 1, 2021).

Gallese, Vittorio (2017a), "Mirroring, a Liberated Embodied Simulation and Aesthetic Experience," in Helen Hirsch and Alessandra Pace (eds.), *Mirror Images*, 27–37, Wien: Verlag für moderne Kunst.

Gallese, Vittorio (2017b), "Visions of the Body: Embodied Simulation and Aesthetic Experience." Humanities Futures, June 1. https://humanitiesfutures.org/papers/visions-body-embodied-simulation-aesthetic-experience/.

Gallese, Vittorio (2018), "The Problem of Images: A View from the Brain-Body," *Phenomenology and Mind* 14: 70–9. https://doi.org/10.13128/Phe_Mi-23626.

Gard, Tim, Jessica J. Noggle, Crystal L. Park, David R. Vago, and Angela Wilson (2014), "Potential Self-Regulatory Mechanisms of Yoga for Psychological Health," Frontiers in Human Neuroscience 8 (September): 770. https://doi.org/10.3389/fnhum.2014.00770.

Gauthier, François (2017), "Consumer Culture and the Sensory Remodeling of Religion," in Alexandra Grieser and Jay Johnston (eds.), *Aesthetics of Religion: A Connective Concept*, 447–56, Berlin: De Gruyter. https://doi.org/10.1515/9783110461015-020.

Gauthier, François, and Tuomas Martikainen (2013), "Introduction: Consumerism as the Ethos of Consumer Society," in François Gauthier and Tuomas Martikainen (eds.), *Religion in Consumer Society: Brands, Consumers and Markets*, 1–26, Farnham: Ashgate.

Gesler, Wilbert M. (2003), *Healing Places*, Lanham: Rowman & Littlefield.

Gilman, Sander (1991), *The Jew's Body*, New York: Routledge.

Gore, Georgiana, Géraldine Rix-Lièvre, Olivier Wathelet, and Anne Cazemajou (2012), "Eliciting the Tacit: Interviewing to Understand Bodily Experience," in Jonathan Skinner (ed.), *The Interview: An Ethnographic Approach*, 127–42, London: Berg.

Grieser, Alexandra, and Jay Johnston, eds. (2017a), *Aesthetics of Religion: A Connective Concept*, Berlin: De Gruyter. https://doi.org/10.1515/9783110461015.

Grieser, Alexandra, and Jay Johnston (2017b), "What Is an Aesthetics of Religion? From the Senses to Meaning—And Back Again," in Alexandra Grieser and Jay Johnston (eds.), *Aesthetics of Religion: A Connective Concept*, 1–50, Berlin: De Gruyter. https://doi.org/10.1515/9783110461015-001.

Griffiths, Mark (1997), "Exercise Addiction: A Case Study," *Addiction Research* 5 (2): 161–8. https://doi.org/10.3109/16066359709005257.

Grimes, Ronald L. (2014), *The Craft of Ritual Studies*, Oxford: Oxford University Press.

Guest, Ann Hutchinson (2005), *Labanotation: The System of Analyzing and Recording Movement*, 4th ed., New York: Routledge.

Gugutzer, Robert, Gabriele Klein, and Michael Meuser (2017), "Vorwort," in Gugutzer Robert, Gabriele Klein, and Michael Meuser (eds.), *Handbuch Körpersoziologie*, v–viii, Wiesbaden: Springer Fachmedien Wiesbaden. https://doi.org/10.1007/978-3-658-04136-6.

Haas, Jacqui Greene (2018), *Dance Anatomy*, 2nd ed., Champaign: Human Kinetics.

Halliday, M. A. K. (1987), "Language and the Order of Nature," in Nigel Fabb, Derek Attridge, Alan Durant, and Colin MacCabe (eds.), *The Linguistics of Writing*, 135–54, Manchester: Manchester University Press.

Hamera, Judith (2007), *Dancing Communities: Performance, Difference and Connection in the Global City*, Studies in International Performance, London: Palgrave Macmillan.

Hanna, Thomas (1986), "What Is Somatics?" https://somatics.org/library/htl-wis1.

Heyes, Cecilia, and Caroline Catmur (2022), "What Happened to Mirror Neurons?" *Perspectives on Psychological Science* 17 (1): 153–68. https://doi.org/10.1177%2F1745691621990638.

Ingber, Judith Brin (2009), "Yardena Cohen," in *Jewish Women: A Comprehensive Historical Encyclopedia*. Jewish Women's Archive. https://jwa.org/encyclopedia/article/cohen-yardena (accessed October 1, 2021).

Ingber, Judith Brin (2011a), "Shorashim: The Roots of Israeli Folk Dance," in Judith Brin Ingber (ed.), *Seeing Israeli and Jewish Dance*, 99–169. Detroit: Wayne State University Press.

Ingber, Judith Brin (2011b), "The Unwitting Gastrol: Touring the Soviet Union, France, the United States, Canada, Israel, South America, Europe, and Back to Poland," in Judith Brin Ingber (Ed.), *Seeing Israeli and Jewish Dance*, 43–55. Detroit: Wayne State University Press.

ISMETA (2019), "Home." https://ismeta.org/ (accessed October 1, 2021).

Johnston, Jay (2013), "The Body in Wellbeing Spirituality," *Scripta Instituti Donneriani Aboensis* 23: 174–85. https://doi.org/10.30674/scripta.67385.

Kaplan, Dana, and Rachel Werczberger (2017), "Jewish New Age and the Middle Class: Jewish Identity Politics in Israel under Neoliberalism," *Sociology* 51 (3): 575–91. https://doi.org/10.1177/0038038515595953.

Kaschak, Michael P., John L. Jones, Julie Carranza, and Melissa R. Fox (2014), "Embodiment and Language Comprehension," in Lawrence Shapiro (ed.), *The Routledge Handbook of Embodied Cognition*, 118–26, New York: Routledge.

Katan-Schmid, Einav (2016), *Embodied Philosophy in Dance: Gaga and Ohad Naharin's Movement Research*, Performance Philosophy, London: Palgrave Macmillan.

Katan-Schmid, Einav (2017), "Dancing Metaphors: Creative Thinking within Bodily Movements," in Dan-Eugen Ratiu and Connell Vaughan (eds.), *Proceedings of the European Society for Aesthetics*, 9:275–90, Fribourg: The European Society for Aesthetics.

Kaufman, Haim, and Yair Galily (2009), "Sport, Zionist Ideology and the State of Israel," *Sport in Society* 12 (8): 1013–27. https://doi.org/10.1080/17430430903076316.

Klein, Gabriele, Gitta Barthel, and Esther Wagner (2011), *Choreografischer Baukasten*, Bielefeld: transcript.

Koch, Anne (2007), *Körperwissen: Grundlegung einer Religionsaisthetik*, München: Ludwig-Maximilians-Universität. https://epub.ub.uni-muenchen.de/12438/1/Habilitation-Koch-02.03.07.pdf (accessed October 1, 2021).

Koch, Anne (2012), "Reasons for Boom of Body Discourses in the Humanities and the Social Sciences since the 1980s," in Angelika Berlejung, Jan Dietrich, and Joachim Friedrich Quack (eds.), *Menschenbilder und Körperkonzepte im Alten Israel, in Ägypten und im Alten Orient*, 3–42, Orientalische Religionen in der Antike/Oriental Religions in Antiquity 9, Tübingen: Mohr Siebeck.

Koch, Anne (2014), "Ganzheitsmedizin zwischen Religion und Wissenschaft," in Michael Utsch (ed.), *Spirituelle Lebenshilfe*, 7–19, EZW Texte 229, Berlin: EZW.

Koch, Anne (2015), "'Körperwissen': Modewort oder Grundstein einer Religionssomatik und Religionsästhetik?," in Oliver Krüger and Nadine Weibel (eds.), *Die Körper der Religion/Corps de la religion*, 21–45, Zürich: Pano.

Koch, Anne (2017), "The Governance of Aesthetic Subjects through Body Knowledge and Affect Economies: A Cognitive-Aesthetic Approach," in Alexandra Grieser and Jay Johnston (eds.), *Aesthetics of Religion: A Connective Concept*, 58:389–412, Berlin: De Gruyter. https://doi.org/10.1515/9783110461015-017.

Koch, Ann (2018), "Übungswissen: Subjekttheoretische Bemerkungen zu somatischer Konditionierung, Widerständigkeit und Externalisierung," in Almut-Barbara Renger and Alexandra Stellmacher (eds.), *Übungswissen in Religion und Philosophie: Produktion, Weitergabe, Wandel*, 1–18, Münster: LIT.

Koch, Anne (2020), "Epistemology," in Anne Koch and Katharina Wilkens (eds.), *The Bloomsbury Handbook of the Cultural and Cognitive Aesthetics of Religion*, 23–32, London: Bloomsbury Academic. https://doi.org/10.5040/9781350066748.

Koch, Anne, and Karin Meissner (2015), "Imagination, Suggestion und Trance: Suggestionsforschung und Religionsästhetik zu Heilung," in *Religion–Imagination–Ästhetik: Vorstellungs- und Sinneswelten in Religion und Kultur*, 131–54, Critical Studies in Religion/Religionswissenschaft 7, Göttingen: Vandenhoeck & Ruprecht. https://doi.org/10.13109/9783666540318.131.

Koch, Anne, and Katharina Wilkens, eds. (2020), *The Bloomsbury Handbook of the Cultural and Cognitive Aesthetics of Religion*, London: Bloomsbury Academic. https://doi.org/10.5040/9781350066748.

Kohls, Niko, Harald Walach, and George Lewith (2009), "The Impact of Positive and Negative Spiritual Experiences on Distress and the Moderating Role of Mindfulness," *Archive for the Psychology of Religion* 31 (3): 357–74. https://doi.org/10.1163/008467209X12524724282032.

Krivoschekov, S. G., and O. N. Lushnikov (2011), "Psychophysiology of Sports Addictions (Exercise Addiction)," *Human Physiology* 37 (4): 509–13. https://doi.org/10.1134/S0362119711030030.

Laack, Isabel, and Petra Tillessen (2020), "Aesthetics of Religion in the Classroom," in Anne Koch and Katharina Wilkens (eds.), *The Bloomsbury Handbook of the Cultural and Cognitive Aesthetics of Religion*, 285–94, London: Bloomsbury Academic. https://doi.org/10.5040/9781350066748.

Lakoff, George, and Mark Johnson ([1980] 2003), *Metaphors We Live By*, Chicago: University of Chicago Press.

Lea, Jennifer (2008), "Retreating to Nature: Rethinking 'Therapeutic Landscapes,'" *Area* 40 (1): 90–8. http://doi.org/10.1111/j.1475-4762.2008.00789.x.

Leigh Foster, Susan (1997), "Dancing Bodies," in Jane Desmond (ed.), *Meaning in Motion: New Cultural Studies of Dance*, 235–58. Durham: Duke University Press.

Lexico (2019), "Stage." https://www.lexico.com/en/definition/stage.

Luhrmann, Tanya Marie (2020), "Absorption," in Anne Koch and Katharina Wilkens (eds.), *The Bloomsbury Handbook of the Cultural and Cognitive Aesthetics of Religion*, 85–96, London: Bloomsbury Academic. http://doi.org/10.5040/9781350066748.ch-008.

Maehle, Gregor (2011), *Ashtanga Yoga: Practice and Philosophy*, Novato: New World Library.

Manor, Giora (2009), "Gertrud Kraus," in *Jewish Women: A Comprehensive Historical Encyclopedia*. Jewish Women's Archive. https://jwa.org/encyclopedia/article/kraus-gertrud (accessed October 1, 2021).

Mauss, Marcel (1973), "Techniques of the Body," *Economy and Society* 2 (1): 70–88. https://doi.org/10.1080/03085147300000003.

Mazzella di Bosco, Marie (2021), "'Danser la relation.' Interactions en mouvement dans les danses libres en conscience," *Ateliers d'anthropologie (En Ligne)* 50 (July). https://doi.org/10.4000/ateliers.14618.

Meckel, Daniel (2016), "Peak Experience," in Robert A. Segal and Kocku von Stuckrad (eds.), *Vocabulary for the Study of Religion*. https://referenceworks-brillonline-com.emedien.ub.uni-muenchen.de/entries/vocabulary-for-the-study-of-religion/peak-experience-COM_00000406 (accessed October 1, 2021).

Menon, Sangeetha (2014), *Brain, Self and Consciousness: Explaining the Conspiracy of Experience*, Studies in Neuroscience, Consciousness and Spirituality, New Delhi: Springer India.

Merleau-Ponty, Maurice ([1962] 2002), *Phenomenology of Perception*, translated by Colin Smith, Routledge Classics, London: Routledge.
Merriam-Webster (2019a), "Heal." https://www.merriam-webster.com/dictionary/heal (accessed October 1, 2021).
Merriam-Webster (2019b), "Script." https://www.merriam-webster.com/dictionary/script (accessed October 1, 2021).
Merriam-Webster (2019c), "Silly." https://www.merriam-webster.com/dictionary/silly (accessed October 1, 2021).
Merriam-Webster (2022), "Flesh." https://www.gagapeople.com/en/gaga-seated-classes/ (accessed April 29, 2022).
Merta, Sabine (2003), *Wege und Irrwege zum modernen Schlankheitskult: Diätkost und Körperkultur als Suche nach neuen Lebensstilformen 1880–1930*, Stuttgart: Franz Steiner.
Meyer, Birgit (2012), "Religious Sensations: Why Media, Aesthetics and Power Matter in the Study of Contemporary Religion," in Gordon Lynch, Jolyon Mitchell, and Anna Strhan (eds.), *Religion, Media and Culture: A Reader*, 159–70, New York: Routledge.
Meyer, Birgit (2015), "How to Capture the 'Wow': R.R. Marett's Notion of Awe and the Study of Religion," *Journal of the Royal Anthropological Institute* 22 (December): 7–26. https://doi.org/10.1111/1467-9655.12331.
Mignolo, Walter, and Rolando Vázquez (2013), "Decolonial AestheSis: Colonial Wounds/Decolonial Healings." SocialText Online (blog), July 15. https://socialtextjournal.org/periscope_article/decolonial-aesthesis-colonial-woundsdecolonial-healings/ (accessed April 29, 2022).
Mr. Gaga (2015) [film] Dir. Tomer Heymann, Israel.
Mullan, Kelly Jean (2017), "Somatics Herstories: Tracing Elsa Gindler's Educational Antecedents Hade Kallmeyer and Genevieve Stebbins," *Journal of Dance & Somatic Practices* 9 (2): 159–78. https://doi.org/10.1386/jdsp.9.2.159_1.
Mullan, Kelly Jean (2020), "Forgotten 'New' Dancer of New York City's Gilded Age: Genevieve Lee Stebbins and the Dance as Yet Undreamed," *Dance Research Journal* 52 (3): 97–117. https://doi.org/10.1017/S0149767720000327.
Newth, Glenn D. (2006), *Hwa Yu Tai Chi Ch'uan: Unlocking the Mysteries of the Five-Word Song*, Berkley: Blue Snake Books.
Oosterwijk, Suzanne, and Lisa Feldman Barret (2014), "Embodiment in the Construction of Emotion Experience and Emotion Understanding," in Lawrence Shapiro (ed.), *The Routledge Handbook of Embodied Cognition*, 250–60, New York: Routledge.
Otto, Rudolf (1920), *Das Heilige*, Breslau: Trewendt und Granier.
Patel, Vikram (1993), "Crying Behavior and Psychiatric Disorder in Adults: A Review," *Comprehensive Psychiatry* 34 (3): 206–11. https://doi.org/10.1016/0010-440X(93)90049-A.

Payne, Peter, and Mardi A. Crane-Godreau (2013), "Meditative Movement for Depression and Anxiety," *Frontiers in Psychiatry* 4: 71. https://doi.org/10.3389/fpsyt.2013.00071.

Payne, Peter, and Mardi A. Crane-Godreau (2015), "The Preparatory Set: A Novel Approach to Understanding Stress, Trauma, and the Bodymind Therapies," *Frontiers in Human Neuroscience* 9. https://doi.org/10.3389/fnhum.2015.00178.

Popp-Baier, Ulrike (2001), "Narrating Embodied Aims. Self-Transformation in Conversion Narratives—A Psychological Analysis," *Forum Qualitative Sozialforschung/Forum: Qualitative Social Research* 2 (3). http://doi.org/10.17169/fqs-2.3.911.

Preston, Stephanie D., and Frans B. M. de Waal (2002), "Empathy: Its Ultimate and Proximate Bases," *Behavioral and Brain Sciences* 25 (1): 1–20. https://doi.org/10.1017/S0140525X02000018.

Quinlan, Meghan (2016), "Gaga as Politics: A Case Study of Contemporary Dance Training," PhD thesis, University of California, Riverside. https://escholarship.org/uc/item/5mk66482 (accessed October 1, 2021).

Quinlan, Meghan (2017), "Gaga as Metatechnique: Negotiating Choreography, Improvisation, and Technique in a Neoliberal Dance Market," *Dance Research Journal* 49 (2): 26–43. https://doi.org/10.1017/S0149767717000183.

Ram, Uri (2008), *The Globalization of Israel: McWorld in Tel Aviv, Jihad in Jerusalem*, New York: Routledge.

Raz, Amir, and Jason Buhle (2006), "Typologies of Attentional Networks," *Nature Reviews Neuroscience* 7 (5): 367–79. https://doi.org/10.1038/nrn1903.

Riener, Cedar, and Jeanine Stefanucci (2014), "Perception and/for/with/as Action," in Lawrence Shapiro (ed.), *The Routledge Handbook of Embodied Cognition*, 99–107, New York: Routledge.

Roberts, R. E., P. G. Bain, B. L. Day, and M. Husain (2013), "Individual Differences in Expert Motor Coordination Associated with White Matter Microstructure in the Cerebellum," *Cerebral Cortex* 23 (10): 2282–92. https://doi.org/10.1093/cercor/bhs219.

Robinson, Simon (2007), "Spirituality: A Story so Far," in Jim Parry, Simon Robinson, Nick Watson, and Mark Nesti (eds.), *Sport and Spirituality: An Introduction*, 7–21, New York: Routledge.

The Roestone Collective (2014), "Safe Space: Towards a Reconceptualization," *Antipode* 46 (5): 1346–65. https://doi.org/10.1111/anti.12089.

Ronen, Dan (2009a), "Leah Bergstein," in Jewish Women: A Comprehensive Historical Encyclopedia. Jewish Women's Archive. https://jwa.org/encyclopedia/article/bergstein-leah (accessed October 1, 2021).

Ronen, Dan (2009b), "Rivka Sturman," in Jewish Women: A Comprehensive Historical Encyclopedia. Jewish Women's Archive. https://jwa.org/encyclopedia/article/sturman-rivka (accessed October 1, 2021).

Ruah-Midbar, Marianna (2013), "'Everything Starts Within': New Age Values, Images, and Language in Israeli Advertising," *Journal of Contemporary Religion* 28 (3): 421–36. https://doi.org/10.1080/13537903.2013.831652.

Rühlemann, Christoph (2013), *Narrative in English Conversation: A Corpus Analysis of Storytelling*, Cambridge: Cambridge University Press.

Russell, Tamara Anne, and Silvia Maria Arcuri (2015), "A Neurophysiological and Neuropsychological Consideration of Mindful Movement: Clinical and Research Implications," *Frontiers in Human Neuroscience* 9 (May). https://doi.org/10.3389/fnhum.2015.00282.

Schmalzl, Laura, Mardi A. Crane-Godreau, and Peter Payne (2014), "Movement-Based Embodied Contemplative Practices: Definitions and Paradigms," *Frontiers in Human Neuroscience* 8. https://doi.org/10.3389/fnhum.2014.00205.

Schmalzl, Laura, Chivon Powers, and Eva Henje Blom (2015), "Neurophysiological and Neurocognitive Mechanisms Underlying the Effects of Yoga-Based Practices: Towards a Comprehensive Theoretical Framework," *Frontiers in Human Neuroscience* 9. https://doi.org/10.3389/fnhum.2015.00235.

Schröder, Anna-Konstanze (2013), "Konversionserleben als Schnittpunkt der psychologischen und soziologischen Forschungsperspektive auf den Konversionsprozess," PhD thesis, Universität Leipzig, Leipzig.

Scorolli, Claudia (2014), "Embodiment and Language," in Lawrence Shapiro (ed.), *The Routledge Handbook of Embodied Cognition*, 127–38, New York: Routledge.

Shapiro, Lawrence, ed. (2014), *The Routledge Handbook of Embodied Cognition*, London: Routledge.

Shavit, Zohar, and Yaacov Shavit (2016), "Israeli Culture Today: How Jewish?" in Eliezer Ben-Rafael, Julius H. Schoeps, Yitzhak Sternberg, and Olaf Glöckner (eds.), *Handbook of Israel: Major Debates*, 22–38, Berlin: De Gruyter. https://doi.org/10.1515/9783110351637.

Singleton, Mark (2010), *Yoga Body: The Origins of Modern Posture Practice*, Oxford: Oxford University Press.

Sklar, Deidre (2000), "Reprise: On Dance Ethnography," *Dance Research Journal* 32 (1): 70–7. https://doi.org/10.2307/1478278.

Soliman, Tamer, and Arthur M. Glenberg (2014), "The Embodiment of Culture," in Lawrence Shapiro (ed.), *The Routledge Handbook of Embodied Cognition*, 197–219, New York: Routledge.

Spiegel, Nina S. (2013), *Embodying Hebrew Culture: Aesthetics, Athletics, and Dance in the Jewish Community of Mandate Palestine*, Detroit: Wayne State University Press.

Stahl, Jennifer (2017), "The Most Influential People in Dance Today," *Dance Magazine*, June 19. https://web.archive.org/web/20191031220707/https://www.dancemagazine.com/the-most-influential-people-in-dance-today-2440965004.html.

Streib, Heinz, and Barbara Keller (2015), *Was bedeutet Spiritualität? Befunde, Analysen und Fallstudien aus Deutschland*, Göttingen: Vandenhoeck & Ruprecht.

Stromberg, Peter G. (1993), *Language and Self-Transformation: A Study of the Christian Conversion Narrative*, Cambridge: Cambridge University Press.

Sutton, John, and Kellie Williamson (2014), "Embodied Remembering," in Lawrence Shapiro (ed.), *The Routledge Handbook of Embodied Cognition*, 315–25, New York: Routledge.

Taves, Ann (2018), "Finding and Articulating Meaning in Secular Experience," in Ulrich Riegel, Eva-Maria Leven, and Daniel Fleming (eds.), *Religious Experience and Experiencing Religion in Religious Education*, 13–22, Münster: Waxmann.

Taves, Ann (2020a), "Mystical and Other Alterations in Sense of Self: An Expanded Framework for Studying Nonordinary Experiences," *Perspectives on Psychological Science* 15 (3): 669–90. https://doi.org/10.1177/2F1745691619895047.

Taves, Ann (2020b), "From Religious Studies to Worldview Studies," *Religion* 50 (1): 137–47. https://doi.org/10.1080/0048721X.2019.1681124.

Taves, Ann, and Egil Asprem (2016), "Experience as Event: Event Cognition and the Study of (Religious) Experiences," *Religion, Brain & Behavior* 7 (1): 43–62. https://doi.org/10.1080/2153599X.2016.1150327.

Taves, Ann, and Egil Asprem (2018), "Scientific Worldview Studies: A Programmatic Proposal," in Anders Klostergaard Petersen, Ingvild Sælid Gilhus, Luther H. Martin, Jeppe Sinding Jensen, and Jesper Sørensen (eds.), *Evolution, Cognition, and the History of Religion: A New Synthesis: Festschrift in Honour of Armin W. Geertz*, 297–308, Supplements to Method & Theory in the Study of Religion 13, Leiden: Brill. https://doi.org/10.1163/9789004385375_020.

Tiggemann, Marika (2012), "Sociocultural Perspectives on Human Experience and Body Image," in Thomas F. Cash and Linda Smolak (eds.), *Body Image: A Handbook of Science, Practice, and Prevention*, 12–19, New York: Guilford.

Traut, Lucia, and Annette Wilke (2014), "Einleitung," in Lucia Traut and Annette Wilke (eds.), *Religion–Imagination–Ästhetik. Vorstellungs- und Sinneswelten in Religion und Kultur*, 17–70, Critical Studies in Religion/Religionswissenschaft 7, Göttingen: Vandenhoeck & Ruprecht. https://doi.org/10.13109/9783666540318.17.

Vega, Ricardo de la, Irini S. Parastatidou, Roberto Ruíz-Barquín, and Attila Szabo (2016), "Exercise Addiction in Athletes and Leisure Exercisers: The Moderating Role of Passion," *Journal of Behavioral Addictions* 5 (2): 325–31. https://doi.org/10.1556/2006.5.2016.043.

Verrel, Julius, Eilat Almagor, Frank Schumann, Ulman Lindenberger, and Simone Kühn (2015), "Changes in Neural Resting State Activity in Primary and Higher-Order Motor Areas Induced by a Short Sensorimotor Intervention Based on the Feldenkrais Method," *Frontiers in Human Neuroscience* 9 (April). https://doi.org/10.3389/fnhum.2015.00232.

Vignemont, Frederique de (2014), "Acting for Bodily Awareness," in Lawrence Shapiro (ed.), *The Routledge Handbook of Embodied Cognition*, 272–86, New York: Routledge.

von Steinaecker, Karoline (2000), *Luftsprünge. Anfänge Moderner Körpertherapien*, München: Urban & Fischer.

Weissbrod, Lilly (2014), *Israeli Identity: In Search of a Successor to the Pioneer, Tsabar and Settler*, New York: Routledge.

Werczberger, Rachel, and Boaz Huss (2014), "Guest Editors' Introduction: New Age Culture in Israel," *Israel Studies Review* 29 (2): 1–16. https://doi.org/10.3167/isr.2014.290202.

Wicher, Dieter (2010), "Design Principles of Sensory Receptors," *Frontiers in Cellular Neuroscience* 4. https://doi.org/10.3389/fncel.2010.00025.

Index

action, *see* animation
active vs. passive 112, 130–1, 138, 139–43, 147–8, 193–4
addiction 200–3, 223, 239–41, 249, *see also* time and amount of practice
aesthetic analysis 17, 242
aesthetic cognizing subject 9, 248
aesthetics
  and body knowledge 155–6
  definition of 7–8
  individual and collective 155–6
  narration of 159
  neo-spiritual 31, 244–9
Aesthetics of Religion 8
aestheticization 3–6, 247, 249
affects, *see* relationality 194–9
agency 66–7, 73–6, 113, 184, 193–9
  of Ohad Naharin 198
  of participants 193–6
  of teachers 184, 195–8, 243
Alexander technique 39, 70, 245
Anatomy 9, 10, 23, 90–9, 245, *see also* body concept *and* body topography
animation 60–2, 64–6, 76, 78–80, 103–4, 155–6, 187
AoR, *see* Aesthetics of Religion
archive(s) 31, 34–5, 40, 48, 89
attention 106, 122–7, *see also* awareness
availability 126–8, *see also* awareness
awareness
  as achievable state and identity 217, 220–1, 224–5, 228–31, 242
  as body knowledge 206, 210–12
  characteristic to the Gaga body 90–1
  history of 35–41, 169–70
  instructions of 79, 85–6, 185, 199
  role of 112, 152
  as technique 122–8, 135, 210–11, 244
awe 179

balanced tone 121, 126, 129, 140, 142–3, 149, 243–4

Batsheva 2, 32, 49–50, 52–7, 67–8, 71–2, 75, 107, 199–200, 225, 228, 243
behavior 1, 9, 15, 84–7, 107, 218
belief, *see* worldview
blood flow, *see* thermoregulation
body concept 10, 82, 88–9, 128, 131, 143, 147, 150, 152, 245–7
  characteristic to Gaga 169–70, 206, 217, 220, 242–4
body-focused ethnography 20–7
body image, *see* body topography
body knowledge
  collective 149–50, 155, 159, 169–70, 246–7
  definition of 10–14
  embodiment of 119–56, 206–8, 217, 219–22, 224
  explicit and implicit 121–2, 128, 217, 225
  extraordinary 167, 181
  narration 159–77, 204, 221–2, 240
  research of 20–4
  transformation of 119, 206–8, 217, 221–2, 237–9, 243–4, 247
body knowledge vocabulary, *see* body concept, body scheme, body topography, focused attention, kinesthesia, (embodied) imagination, movement quality, movement range, movement source, movement style, muscle tone, open monitoring, peripersonal space, posture, proprioception, prosthetic perception, stamina, strength, tattooing, thermoregulation
body parts 103, 112
  area behind the ears 122, 132
  armpits 122, 132
  arms 37–8, 61, 96, 106, 120–2, 140, 136, 141, 143–6
  back 33–4, 36, 61, 96–7, 122, 125, 129, 132–4, 141, 143–6, 148

back of the neck 132
belly button, *see* navel
between the shoulder blades 122, 132–3
bones 93–4, 131, 148
center 98, 133, 136, 142, 145
chest 96–7, 123, 133–4, 143, 148
coccyx (tail) 95, 97, 145
collarbones 94, 96, 123
eyes 85, 91, 94, 124, 129, 131, 170
feet 94, 96, 98, 120, 122, 124, 140, 142, 144, 146–7, 153–4, 169, 171, 206, 212
flesh 92–4, 103–5, 118, 131, 135, 137, 139, 141, 144
Gaga, *see* vocabulary, Gaga (selection)
hands 79, 94, 96, 98, 117, 120, 124, 133, 136, 141–2, 146–8, 154
head 36, 38, 41, 91, 95, 128–9, 141, 145, 148–9, 166, 183, 211, 246, 248
hip 37, 138, 148
joints 79, 91, 97, 124, 127, 129, 138, 141–5, 147–8, 169
knees 91, 97, 104, 124, 127, 129, 136, 143, 146, 149, 246
legs 37, 68, 141, 144–8
navel 142, 145
pelvis 133–4, 143, 146–8, 154
ribcage 145, 133
sacrum 97, 148
shoulder (area) 37, 41, 61, 105, 143, 145
shoulder blades 91, 96–7, 129, 148, 211, 148–9, 206–7
sitting bones 122, 245
skin 93, 124, 131–3, 147, 211, 243, 245
spine 128, 129, 143–6, 148, 211, 246
torso 36, 141–2, 145–6, 149
voice 36, 55, 74, 83, 85, 98–9, 150, 154, 161, 164, 182, 194, 214–15
body scan 125
body scheme 15, 40, 89, 115, 123, 130, 152, 159, 167, 174, 204, 208, 210, 215, 222, 243, 245, 247
body topography 10, 88–99, 105–6, 138, 142, 147, 150–1, 168, 205–9, 245–8
Gaga 169–70, 205–9, 217, 220, 242–4
body-turn 7, 248
Bourdieu, Pierre 7
Butler, Judith 7, 108–9, 114

centralization 218–19, 221, 223, 238–9, 239–40, 249
change, *see* transformation
cognition, embodied 7–10, 210, 225, 248
conceptual system 159–60
connecting *see* simulation, embodied
control, movement 115–18, 124, 126–8, 130–1, 139–43, 184–5, 211–12, 229–31, 240, 244
consumerism 4–5, 17, 43–7
consumption, *see* consumerism
contact, *see* touch
conversion 218–19, 239–41
copying, *see also* simulation, embodied
countdown 82–3, 141, 144–5, 150
covert imitation 12, 125, 149–50, 184
crying 189–90, 213
Csordas, Thomas 7

Dalcroze, *see* Jacques-Dalcroze, Émile
dance 181, 199–200
dance biographies 1, 199–200, 226–8, 238–9
Dawson, Andrew 25, 45–6, 173, 176
Delsarte, François 36–7
discourse(s)
  on body and movement 41–2, 169, 229–31
  cultural and social 31, 48, 143, 172–7, 244
  definition of 15, 225
  embodiment of 88–99, 43
  of Gaga 90–9, 143, 204
  neo-spiritual 4, 172–7, 236–7, 247–8
drugs 191, 228, 230

echo 125, 204–5
effort, Laban Movement Analysis 100–1, 104, 105–6, 129, 135–8
  flow, *see* flux
  flux 106, 135, 138
  space 105, 135–6
  time 105–6, 135–7
  weight 105, 135–7, 140
embodiment, *see* body knowledge *and* cognition, embodied
emotions
  embodied 174, 189–91, 210, 235, 245

and extraordinary experience 178–9, 189–92, 195
narration of 161–8, 170, 175
negative 64, 210, 214–15, 234
positive 13, 210, 215, 235, 242, 245
research on 22–3, 26–7
techniques of 123–4, 143, 151–5, 243
energy 97–8, 175, 246
environment
  ritual 49–87, 243, 246
  sensory 7–9, 22–3, 108, 113, 219
  social and cultural 32–4, 218, 238, 245
  as technique 123, 126–7, 131–4, 149, 199
event
  model 159
  schema 159
experience 159
  aesthetization of 6, 45
  collective 113, 149–50, 177, 246
  event 159–60
  individual 153, 177
  mystical 179–80
  negative 197–8
  peak 179, 237, *see also* wow-moments
  verbalization 167
experience diaries 26–17, 159, 164–7
experience filters 13, 47, 88–9, 110, 153, 159, 164, 172–7, 193, 204, 209, 233
  collective 172–7, 193–4, 204
  individual 176–7, 196–7, 203, 204
experience narration of 159–77, 178, 181–3, 217, 240–1
  oral 160–4, 177
  written 164–8, 177
extraordinary experience 5–6, 64–5, 74–6, 153–4, 167, 178–82, 217, 237, 239–40, 242–3, 247

fast reaction 127, 128, 129, 143
feeling, *see* awareness
Feldenkrais 40–1, 245
flexibility, *see* movement range
floating 91, 120–2, 135–6, 205, 208, 232–4
flow 13, 116–17, 185–6, 243, 245
FA, *see* focused attention
focused attention 122, 243–4
  as technique 122–6, 132, 136, 138, 186
Foucault, Michel 7, 15

freedom 154, 186–7, 245, *see also* body knowledge category, movement range
Friedes Galili, Deborah 2, 16, 32–4, 81–2, 88–9

Gaga
  about 2, 242–4
  class 2–3, 49–50, 67, 77–80
  participants 3, 25, 43–8, 49, 52, 58–9, 67–70, 71–2, 74
  story (biography) 220–4
  teachers 50, 55, 70–1, 73–4, 78
  vocabulary, *see* vocabulary, Gaga
Gaga Movement Ltd. 2–3, 32, 44, 49–50, 68, 71, 84–7, 239
Gauthier, François (and Tuomas Martikainen) 5–6, 43–6
gaze 76, 94, 124
global 25, 44, 50
gravity 125
Grimes, Ronald L. 15, 50–2, 53, 66–7, 76, 80, 84
guru 72–4, 175, 226

habitus 7, 15–16
happiness 190–2, 212, 215, 221, 235
healing
  as body knowledge category 13
  in consumerist neoliberal society 5, 247
  as experience 178, 222, 242
  history of 35
healthism 35–6, 46–7, 91–2, 209
heartbeat, *see* thermoregulation
holistic body 35–8, 46, 91, 93–4, 120, 144, 174, 244, 248

identity 214–15, 221, 224–5, 237–8, 241–2
imagery 40, 109, 112–13, 131, 138, 147–8, 150, 152–3, 165–6, 188, 194, 211
  embodiment of 115–16, 134, 139, 144, 146–7, 185, 193
imagination (embodied) 11, 109, 110–11, 131, 132, 133–4, 149, 173, 245
injury 127
instructions
  design of 99–100, 103–6, 111–13, 135, 150–3, 194, 243, 246
  embodied effect 11–12, 82–3, 150–2, 184–5, 192–4, 243

embodiment by participants 106, 113, 113–14, 117–18, 149–52, 155, 184–5, 243, 246
enactment by teachers 110, 113, 149–50, 152, 196–7, 234–5, 243, 246
role in class 3, 85, 151–2
as vocabulary 231–6, *see also* metaphor
interdisciplinarity 8, 219
interview 26, 159, 160–4

Jacques-Dalcroze, Émile 37, 39
Jewish, *see* Judaism
Judaism 41–3, 44

Katan-Schmid, Einav 11, 16, 104, 109–10
kinesphere, *see* movement range
kinesthesia 124–5, 138, *see also* proprioception
Koch, Anne 9–14, 22, 131, 152

Laban Movement Analysis 100–1, 134–8
Lakoff, George and Mark Johnson 11, 109–10, 114–15, 159, 193–4, 233–4
language 80–4, 84–7, 160–77, 182
 comprehension 114–15
 Gaga 168–72, 231–6
 neo-spiritual 174–5
 performative effect 82–3, 108, 193
Language of Dance 100
leisure time activities 2–4, 32, 240, 248–9
listening, *see* awareness
LMA, *see* Laban Movement Analysis
LOD, *see* Language of Dance

Mauss, Marcel 7, 15
meaning-making 1, 8, 11, 219, 225, 233, 243, *see also* worldview
meaning system 27, 218–19, 230, *see also* worldview
memory, autobiographical 168, 241
Merleau-Ponty, Maurice 7
metalanguage 10–14, 99–100, 102, 168
metaphor 16, 69, 82, 104, 109–10, 165–6, 169–72, 185, 193–4, 232–6
methodology 10–14, 20–7, 159–60, 183
Meyer, Birgit 11–12, 179, 224
mind wandering 117, 128, 186, 211
mirrors 3, 57, 59, 63, 66, 155, 187

mobilization 79, 129, 133–4, 143, 147–8, *see also* movement range
monthly pass 58, 68, 220–1
movement efficiency 40, 124, 134, 143, 243–4
movement mode 99, 105–6, 126
movement notation 100
movement quality 99, 101, 104, 105–106, 124, 125, 126, 129, 134, 134–8, 146, 151, 187–8, 211, 243–4
movement range 101, 104–5, 129, 133–4, 136, 143, 145, 147–9, 186–7, 211, 212–13, 215, 222, 243–5
movement source 133–4, 136, 146
movement style 10, 89–90, 103–6, 138, 143, 149, 150, 152, 205, 220, 247
 Gaga 242–3
muscle groups (selection), *see also* body parts
 abdominal/core 95, 122, 127, 133–4, 144–6, 149, 245, *see also* vocabulary, Gaga, lena *and* yoyo
 arms 144, 146
 back muscles 129, 144
 deltoid 122
 feet 147
 intrinsic 127
 joint area 147
 legs 144, 146
 pelvic floor 91, 94–5, 97, 133–4, 145–6, 245, *see also* vocabulary, Gaga, pika *and*
 skeletal 144
 trapezius 122
 upper body 146
muscle tone 11, 91–2, 128, 129, 131, 136–7, 144, 146, 210, 243
muscular
 contraction 131, 134, 137, 139–45, 190
 effort 121–2, 141, 235, 243
 isolation 141–3
 relaxation 125, 127, 131, 137–43, 145–6, 148, 190
music 2, 54–6, 74, 78–9, 98, 150, 184, 191–7, 199–200

Naharin, Ohad 2, 31, 32–4, 72, 74–6, 198, 199, 225–6, 228, 235

narrative
  of conversion 217–19
  data and analysis 23–6, 159–77, 184–5, 220–4, 226–31, 241
  of healing 34, 204–5
  oral 160–4
  written 164–18
national body 35, 40–3
neoliberal, see neoliberalism
neoliberalism 4–5, 17, 44–7, 236–7
neo-spiritualities, see neo-spirituality
neo-spirituality 3–6, 45–6, 47, 48, 156, 174–5
neo-spiritual practices, see neo-spirituality
nonordinary, see extraordinary experience

OM, see open monitoring
open monitoring 122, 243–4
  as technique 122–7, 132–3, 136, 138, 142, 184–5, 210–11
othering 224–5, 229–31, 238

pain 143, 148, 234
  relief 148, 204, 212–13, 221, 243
participant observation
participants 25
party 230
passion 240–1, 249
perception, see (embodied) cognition
perceptual (cultural) order 159, 219, 243, 247, see worldview
peripersonal space 12–13, 101, 104–5, 123, 128, 132, 134, 199, 243, 245
Pilates 33, 245
play 40–1, 152–5
pleasure 185, 243
posture
  as body knowledge 11
  characteristic to Gaga 91–2, 94–9, 127, 143, 149
  problematic 148, 210
  as technique 127, 128, 129, 133–4, 136, 138, 143, 148–9, 210–11, 243, 245
power 66, 114, 117, 197
practices 14–15
preconditions
  collective 155, 176–7, 244, 246
  individual 58–9, 64, 66, 67–70, 117, 149, 155, 159–60, 176–7, 193, 203, 243, 244, 246–7

proprioception 11, 124, 126, 128, 134, 138, 142–3, 146, 211, 244
prosthetic perception 12, 132, 134, 199, 211, 243

qigong 39, 245
Quinlan, Meghan 16–17, 43

relationality 66, 87, 155, 194–9, 243, 246
relations 65, 92–3, 222–4
release 189–90, 192
  emotional 189, 212–16
  physical 189, 212–13
religion 5–6, 45–6, 217–20, 248–9
ritual
  definition of 15, 50–2
  dynamics 51–2
  elements 51–2
  Gaga 49–87
runner's high 192, 243

Schröder, Anne-Konstanze 218–19
secular 4, 47, 241, 248–9
sensation, verbalization 160–77
senses
  definition of 15
  Gaga concept 94, 98, 244
sensing, see awareness
sensory stimuli, see stimuli, sensory
self, see subjectivity
self-optimization
  in consumerist neoliberal society 5, 236–7, 247
  in Gaga 91–2
self-reflected, self-reflecting 22–3, 26–7, 83, 151, 165–4, 173–7, 221, 236
self-responsibility 197, 221
self-sense 13, 117, 130–1, 183–6, 210–11
setting
  religious 218–19
  ritual 537
skin sense 131–3, 147, 211, 243, 245
simulation, embodied 12, 72, 114–16, 184, 198–9
somatic modes of attention 7, 15
somatic pratices, see somatics
somatics 39–40, 122, 172, 174–5, 230–1, 238–9, 248

space
  dance studios 53–7
  qualities (safe, therapeutic, extraordinary) 62–3, 195, 214
  ritual 52–3
speech act 108–10, 218
spiritual 5–6, 46–8, 174–5, 182, 186, 218–20, 241, 248
  endemic use 64, 73, 165, 189, 193, 196, 234
stamina 91–2, 128, 133, 143–4, 192, 245
stimuli, sensory, *see* body knowledge *and* environment
strength 91–2, 127, 128, 133, 143, 144–7, 243, 245
subjectivity, Gaga 90, 103

tattooing 11, 131
Taves, Ann (and Egil Asprem) 13, 159–60, 179–80, 183, 203, 219, 231, 240–1
technique(s), movement
  definition of 15, 119
  Gaga 119–45, 243–4
  neo-spiritual 245–8
  techniques of the body 7, 15
therapy 191, 209–16, 223
thermoregulation 11, 128, 141, 144, 192, 245
time and amount of Gaga practice 70, 220–1, 240–1 *see also* addiction and passion
touch 131–2, 140–1, 194, 228, 245
transcendence 5, 179–80, 183–6, 200, 243, 245
t'ai chi 33, 39, 245–6

vocabulary 24, 81–2, 86–7, 112
  used by participants 82, 168–72, 178–9, 220
vocabulary, Gaga (selection)
  activate 94–5, 139
  animal 91–2, 127–30, 142–3, 153–4, 246
  ball joints 97, 147–8
  balls 125, 142
  blanket 136, 147
  body builder 91, 104, 139, 145, 137
  bones 93–4, 131, 148
  box of the chest 96–7, 123, 134
  break patterns 128–30, 154, 190

  bumpy road 113, 138, 153
  caress 97, 207
  change habits 92, 128
  circles and curves 104, 113, 135, 148
  clay 92, 135, 139–40
  cold shower 69, 79, 92, 133, 139, 153
  collapse 125, 129, 131, 194
  connect 86, 112, 124, 130, 136, 139, 155
  crawl 146, 154, 246
  delicate 101, 105, 133, 137
  dolfi 82, 126
  drill 146
  drum 79, 141
  earthquake 111, 138, 153
  effort 19, 85–6, 92, 98, 120, 125, 145, 147, 155, 129
  energy 61, 91, 98, 105, 125, 133
  engage 137–9
  engine 90, 95–7, 127, 130–4, 136–7, 139
  envelope of the skin 131
  evaporate 131–2
  exaggerate 144
  excess force 132
  explode 106, 127, 137–8, 142
  explosive power 85
  external forces 199, 254
  feathers 92, 140
  flesh 92–4, 103–5, 118, 131, 135, 137, 139, 141, 144
  flexible 129, 143
  flipper machine 138
  fold and unfold 96
  freedom 92
  generous 61, 133
  give 94, 132, 140
  grab 104, 130, 138–40, 143–4, 146–7
  gravity 91, 120–1, 125, 135, 149
  groove 92, 98
  happy feet 144
  highway 97, 125
  home 96–7, 149
  honey 92, 98, 112, 139–42, 153, 193
  horizon 136
  information 90–1, 97–8, 125
  juicy 140
  knead (like dough) 140, 147
  laugh 92, 130
  lava 98, 112–13, 139
  layer 85–6, 93, 98, 135, 151–2

lena 95, 133–4, 246
let go 140
magma 98, 112–13, 139
making faces 130, 145
mama 97
melt 105, 125, 140
mermaid 145
moons 147
motor 133–4
movement habits 128, 211
Nutella 112, 140, 153, 193
oil 97, 148, 169–70
overwhelmed 90, 104, 123, 130
piece of cake 155, 234–5
pika 94–5, 133–4, 145
pleasure 85–6, 92, 128–9, 147, 155
pull 106, 130, 139, 143, 169
punch 127, 136–7
quake 104, 113, 130
receive 132, 136, 140
rope of the arms 96, 120
run 79, 144
seaweed spine 95–6, 149
sense 124
separate 141
shake 98, 104, 112, 130, 138, 141, 151
skin 93, 124, 131–3, 147, 211, 243, 245
silly 90, 92, 153, 162, 235
slide 90, 93–4, 96, 98, 130, 140, 143, 146
slippery 93, 131, 148
snake (of the spine) 95–6
snap 82, 126, 135–6, 138, 142, 155
soap 131
soft 82, 86, 93, 95–6, 105, 120, 123, 128–9, 135–7, 139–41, 145
spaghetti in boiling water 92, 104, 112, 140
spaghetti, overcooked 153–4
squeeze 140
stick the tongue out 130, 154
swallow 98, 141, 153
sweet 153

switch 135–7
tail 95, 97
tama 97
tap dancing 144
taste 153
texture 92, 139, 144
thick 81–2, 86, 93, 98, 103, 125, 135, 137, 139–40, 144
thickness 105
tickling sensation 131, 141
tight 133, 136, 144–5
travel 94–6, 105, 120, 135, 137, 139, 141
travelling stuff 97–8, 125, 142
water 112, 17, 120–1, 137, 140
waves 95, 145
wear 139
yawn 90, 133, 139, 147, 154
yoyo 95, 133–4, 145, 246
volatility 76, 87, 121, 187–8, *see also* animation

well-being
  evolution of 35
  as a neo-spiritual characteristic 4, 46–7, 247–8
  perceived 143, 200, 204, 212, 217, 242
  in somatics 40, 174
worldview
  as body knowledge 87, 89, 159, 170–2, 204
  definition of 13, 218–20
  embodiment of 110, 217–41
  neo-spiritual 107, 175, 247–9
wow-moments 13, 167, 178–203, 223, 232, 237, 239, 240, *see also* extraordinary experience
  definition of 13, 178–9, 180–3
  history of 179–80

yoga 172, 174, 206, 220, 223–4, 229, 237, 245

www.ingramcontent.com/pod-product-compliance
Lightning Source LLC
Chambersburg PA
CBHW052216300426
44115CB00011B/1709